REAL
VS.
RUMOR

REAL VS. RUMOR

HOW TO DISPEL
LATTER-DAY MYTHS

KEITH A. EREKSON

DESERET
BOOK

SALT LAKE CITY, UTAH

Library of Congress Cataloging-in-Publication Data

Names: Erekson, Keith A., author.
Title: Real vs. rumor : how to dispel latter-day myths / Keith A. Erekson.
Description: Salt Lake City, Utah : Deseret Book, [2021] | Includes bibliographical references and index. | Summary: "Author Keith Erekson shares strategies and methods to determine the truth in historical and doctrinal accounts pertaining to The Church of Jesus Christ of Latter-day Saints"—Provided by publisher.
Identifiers: LCCN 2021000429 | ISBN 9781629729091 (trade paperback)
Subjects: LCSH: The Church of Jesus Christ of Latter-day Saints—Apologetic works. | The Church of Jesus Christ of Latter-day Saints—History. | The Church of Jesus Christ of Latter-day Saints—Doctrines. | Mormon Church—Apologetic works. | Mormon Church—History. | Mormon Church—Doctrines. | Research—Methodology—Handbooks, manuals, etc. | Critical thinking—Handbooks, manuals, etc.
Classification: LCC BX8635.5 .E74 2021 | DDC 289.3—dc23
LC record available at https://lccn.loc.gov/2021000429

Printed in the United States of America
Brigham Young University Press, Provo, UT

10   9   8   7   6   5   4   3   2   1

Contents

PART III. DISPEL THIS

APPENDICES

INTRODUCTION

Our Day of Rumors

The rumors shot through the crowd like lightning. *Murder! Enemy infiltration! The tyrant got what he deserved!* Each newcomer gaped in horror at the motionless bodies scattered on the ground— the king, the queen, their servants, and also . . . the foe. *Nasty outsider! Evil specter! More like a monster!* Speculation mounted into sharp contention as a woman arrived. Everything was wrong! She had seen what really happened; it was she who had run excitedly to call the crowd. Knowing she could only quash the rumors with something real, Abish reached out and took the queen by the hand (see Alma 19:17–29).

We, too, live in a day when rumors and myths mingle with reality and cause confusion, concern, and contention. To survive, we must find and grab hold of the real from amid the rumor, but frequently the two are closely entangled. Forgers write fake words on actual historical paper; con artists couch a long lie in many short truths; spokespeople offer finely parsed words that sound like a lot but commit only a little. Today *rumors* appear as errors, falsehoods, legends, family lore, false quotes, lies, misleading misinformation, and deliberately distorted disinformation. Sometimes the word *myth* is used to describe simple errors that stand in opposition to facts. But a myth can also be a sweeping cultural story that lives

1

deep in our minds and underlies our actions. Surrounded as we are by myths and rumors, the best protection lies not in memorizing every possible fact or in debunking simple errors but rather in knowing how good thinking works. Just as Adam and Eve needed to "taste the bitter, that they may know to prize the good" (Moses 6:55), so can we dissolve rumors by recognizing what is real.

Though misinformation exists in every arena, *Real vs. Rumor* focuses on making sense of the rumors, myths, and complicated twists of Church history. As members of The Church of Jesus Christ of Latter-day Saints, we regularly engage history in our devotions. We read and "liken" writings of ancient and historical scripture to our present day, study Church history as part of our Sunday curriculum, give talks and teach lessons about historical events, study our family's history, sing hymns about Joseph Smith and the pioneers, and share quotations from past leaders online and on handouts. Indeed, the doctrine and practices of our Church are rooted in our history and have been revealed over time, line upon line—an ongoing process of restoration that continues in our time.

Given that history is nearly everywhere in Latter-day Saint life, it's no surprise that we frequently encounter rumors and myths. "It never ceases to amaze me," President Harold B. Lee observed, "how gullible some of our Church members are in broadcasting sensational stories, or dreams, or visions, or purported patriarchal blessings, or quotations, or supposedly from some person's private diary."[1] Scammers appeal to history in efforts to sell us scriptural herbs or energized healing methods.[2] Antagonists distort the Church's history, and some Saints abandon their faith because they can't make sense of the past or discern present manipulations.

Such distortions are certainly not unique to the Saints. Social media floods our streaming consciousness with photoshopped images, deep-faked videos, and unattributed texts. Politicians tell bald-faced lies in public and then dismiss fact checkers as liars.

Studies reveal that few Americans know how to verify information they encounter on the internet. Belonging to the same "group" in person or online makes us *less* likely to check the facts shared by our peers, and one recent study found that false headlines travel even *faster* on social media than true ones![3]

Real vs. Rumor offers practical advice for both developing good thinking skills and receiving divine inspiration, for investigating "by study and also by faith" (D&C 88:118). President M. Russell Ballard exhorted gospel teachers to train learners in "the skills and attitudes necessary to distinguish between reliable information that will lift them up and the half-truths and incorrect interpretations of doctrine, history, and practices that will bring them down."[4] This book presents many concrete examples from history, scripture, and popular culture to clarify what we know as well as to prepare you for the next rumor you encounter, whether it be an exaggerated story or a forged website or antagonistic writing or a false quote in class.

The strategies and skills I share in here are techniques I use each day as a public historian. I have researched, written about, and taught these skills for nearly two decades. I know the techniques work because I've witnessed their impact in the lives of so many people.

Real vs. Rumor is organized into three parts. We begin to improve our thinking by exposing the "myths within us" that keep us from seeing what is real. Most of these errors lie hidden within our cultures, traditions, and thinking. "Even the Saints are slow to understand," Joseph Smith observed. "We frequently see some of them, after suffering all they have for the work of God will fly to pieces like glass, as soon as anything comes that is contrary to their traditions."[5] We think we know everything, we don't ask for evidence, we assume, we fail to see the interpretations made by others, we limit our options, and we get distracted by insignificant details.

This book teaches you how to investigate rumors and realities by learning to survey the situation, analyze the contents, connect the contexts, and evaluate the significances.

Situation

Contents 🔍	Contexts

Significances ⚖️

Part II applies the skills and habits learned in part I to investigate three meanings of the English word *history*. Sometimes people use the word to refer to the past, as when speaking of the people and places and things of "the olden days" that happened "in our history." All that survives of the past are pieces, such as old letters, photographs, and diaries, which we call *sources*. Other times, people use the word *history* to refer to *stories* about the past, as when saying "I read a history of the early Church." Finally, the word *history* can be used to describe a formal *study* of the past that surveys all relevant sources and previous stories. Sources, stories, and studies may contain rumors and myths, so to discern if we can trust them, we investigate to corroborate accuracy, verify authenticity, and judge reliability, fairness, and comprehensiveness.

Part III extends the investigative skills and habits into personal efforts to dispel the rumors and myths around us. We are responsible to learn all that we can, quote responsibly, help others who struggle, and understand God's dealings.

To help you learn and remember, *Real vs. Rumor* features repeated elements. Each chapter opens with a vignette of a modern rumor from Church history and features abundant examples. Throughout the book, I introduce simple, memorable, and descriptive sayings about how good thinking works. *Thinking habits* are skills that combine study and faith to make sense of rumors, myths, and history. Along the way, you'll also find my recommendations on the *best resources* to improve your skills as well as *everyday encounters* that translate the concepts and habits to everyday life. Every chapter ends with a "You Try It" section that summarizes *key concepts* and introduces *sniff tests*, or clues that something just isn't right. You need not become an expert on every subject to recognize when good thinking is not being used. Like Abish's Lamanite queen who asked Ammon about her husband Lamoni's health, you may not be a medical expert, but you can tell when something stinks or not (see Alma 19:1–12).

Repeated Elements in *Real vs. Rumor*

Thinking Habits—Skills that combine study and faith to make sense of history.

Everyday Encounters—Examples of how to apply thinking habits to daily experiences.

Best Resources—Recommendations offered in the spirit of finding the "best books" (see D&C 88:118; 90:15).

You Try It—Summaries of *key concepts* and *sniff tests* that suggest something just isn't right.

Perhaps a word of warning is in order. It requires careful exertion and vigilance to expose and correct the myths and rumors around us. We must think about how we think, analyze our thought processes, and improve the way that we evaluate the world around us. We should also invite the Holy Spirit into our process of remembering, evaluating, and knowing to help us overcome our natural impulses. We need, as President M. Russell Ballard put it, "the help of the Holy Ghost to think straight."[6]

In addition to your mind, this effort will also require your heart, might, and strength. It requires humility to admit we don't know everything and courage to change what we have long incorrectly thought or assumed. Diligence, perseverance, and patience carry us through complex topics and challenging questions. We need empathy to try to understand the experiences of others, temperance to avoid extremes, and faith not to waver as we work to sort things out. Sometimes the answers to the toughest questions come not when we're actively studying or praying but when we're serving others.

It is my sincere hope that the concepts and examples in this book leap out of these pages and into your daily life. I truly believe that learning how to analyze rumors, myths, and Church history will improve our lives, making us better friends and neighbors, learners and teachers, parents and children, disciples and Saints. The study of things "as they were" helps us understand "things as they are" and prepares us for things that "are to come," all "for the salvation of Zion" (D&C 93:24, 53). Good thinking is both a habit of good living and a divine pursuit that helps us serve one another and draw closer to God by understanding His words and dealings.

Notes

1. Harold B. Lee, *The Teachings of Harold B. Lee*, ed. Clyde J. Williams (Salt Lake City: Bookcraft, 1996), 399.
2. M. Russell Ballard, "The Trek Continues!" *Ensign*, November 2017, 106n11; Dennis Romboy, "Does Utah Deserve the Title 'Fraud Capital of the United States'?" *Deseret News*, April 29, 2019.
3. Rachel Meng and others, "Being in a Group Makes Us Less Likely to Fact-Check," *Harvard Business Review*, August 1, 2017; Steve Lohr, "It's True: False News Spreads Faster and Wider. And Humans Are to Blame," *New York Times*, March 8, 2018.
4. M. Russell Ballard, "By Study and by Faith," *Ensign*, December 2016, 25.
5. Joseph Smith, in "History, 1838–1856, volume E-1 [1 July 1843–30 April 1844]," p. 1867, The Joseph Smith Papers, https://www.josephsmithpapers.org/paper-summary/history-1838-1856-volume-e-1-1-july-1843-30-april-1844/239.
6. M. Russell Ballard, "Let Us Think Straight" (address, BYU Education Week, Provo, UT, August 20, 2013), https://speeches.byu.edu/talks/m-russell-ballard_let-us-think-straight-2/.

PART I
THE MYTHS WITHIN US

CHAPTER 1

We Know Everything

"What about those different accounts of the First Vision? They're a myth, right?"

I am asked this question regularly, often by people who are troubled by the idea that there could be multiple accounts. One person refused even to look at the accounts because several family members had left the Church over this subject.

My answer typically goes something like this: "Let me tell you about one of the most important events in history. It occurred at a time when families and neighbors were divided by a tumult of opinions. On this occasion, only a few simple words were uttered about the human condition, about life and death. Little noted at the time, the words today provide inspiration to millions and many have committed them to memory. Very few know, however, that there is more than one account of this event. Later accounts differ from earlier ones, in small ways dealing with grammar and word choice, but also in other ways, such as the mention of deity. The words are all that have survived—their author is dead, video technology did not exist, not even a photograph was taken. Of course, I'm talking about Abraham Lincoln's Gettysburg Address."

"Wait! What?" the person sputters. "I thought you were talking about the First Vision."

———————————— Q ————————————

The First Vision—like *every* event that happened in the past—is over. It's done. It's history. We do not know everything about the past. Past events are only known to us today in the present because records survived. Those records are fragmentary, partial, and—if we're lucky—multiple. In the case of the Gettysburg Address, Lincoln penned five differing versions of the speech, one before the event and four after, with the words "under God" appearing in only the later versions.[1] And similar descriptions could be written about myriad other historical events and documents. We expect that "multiple conflicting perspectives are among the truths of history."[2] The past is gone. Information gets lost over time. That's how history works. Our task is to piece together what we know and what we don't and then develop the humility both to wait for more knowledge and to revise our understanding when we learn it.

The Past Is Gone

The events of the past have ended. The people who lived there are dead. Yet pieces of the past remain into the present. The pieces take the form of private letters and diaries, public records of businesses and governments, published memos and private plans, advertisements and household objects, and abstract social institutions and traditions. These pieces of the past serve as "its residues, its remnants, its remainders and reminders."[3] Though gone, the past influences how we think, how we act, where we live, and what we know.

Imagine Joseph Smith preaching a sermon to the Saints in Kirtland or Nauvoo. When he spoke, he typically spoke extemporaneously with no prepared text, so no notes survive. No audio or video recording was made (because the technologies had not been invented), and he never had a scribe present who could record all of what he spoke in shorthand. So we must rely on the listeners.

Hundreds of people may have been in the crowd but perhaps only a few dozen recorded the experience—maybe in a letter to a friend or in a journal or in a recollection written many years later. Here's one of my favorite records of a sermon given by Joseph Smith: William W. Phelps wrote a letter to his wife, saying, "President Smith preached last Sabbath and I gave him the text: 'This is my beloved Son; hear ye him!' He preached one of the greatest sermons I ever heard—it was about 3½ hours long—and unfolded more mysteries than I can write at this time." Phelps left no additional record of the sermon, nor did anyone else. Other records read like this one from the minutes of the very first conference of the Church: "exhortation by Joseph Smith."[4] That's it. More records have survived for his sermons in the 1840s than in earlier times, but his original words are largely missing, incomplete, with no verbatim account. The past is gone.

The fact that most of the past is gone challenges our understanding of the lives and experiences of most people who ever lived. Consider Joseph Smith's wife, Emma. She participated in many of the events of the Restoration. An early revelation described her as "an elect lady" ordained "to expound scriptures, and to exhort the church" (D&C 25:3, 7). She edited the Church's first hymnal and served as the first president of the Relief Society. And yet, she kept no journal. About two dozen letters between her and Joseph survive, as do a few additional letters to others after his death in 1844. The pages she wrote as scribe for the Book of Mormon were lost with the 116 pages. She gave a few interviews later in life, and she is mentioned briefly in family papers.[5] As a result, we can reconstruct her activities and experiences, but we know far less about her inner thoughts and feelings.

Today, we can learn about the past only indirectly, through the remaining pieces. We cannot examine the past firsthand in a laboratory as if it were rocks or plants; we cannot visit the past as if it were another country. We must study the records that survive while remembering that they do not represent the entirety of the past. Sometimes, as Lin-Manuel Miranda's Aaron Burr sang in the musical *Hamilton*, "No one else was in the room where it happened," so we may know very little and some things remain unknown. A sixteenth-century English settlement on Roanoke Island in what is now the Outer Banks of North Carolina vanished, leaving only the word "Croatoan" carved onto a fence post and "CRO" on a tree. We do not have records of the visit of Peter, James, and John to Joseph Smith that are as detailed as the accounts of John the Baptist's visit (see JS—H 1:66–75). We don't know who the six original members of the Church were. Only eleven fragments remain of the scrolls from which Joseph translated the Book of Abraham. Terryl and Fiona Givens stated our conundrum simply: "we know less than we want," yet "we crave closure and certainty, wholeness and equilibrium."[6]

These problems are magnified when talking about spiritual events. In a history that is now part of the Pearl of Great Price, Joseph Smith described his visits from Moroni in only 900 words. Later, Oliver Cowdery related what Joseph had told him about the visit in 2,400 words—almost three times as many as Joseph left. Yet, Oliver still concluded, "You are aware of the fact, that to give a minute rehearsal of a lengthy interview with a heavenly messenger, is very difficult, unless one is assisted immediately with the gift of inspiration."[7] The Apostle Paul explained that in the present "we see through a glass, darkly" and only "know in part"; in the future, we will know more (1 Cor. 13:12). Through Joseph Smith comes the promise that "in that day when the Lord shall come, he shall reveal all things—Things which have passed, and hidden things which no man knew" (D&C 101:32–33). Until then, we must accept that the past is gone, some things are unknown, and we have to do the best we can with what has survived.

💬 Everyday Encounter:
"History" Does Not Mean What You Think It Means

History is not what you learned in school, where it was presented as a list of facts and dates in chronological order. A textbook presents one official and unchanging story about important people that students are supposed to learn. After memorizing and reciting, students move on to the next chunk of information. But outside of the classroom, history turns out to be almost the exact opposite. Instead of facts sitting on a textbook page, history is hidden in old records. Instead of one official story, there are myriad experiences, perspectives, and stories. Instead of knowing everything about the past, we know very little about people and cultures that are gone. Instead of memorizing, we need to think, search, and discover.

History is also not an empirical science whose results can be tested and replicated. For example, if you and I were to debate how many stomachs a cow has, we would resolve our differences by cutting open a cow, counting four stomachs, and then holding a barbeque to celebrate our common understanding. But if we disagree about Abraham Lincoln's views on a subject, how do we resolve that? How can we cut him open? (Honestly, his remains are encased in concrete.) And even if we could cut him open, where would we look? The scientific method provides no help for answering the most important questions of history.

How the Past Got Gone

Information is always lost between the past and the present through processes that are entirely normal. Imagine a large circle that represents the entirety of the past. A person in history *experienced* only a portion of the *past*, a smaller circle within a larger one. Not everything that a person experiences is perceived, comprehended, or *remembered*. What is remembered may become merged with other memories, distorted, or invented. Many people never record anything about their experiences, but some do. However, no person has ever been able to record everything he or she experienced, so an even smaller circle represents the parts of the past that get *recorded*. Most records are then eventually lost—some get misplaced, others are destroyed in natural disasters, and still more are discovered in attics or basements and then sent to the trash. Only precious few records end up being *preserved* in a format and a storage facility, such as a library or archive, that can ensure the record survives more than one generation. Yet the information in the record will still be of no use unless someone can find it, so records must be organized in such a way that they can be *discovered*. Upon examination, someone can decide if the information is credible and helpful, and, if so, the person will cite the record as a *source*.

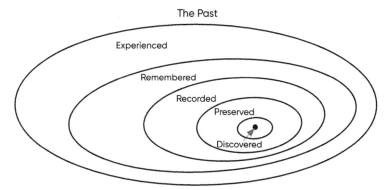

The Past

Experienced

Remembered

Recorded

Preserved

Discovered

Each source constitutes only a small speck of the past, and so we rejoice when multiple pieces of the past survive. Thus we are blessed by the fact that Joseph Smith repeatedly testified of the First Vision and that multiple accounts have survived.

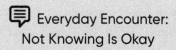 Everyday Encounter:
Not Knowing Is Okay

Because the past is gone and only pieces remain, it is okay that we don't know everything. To not know something is not a sign of sin, or stupidity, or laziness. That's just the way that some things are. This is certainly true about the mysteries of God. Jacob explained: "Behold, great and marvelous are the works of the Lord. How unsearchable are the depths of the mysteries of him; and it is impossible that man should find out all his ways. And no man knoweth of his ways save it be revealed unto him" (Jacob 4:8).

Many prophets have confessed in scripture that they do not know all things but they do know that God loves us, that He has all power, that He gives us commandments, and that He will provide a way when we cannot see it (see 1 Ne. 11:17; 9:6; Alma 7:8; Moses 5:6–7). Joseph F. Smith observed, "It is no discredit to our intelligence or to our integrity to say frankly in the face of a hundred speculative questions, 'I do not know.'"[8] It requires humility to admit we do not know everything, to wait patiently for more answers, and to continue learning. Not knowing is okay; declaring that we don't know demonstrates our humility and trust in the Lord.

What We Know and What We Don't

To make sense of a past that is mostly gone, we begin by identifying what we know and what we don't. This process applies to *everything* that occurred in the past. We know that the Second Continental Congress adopted a resolution of freedom on July 2, 1776 (not July 4), but most of the thoughts, feelings, and intentions of John Adams, Benjamin Franklin, and Thomas Jefferson are forever gone. We have records of George Washington's public addresses and letters, but his wife, Martha, burned the letters written between them.

A simple way to begin investigating a topic about the past is to list in two columns "What We Know" and "What We Don't." The Book of Mormon prophet Alma modeled this skill of seeking knowledge by identifying what is known and unknown in an extended explanation about resurrection. He began by acknowledging that "there are many mysteries which are kept, that no one knoweth them save God himself." All Alma knew was that all die and that "there is a time appointed that all shall rise from the dead." But there was a gap of knowledge between these two knowns, between death and resurrection, and "concerning this space of time, what becometh of the souls of men is the thing which I have inquired diligently of the Lord to know." Alma sized up what he knew, identified what he did not, and asked questions. In this case, the answer to his question was later "made known unto [Alma] by an angel," and he shared the truths with his son (Alma 40:3–11). Identifying what was *unknown* became a stepping-stone to eventually *knowing* it.

⦂💡⦂ Thinking Habit:
Identify What We Know and What We Don't

What We Know	What We Don't

Here's an example of identifying what is known and unknown about the origins of the ban on Black priesthood ordination and temple participation. You'll see that we can identify the person (Brigham Young) and date the policy was publicly announced (1852). We can note that the policy changed the previous practice and that President Young used racialized language common to his time. But we don't know how his personal thoughts took shape into a formal policy of restriction. The issue was debated publicly, but was the change initiated by personal inquiry, through deliberation, or by legislative compromise? We don't know.[9]

What We Know and What We Don't:
Origins of the Priesthood Ban

What We Know	What We Don't
• A few Black men were ordained to the priest-hood during the 1830s and 1840s, including Elijah Able and Q. Walker Lewis (called "one of the best Elders" by Brigham Young[10]).	• How the procedural change was introduced: did it come through response to individual inquiry, the decision of a council, a discussion within the territorial gov-ernment, or some other way?
• Joseph Smith reviewed Able's ordination record and certified its validity.	• If the restriction was enacted privately before the public announcement.
• The earliest private record of a discussion about the priesthood-ordination status of Black men was made in 1847.	• If early advocates of the ban saw it as a change from previous practice.
• Brigham Young an-nounced publicly at an 1852 meeting of the Utah territorial legislature that Black men could no lon-ger be ordained to the priesthood.	
• Brigham Young invoked common racialized ideas about Blacks inheriting a curse of Cain.	

• Contemporaries of Brigham Young, including Apostle Orson Pratt, disagreed with the ban, arguing against multigenerational curses and slavery in Utah Territory. • Brigham Young stated Black men would be ordained at a future day.	

Some of the most harmful myths in all of Church history stem from efforts—official and otherwise—to fill in the gaps of what we don't know about how the priesthood ban was introduced. A statement approved by the First Presidency and Twelve declares: "Today, the Church disavows the theories advanced in the past that black skin is a sign of divine disfavor or curse, or that it reflects unrighteous actions in a premortal life; that mixed-race marriages are a sin; or that blacks or people of any other race or ethnicity are inferior in any way to anyone else." President Dallin H. Oaks described all of these so-called reasons as being "spectacularly wrong." And Elder Jeffrey R. Holland counseled, "Don't perpetuate explanations about things we don't know."[11] When pieces of the past are missing, we must avoid the temptation to fill in the gaps.

Another good reason not to try to fill in the gaps is that sometimes long-missing pieces of the past resurface and change our understanding. In historical study, this happens frequently—a rare copy of the Declaration of Independence, hidden behind a wall during the Civil War, was found; a Bible owned by Abraham Lincoln reappeared after more than a century; a map drawn by a Native American leader for Lewis and Clark was discovered by a graduate student in a French library. For many years, the recollections of participants placed the founding of the Church's young women's organization in November 1869. Later, a contemporary journal and newspaper report were discovered that showed the event really occurred six months later, on May 27, 1870.[12]

In history, this process unfolds over time, with each generation. Consider the example of Nephi who was commanded to make two sets of plates "for a wise purpose . . . , which purpose I know not" (1 Ne. 9:5). Later, he revised that view by adding that the records "should be kept for the instruction of my people" and "for other wise purposes" (1 Ne. 19:3). Five hundred years later Alma observed that the records had been used by Ammon to instruct the Lamanites, but there yet remained another "wise purpose" by which God "may show forth his power unto future generations" (Alma 37:14; see also vv. 8–9). After nearly another five hundred years, Mormon still did not know this "wise purpose" as he included Nephi's small plates to his record (W of M 1:7), but after Joseph Smith lost the 116 manuscript pages, the Lord revealed that Nephi's second, smaller record had been preserved in His "wisdom" because they "throw greater views upon my gospel" (D&C 10:39–45). The best understanding of the purpose of the plates developed over time, through observation and revelation, by study and by faith.

💬 Everyday Encounter: Making Sense of Tough Modern Issues

The practice of identifying what we know and what we don't proves useful in understanding tough modern issues. For example, President M. Russell Ballard used this framework to examine suicide, observing that while we know the seriousness of suicide, we don't know the full circumstances surrounding every act of suicide. Thankfully, God does know all of the circumstances and considers them all in His merciful judgment. President Ballard drew his conclusions by reading widely; he cited the Book of Mormon, the New

Testament, the Doctrine and Covenants, Joseph Smith, George Q. Cannon, Bruce R. McConkie, and Spencer W. Kimball.[13]

You Try It

Rumor

We know everything.

Sniff Tests

1. *"History is like school and science."* History is not a tidy list of facts in a textbook, nor is it the work for hypotheses and replication. History requires evidence, investigation, and discovery.
2. *Nothing missing.* Beware of histories that fill in all of the gaps. It is okay that we don't know everything. Be suspicious of a history that does not confess that some things remain unknown.
3. *"Hindsight is 20/20."* This common saying is wrong. Because the past is gone and because so many pieces are missing, there is no event from history about which we know everything. We do know some things that people in the past did not know, such as the outcome of decisions and events. But in other ways, we know far less. While we may know *what* happened, often the *how* and *why* is far harder for us to discern today. And there is no way to know *the alternate outcome if* something had not happened. You should be suspicious of any presentation of history that states or implies that we know everything.
4. *"The past is in the past."* Pieces of the past get woven into present expressions of culture, power, and faith. We must deal with the legacy of the past every day.

Real

The past is gone; only pieces remain.

Key Concepts

1. We do not know everything about the past.
2. Information is always lost between the past and the present through the processes of remembering, recording, preserving, discovering, and using. Thus, we can learn about the past only indirectly, through the pieces that survive, always remembering that they do not represent the entirety of the past.
3. It is okay that we know very little about the past, that some things remain unknown, that some unknown things become known, and that we continually revise what we know.
4. To understand the past, we should identify what we know and what we don't know.

Notes

1. Gettysburg Address, Library of Congress, http://www.loc.gov/exhibits/gettysburg-address/.
2. "Statement on Standards of Professional Conduct," American Historical Association, June 2019, https://www.historians.org/jobs-and-professional-development/statements-standards-and-guidelines-of-the-discipline/statement-on-standards-of-professional-conduct.
3. Joyce Appleby, "The Power of History," *American Historical Review* 103, no. 1 (February 1998): 12.
4. William W. Phelps to Sally Phelps, June 2, 1835, "Journal History of the Church," Church History Library, Salt Lake City; "Minutes, 9 June 1830," p. 1, The Joseph Smith Papers, https://www.josephsmithpapers.org/paper-summary/minutes-9-june-1830/1.
5. Jennifer Reeder, *First: The Life and Faith of Emma Smith* (Salt Lake City: Deseret Book, 2021).
6. Terryl Givens and Fiona Givens, *The Crucible of Doubt: Reflections on the Quest for Faith* (Salt Lake City: Deseret Book, 2014), 25; Richard L. Anderson, "Who Were the Six Who Organized the Church on 6 April 1830?" *Ensign*, June 1980, 44–45.
7. Oliver Cowdery, in *Messenger and Advocate* (Kirtland, OH, 1834–37), 1:112.

8. Joseph F. Smith, *Gospel Doctrine: Selections from the Sermons and Writings of Joseph F. Smith* (Salt Lake City: Deseret Book, 1939), 9.

9. "Race and the Priesthood," Gospel Topics Essays, The Church of Jesus Christ of Latter-day Saints, 2013, https://www.churchofjesuschrist.org/study/manual/gospel-topics-essays/race-and-the-priesthood; W. Paul Reeve, *Religion of a Different Color: Race and the Mormon Struggle for Whiteness* (New York: Oxford University Press, 2015), 144–61.

10. Historian's Office General Church Minutes, March 26, 1847, Church History Library.

11. "Race and the Priesthood," Gospel Topics Essays, https://www.churchofjesuschrist.org/study/manual/gospel-topics-essays/race-and-the-priesthood; Dallin H. Oaks, *Life's Lessons Learned* (Salt Lake City: Deseret Book, 2011), 68–69; Jeffrey R. Holland, "Interview," *The Mormons* (transcript of video) (PBS, 2006), https://www.pbs.org/mormons/interviews/holland.html.

12. Susa Young Gates, *History of the Young Ladies' Mutual Improvement Association of the Church of Jesus Christ of Latter-Day Saints from November 1869 to June 1910* (Salt Lake City: Deseret News, 1911); "Young Ladies' Department of the Ladies' Cooperative Retrenchment Association, Resolution, May 27, 1870," in *The First Fifty Years of Relief Society: Key Documents in Latter-day Saint Women's History*, ed. Jill Mulvay Derr and others (Salt Lake City: Church Historian's Press, 2016), 353–57.

13. M. Russell Ballard, "Suicide: Some Things We Know, and Some We Do Not," *Ensign*, October 1987, 6–9.

CHAPTER 2

I Heard . . .

"Have you heard what's happening with mission calls?"

"No. What's happening?"

"People are receiving mission calls that say to wait for general conference for details."

"Do you know a person who has received such a call?"

"Well, not personally, but it happened to someone in my roommate's home ward."

"Have you seen an actual letter saying this?"

"Er, no, but I've seen the message about it on social media."

"But have you actually seen the statement in a letter or email from the First Presidency?"

"No."

"Then it's not happening."

As we seek for what is real, we must look for evidence. Because the past is gone, the pieces of the past that remain into our day must be investigated in order to best understand what happened. The Book of Mormon relates the story of the false prophet Korihor, who attempted to lure others into a battle of opinions by taunting, "Ye say" there is a God and that "Christ shall come," but "behold,

I say" the opposite (Alma 30:24–26). Alma cut to the heart of Korihor's trickery by identifying the principal problem: "What *evidence* have ye," Alma asked, "that there is no God, or that Christ cometh not? I say unto you that ye have none, save it be your word only." Alma then countered Korihor by presenting evidence: "But, behold, I have all things as a testimony that these things are true," including the testimonies of prophets, the scriptures, and the motion of the planets (Alma 30:40–44; emphasis added).

Korihor was struck dumb, cast out, and trampled to death. We can avoid such a fate by learning to think and reason with evidence! And, as the Nephite prophet Jacob taught, by gathering evidence from "all these witnesses we obtain a hope, and our faith becometh unshaken" (Jacob 4:6). In other words, gathering and evaluating evidence is a process of learning by study and by faith.

All Evidence Is Not Equal

All evidence is not equal; some is much better than others. The field of history has not defined formal rules for evidence as in other fields, such as medicine or law. However, there is consensus around some important rules of thumb, each with some qualifications. We might sum up these rules by saying that we prefer records made closer to the participants and closer to the time of the event:

1. We typically *prefer information from witnesses more closely involved with the event.* Stories told by participants and observers are called *firsthand* accounts, while those told by someone who only heard the story from a participant are called *secondhand* accounts or *hearsay.* We prefer firsthand testimony to guard against the distortion of facts that invariably happens when information is passed from one person to another. Some participants may not have observed or remember everything that happened, such as a person who turns to look after hearing a noise and therefore really witnessed only the aftermath. And in

the absence of firsthand accounts, we look to secondhand as the best available option.

2. We typically *prefer information recorded close in time to the event.* This rule applies to accounts of both those who observed and those who only heard about an event. Records made closer to the event guard against memory loss or other errors that arise as events fade into the distance. Although the passage of time can dilute or distort memories, exhilarating moments may be seared into memory. On the other hand, some traumatic memories may be repressed for many years, which could make a later record more complete. Additionally, subsequent events may cause a person to recall and record additional details that were not noted at the time of the event.

3. We can *accept information that is inferred from direct evidence.* Frequently, firsthand sources do not survive that document secretive, sensitive, or traumatic experiences, such as participation in plural marriage, social exclusion, or abusive relationships. Historical experts who study the sources, conditions, and contexts of a given time period may be able to draw conclusions informed by their expertise—to read between the lines or listen within the silences—but the best experts will always distinguish between "proven knowledge and informed inference."[1]

4. We must *provide additional explanation for any other information that is drawn indirectly from context or other sources.* We may gain insight from surrounding circumstances or the backstory of a participant, but such information always needs explanation to link it to the immediate topic at hand.

Different varieties of evidence are summarized in the accompanying table. The strongest approach is to gather all possible evidence from multiple sources.

Varieties of Historical Evidence

Observed	Heard	Inferred
• Reported by a participant, an eyewitness who participated in the event • Reported by a nonparticipant, an eyewitness who watched the event • Reported by someone who observed non-visual sensory information—that is, experiences through hearing, feeling, smelling, or tasting	• Reported by someone who heard a participant or observer • Reported by someone who takes respon-sibility for the reliability of the information • Reported by someone known to be reliable	• Inferred from direct evidence or results • Inferred through informed expertise • Inferred by reasoning from general knowledge or experience with similar situations

Let's apply these rules of thumb to some real-life examples.

How many wives did Joseph Smith have? Footnote 24 of the Church's Gospel Topics Essay on the subject puts the number at thirty to forty. The thirty come from records of women who reported being married to Joseph or from family members or friends with knowledge of the marriage. The additional ten come from second- or thirdhand accounts.[2]

Was the *Star Wars* character Yoda modeled after Church President Spencer W. Kimball? A wise and powerful teacher, Yoda taught Luke Skywalker to "do, or do not. There is no try." President Kimball served as President of the Church at the time the movie was released and kept a sign on his desk that read, "Do it." Though such coincidences may be appealing, the evidence for this one is easy to examine. A firsthand account from the artist Stuart Freeborn reported on multiple occasions that he created Yoda to look like himself and Albert Einstein.[3]

Simply being firsthand is not always enough to make evidence credible. Since the 1960s, several variations of a story have been told about a Japanese pilot and the Laie Hawaii Temple during the attack on Pearl Harbor. In the most common version, the pilot leaves his squadron to attack the temple, but the bomb would not release, so he rejoined the raid and his bomb worked, prompting him to seek an explanation after the war, and he was eventually baptized. In other versions of the story, the pilot was assigned to target the temple but he blacked out, or the temple was suddenly hidden by clouds, or a suicide dive did not work, or a mysterious force prevented the plane from flying. In one variation, the pilot later became the gardener at the temple.

Two firsthand witnesses surfaced to defend two parts of the story. First, Robert Kahawaii was an inactive member in 1941 who came home drunk on the night of December 6 to find his wife had locked him out. He slept outside and reported seeing a plane make three attempts on the temple the next morning, but the bomb would not drop. Two decades later, after returning to Church activity, he began to tell the story. No other Laie residents saw or heard a plane, he did not report the experience to a friend that morning, and he was likely hungover at the time. Second, Robert Stout reported that while serving a mission in Matsumoto City, Japan, in September 1957, he and his companion met a man who became agitated on seeing a photo of the Laie Temple and confessed to trying to bomb, strafe, and suicide dive the building to no avail. Stout had been serving in the mission field for only five months and admitted that he and his companion did not understand Japanese fully.

These two witnesses speak to different variations of the story, but specific details in both accounts don't match known details about the aircraft or bombs used in the raid, and the kamikaze phase of the war occurred after the attack on Pearl Harbor. The raid's flight path did not cross Laie; it was planned and conducted in secrecy, and the likelihood of a rogue pilot flying off course is extremely low. Extensive searching over many decades has not revealed a war veteran among the Saints in Hawaii or Japan; most of the Japanese participants in the raid were killed at the Battle of Midway.[4]

All of the types of evidence apply to the question of the reality of the gold plates. A dozen men and women reported being *eyewitness observers of the plates*—three witnesses were shown them by an angel, eight witnesses were shown them by Joseph Smith, and Mary Whitmer was shown them by a visitor who was later deduced to be Moroni. The formal witnesses made a written record of their testimony that was published *within a year of their experience* in the first edition of the Book of Mormon. Many of them, especially David Whitmer, made additional statements throughout their lifetimes. Other witnesses *drew inferences from direct physical evidence*—Joseph's family felt the plates through cloth, his brother William carried the plates, and his wife Emma traced the outline of the plates and ruffled them through cloth. Even contextual evidence survives that indicates people in the neighborhood heard rumor of the plates and some developed schemes to steal the plates. Contemporary newspapers ridiculed the idea of golden plates but in so doing provide evidence that the idea circulated. Thus, *many sources, produced over many years*, corroborate Joseph Smith's statement that he had gold plates in his possession in 1828 and 1829.[5]

Faith Is Evidence

I always cringe when I hear people say something like "I know such-and-such through science or reason, but the rest I'll have to take on faith." This statement suggests that faith is *not* about evidence—after all of the evidence is gathered and found wanting, then a person turns reluctantly to something called "faith" to patch the holes. Elder Neil L. Andersen explained that faith "is not something ethereal, floating loosely in the air." Instead, our scriptures teach "faith is the *substance* of things hoped for, the *evidence* of things not seen" (Heb. 11:1; emphasis added). Joseph Smith changed the word "substance" to "assurance" in his inspired translation, and the underlying Greek word, *hypostasis*, may also be translated as "confidence." "Assurance comes in ways that aren't always easy to analyze," Sharon Eubank observed, "but there is light in our darkness." Thus, faith is not the absence of certitude, positive thinking, or a weak foundation of flimsy evidence. To have faith, Alma taught, means to "hope for things which are not seen, which are true" (Alma 32:21). Anne C. Pingree described it as a "spiritual ability to be persuaded of promises that are seen 'afar off.'"[6] Faith develops through our relationship with God our Father, by His communications with us through the Holy Ghost.

Faith is a type of evidence that can be strengthened by observations, reports, and inferences, but it also exists independent of them. Remembering the tough times in Kirtland, Ohio, when many rejected Joseph Smith and left the Church, Desdemona Fullmer said that "Oliver Cowdery with others would say to me are you such a fool as still to go to hear Joseph the fallen prophet. I said the Lord convinced me that he was a true prophet. And he has not told me that he is fallen yet."[7]

Placing reason *before* faith also implies that things discovered through scientific or historical inquiry are fully known, but such knowledge is incomplete and experimental. Speaking to Latter-day Saint youth in 1934, Elsie Talmage Brandley noted that we "accept much without criticism and doubt: fruit is eaten without knowing botany; stars are loved in ignorance of astronomy; telegrams are sent with no knowledge of the Morse code." Today we might add smart phones and cloud computing to the list. She urged, "Let us not encourage youth to segregate religion as the only phase of life upon which to concentrate doubtful inquiry."[8]

Instead of seeing study and faith in a sequential relationship, study before faith, I prefer to see them in a contemporary relationship—study *and* faith, working *together* at the same time to address the same issues. There are many metaphors we might choose to describe this relationship: Both are essential for progress and movement, like two oars in a boat or a two-person bicycle. Their combined use amplifies the lone abilities of either one, like two eyes. They provide different views of the same topic, like the big picture view on the box of a jigsaw puzzle and the details of its individual pieces. They are "members" of the same "one body" (1 Cor. 12:20).[9]

Show Me the Evidence

Every time we hear a quote or story or rumor we must respond with "Show me the evidence." After asking about what we know and what we don't, we should also ask "How do we know it?"

💡 Thinking Habit:
Identify What We Know and How We Know It

What We Know	How We Know It

Let me illustrate this process by answering *the most common* question I receive when people learn that I'm the director of the Church History Library—"Do you have the sword of Laban?" The short answer is "No," but there is more to the response. I don't know where the sword is now or whether it has even been used since the late 1820s, but I do know that Joseph Smith saw the sword in the box with the plates, that Moroni showed it to the

Three Witnesses, and that Oliver reported seeing the sword unsheathed on a table in a vision about a cave of records. Once we establish what we know, then we ask, "How do we know it?"

What We Know and How We Know It: The Sword of Laban

What We Know	How We Know It
Joseph Smith saw the sword in the stone box with the plates.	His sister Catherine stated in 1886 that Joseph "went frequently to the hill, and upon returning he would tell us, 'I have seen the records, also the brass plates and the sword of Laban with the breast plate and the interpreters.'"[10]
Moroni showed the sword to the Three Witnesses.	The Lord promised to show the sword to the Three Witnesses in a revelation (D&C 17:1), and in the late 1870s and early 1880s, David Whitmer told multiple interviewers that Moroni "exhibited to them the plates, the sword of Laban, the Directors which were given to Lehi (called Liahona), the Urim and Thummim, and other records."[11]
Joseph and Oliver Cowdery saw the sword on a table in a cave in a vision.	Brigham Young related the story in a talk in June 1877, noting that Oliver and Joseph "walked into a cave" containing "more plates than probably many wagon

loads." The first time they visited, the sword hung on the wall, but "when they went again it had been taken down and laid upon the table across the gold plates; it was unsheathed, and on it was written these words: 'This sword will never be sheathed again until the kingdoms of this world become the kingdom of our God and his Christ.'" Brigham said he heard this story from Oliver and from Joseph's brother Don Carlos. Three people recorded hearing Brigham Young tell this story, two people recorded hearing it from David Whitmer, and one reported hearing it from Martin Harris.[12]

In describing how we know, I named the source of the information and stated the year in which the source told the story. Our evidentiary rules of thumb illuminate two interesting observations. First, the second piece of information comes from a participant in the event (David Whitmer said he saw the sword) but the first and third facts come from people who heard the participants tell the story. Second, all of the stories were told in the 1870s and 1880s, at least fifty years after the events. Our evidence about the sword of Laban comes from persons close to the events (and one participant), but it also comes many years after the events. We would prefer sources created closer in time to the event, but these are the best available. All of the sources describe only seeing the sword—it was never given to someone and thus could never have been handed down to eventually arrive in the Church History Library.

It is also important to peel back the layers of evidence. In the 1890s, Edward Rushton alleged hearing a statement by Joseph Smith in 1843 that has come to be known as the "white horse prophecy." In a sworn and notarized statement, Rushton presented a hodgepodge of ideas that involve the four horses of the Apocalypse (see Rev. 6:1–8), the Saints' move to the Rocky Mountains, and the idea that the Constitution would hang by a thread before being rescued by Latter-day Saints (the white horse). Rushton's prophecy was repudiated by Church leaders at the time and continues to be rejected in the twenty-first century, often by observing that Rushton is a *secondhand* source whose account was prepared *many years after* the event.[13]

But if we dig a little deeper, better sources can be found to support the future fragility of the US Constitution. Martha Coray's notes of a sermon on July 19, 1840, record Joseph Smith saying, "When the constitution is upon the brink of ruin this people will be the Staff up[on] which the Nation shall lean and they shall bear away the constitution away from the <very> verge of destruction." In 1854, Brigham Young remembered Joseph saying, "The destiny of the nation will hang upon a single thread," and in 1870, at a suffrage meeting, Eliza R. Snow recalled him saying, "The Constitution of our country would hang as it were by a thread." Each record extends the idea of an 1832 revelation that prophesied "a full end of all nations" (D&C 87:6).[14] Thus, while it is easy to dismiss Rushton and his horses, the underlying idea rests on better evidence.

Many rumors are passed with only vague or loose evidence. For many years, stories circulated that the persecutors of Joseph Smith and the early Saints suffered gruesome and untimely deaths—they were eaten alive by worms, their eyeballs fell out, their flesh fell off. However, the book that popularized these stories employed a very loose definition of "persecutor" and reported vague secondhand information from persons claiming to know the unnamed persecutors. It is impossible to verify information about unnamed persons. By contrast, lawyer Dallin H. Oaks and historian Marvin S. Hill analyzed the life experience of the named persons who were tried and acquitted for Joseph Smith's murder—each of whom went on to live long lives and have successful careers.[15]

The best speakers and writers discuss the evidence they use. They may refer to their sources in the main body of the work, but most often you'll need to look in other places. Sources can be found in electronic works through hyperlinks (of specific words), and in printed materials through footnotes (at the bottom of the page) or endnotes (at the back of the chapter or book). If the author provides only a general essay about sources or a simple list of sources used in the whole work, it is harder to pinpoint the source of specific information. Beware of works that provide no citations for their evidence. When possible, look for authors who have sought out and evaluated every relevant source regarding a particular topic.

💬 Everyday Encounter:
Making Decisions with Evidence

Early in my career, I worked closely with the vice president of a multinational automobile manufacturing company. He was a shrewd leader, a savvy businessman, and a wise observer of human nature—all traits that had brought him to this influential position and helped him make a lot of money. We were launching seven new plants across Latin America, and we worked with a variety of ad hoc teams that the company brought together from around the world. Frequently, one of the newer team members would recommend a course of action with little thought.

"Why should we do that?" the vice president would ask.

"I don't know," the naïve employee would say, "but I think it will work. Trust me."

Hearing those words, I knew we were in for a show.

"Pull out a dollar bill," the vice president would bark. "Why are we here?"

"To make profit for our shareholders."

"And what does it say on the back of that dollar bill?"

"In God we trust," the employee would read aloud.

"That's right!" the vice president would thunder. "And God is the only one I trust. All else, bring data!"

Learning to seek, evaluate, and use evidence will make you a better decision maker in all aspects of your life.

You Try It

Rumor

I heard . . .

Sniff Tests

1. *No evidence.* Because the past is gone, evidence is *required.*
2. *A single piece of evidence.* Be wary of an author who takes a single source from the past and uses it to the exclusion of all other available and relevant sources.
3. *Narrowly selected evidence.* Sometimes authors distort by selecting a few facts to emphasize while ignoring others. For example, this sentence is factually accurate, but by omission it is misleading: "The English alphabet contains the letters A, E, H, and L." All of those letters are, in fact, part of the alphabet, but by omitting twenty-two other letters, the sentence implies that the alphabet has only four letters. Authors who employ this technique typically emphasize loudly that their "facts" are "correct."

4. *Vague evidence.* Vague information from unnamed actors should always be suspect.

Real

Show me the evidence.

Key Concepts

1. To understand history, we must use the pieces of the past as evidence.
2. All evidence is not equal. In general, we prefer evidence that originates closer to the participants and closer to the event.
3. Faith is evidence; it works with study, thinking, and reasoning.
4. We should expect speakers and authors to show us how they know what they know.

Notes

1. John Demos, "Afterword: Notes from, and about, the History/Fiction Borderland," *Rethinking History* 9, nos. 2/3 (June/September 2005): 334.
2. "Plural Marriage in Kirtland and Nauvoo," Gospel Topics Essays, The Church of Jesus Christ of Latter-day Saints, https://www.churchofjesuschrist.org/study/manual/gospel-topics-essays/plural-marriage-in-kirtland-and-nauvoo.
3. "Make-up Artist Stuart Freeborn Dies," BBC News, February 6, 2013; "Five Stories about Stuart Freeborn That Aren't Made Up," *The Week*, February 7, 2013; Aisha Harris, "Hollywood Visionaries Who Resemble Their Own Creations," *Slate*, February 8, 2013.
4. Kenneth W. Baldridge and Lance D. Chase, "The Purported December 7, 1941, Attack on the Hawai'i Temple," in *Voyages of Faith: Explorations in Mormon Pacific History*, ed. Grant Underwood (Provo, UT: Brigham Young University Press, 2000), 165–90; Robert T. Stout Papers, 1957, 1983, Church History Library, Salt Lake City.
5. Richard Lloyd Anderson, *Investigating the Book of Mormon Witnesses* (Salt Lake City: Deseret Book, 1981); Larry E Morris, "Empirical Witnesses of the Gold Plates," *Dialogue: A Journal of Mormon Thought* 52, no. 2 (Summer 2019): 59–84; *Saints: The Story of the*

Church of Jesus Christ in the Latter Days, 4 vols. (Salt Lake City: The Church of Jesus Christ of Latter-day Saints, 2018–), 1:70–71.

6. Neil L. Andersen, "Faith Is Not by Chance, but by Choice," *Ensign*, November 2015, 65; Wayne A. Meeks, ed., *The Harper Collins Study Bible: New Revised Standard Version* (New York: HarperCollins Publishers, 1993), 2263, note 11.1; Sharon Eubank, "Christ: The Light That Shines in Darkness," *Ensign*, May 2019, 75; Anne C. Pingree, "Seeing the Promises Afar Off," *Ensign*, November 2003, 14; see also Robert L. Millet, *Whatever Happened to Faith?* (Salt Lake City: Deseret Book, 2017), 76–87.

7. Desdemona Wadsworth Fullmer, Reminiscences, 1868, Desdemona Wadsworth Fullmer Papers, Church History Library.

8. Elsie Talmage Brandley, in *At the Pulpit: 185 Years of Discourses by Latter-day Saint Women*, ed. Jennifer Reeder and Kate Holbrook (Salt Lake City: Church Historian's Press, 2017), 141.

9. John W. Welch, "The Role of Evidence in Religious Discussion," in *No Weapon Shall Prosper: New Light on Sensitive Issues*, ed. Robert L. Millet (Provo, UT: Religious Studies Center, Brigham Young University, 2011), 259–94.

10. Katharine Salisbury, "Dear Sisters," *Saints' Herald* 33 (May 1, 1886): 260.

11. George Q. Cannon, "Church History," *Juvenile Instructor* 19 (April 1, 1884): 107; "Interview with David Whitmer," *Deseret News*, August 21, 1878, 461; "Mormonism," *Kansas City (MO) Daily Journal*, June 5, 1881, [1]; "Letter from Elder W. H. Kelley," *Saints' Herald*, March 1, 1882, 66–69. Whitmer's interviews have been published in Lyndon W. Cook, ed., *David Whitmer Interviews: A Restoration Witness* (Orem, UT: Grandin Book, 1991).

12. Brigham Young, June 17, 1877, in *Journal of Discourses*, 26 vols. (Liverpool: F. D. Richards, 1855–86), 19:37–39; Cameron J. Packer, "Cumorah's Cave," *Journal of Book of Mormon Studies* 13, no. 1 (2004): 50–57.

13. Don L. Penrod, "Edwin Rushton as the Source of the White Horse Prophecy," *BYU Studies* 49, no. 3 (2010): 75–131. For repudiations, see Joseph F. Smith, in *Eighty-Ninth Semiannual Conference of The Church of Jesus Christ of Latter-day Saints* (Salt Lake City: The Church of Jesus Christ of Latter-day Saints, 1918), 57–58; Lyman Kirkland, "Church Statement on 'White Horse Prophecy' and Political Neutrality," The Newsroom Blog, The Church of Jesus Christ of Latter-day Saints,

January 6, 2010, https://newsroom.churchofjesuschrist.org/blog/church-statement-on-white-horse-prophecy-and-political-neutrality.

14. "Discourse, circa 19 July 1840," in *Documents, Volume 7: September 1839–January 1841*, The Joseph Smith Papers, 342; Brigham Young, "Celebration," *Deseret News Weekly*, July 13, 1854, 63–64; Eliza R. Snow, in "Minutes of 'Great Indignation Meeting,' January 13, 1870," in *The First Fifty Years of Relief Society: Key Documents in Latter-day Saint Women's History*, ed. Jill Mulvay Derr and others (Salt Lake City: Church Historian's Press, 2016), 331.

15. N. B. Lundwall, *The Fate of the Persecutors of the Prophet Joseph Smith* (Salt Lake City: Publishers Press, 1952); Dallin H. Oaks and Marvin S. Hill, *Carthage Conspiracy: The Trial of the Accused Assassins of Joseph Smith* (Urbana: University of Illinois Press, 1975), 89–90, 155–57, 217–21. Richard C. Poulsen found that a myth with the same storyline had circulated much earlier about Quakers and was retold by Nathaniel Hawthorne; see "Fate and the Persecutors of Joseph Smith: Transmutations of an American Myth," *Dialogue: A Journal of Mormon Thought* 11, no. 4 (Winter 1978): 63–70.

CHAPTER 3

I Assumed . . .

"Would you like rock-solid proof that God inspires His prophets in every detail?" The Sunday School teacher had saved his favorite story for the end of class. "The Salt Lake Temple was designed by a prophet. Brigham Young told workers to leave empty shafts in the interior, but nobody knew why. It was only later that engineers discovered the shafts were the perfect size for elevators. The technology of the future was known beforehand. Heaven had prepared the way."

Two things interest me about this story. First, to paraphrase Luke Skywalker in his later years, it is amazing that everything in the story is wrong—Brigham gave only loose advice on the temple's design and encouraged others to flesh out the detail, the exterior stone shell was built long before anyone even thought about the interior, and elevators had been invented more than one hundred years before the Saints arrived in the valley. Second, this story illustrates the most common reason that myths and rumors persist among us— people *assume* they are true without question. It is easy to assume that the people in black-and-white photographs of the 1800s lived primitive lifestyles, but when the Salt Lake Temple interior was finally designed in the late 1880s, the architect included electricity, elevators, and a telephone in the modern, fireproof building.[1]

———————— Q ————————

Assumptions are things we presuppose or take for granted or assert as true or certain without offering any evidence. Historian Steven C. Harper noted, "Assumptions are not knowledge, but often those who hold them do not discern the difference."[2] Typically, an assumption is the starting place for thinking, an opening premise.

Frequently, so-called challenges with Church history stem from bad assumptions in the present. We assume that other people at Church don't have problems, that the Book of Mormon peoples spread across the entire western hemisphere, that prophets never get tricked, or that things were simpler in the past. We assume one should *never* speak of Mother in Heaven or of temple ordinances or of questions that trouble us. Poor assumptions can cause error and harm. In cases like the temple elevators, a person who first feels impressed by this story may later feel betrayed when learning the truth. As we identify and address the assumptions in our thinking, we follow Paul's counsel to "prove all things; hold fast that which is good" (1 Thes. 5:21). It takes humility to change our assumptions after we learn they are incorrect.

Present Assumptions Distort the Past

Assumptions can reveal our present perspectives. Consider the case of a man lying in a gutter. One person sees the man and thinks, "There's a drunken bum." A second person sees the man and thinks, "There's a man who needs help." The facts were the same for each viewer—a man and a gutter—but the assumptions drawn about the situation reflect different viewpoints. The first person assumes that "only drunks are found in gutters," while the second assumes that "people lying in gutters need help." The first person likely believes that individuals are responsible for all that happens to them, whereas the second may believe that problems are also caused by events and forces outside of individual control.[3]

Assumptions often spring from things we deeply value—family, service, truth, fairness. Assumptions are not typically wholly "right" or "wrong," nor can they be proven. Often, we use assumptions as shortcuts to leap to a solution we already desire. For example, when a large wooden vessel of "mammoth size" and "fine craftsmanship" was discovered in the Chicago River in the late 1990s, some Latter-day Saints *assumed* (and greatly desired) that it was one of the barges built by the brother of Jared. This conclusion was desirable because it helped prove the truth of the Book of Mormon. The idea spread quickly on the internet and email lists of the time, and the story resurfaces every now and again. However, closer examination revealed the device to be a prototype fuel tanker that was built and tested by the US Navy in 1942.[4]

Assumptions become embedded in cultures—including our own. For example, in many modern cultures, whiteness is *assumed* to be the default skin color—one might describe a "Hispanic man" or "Black hair," but white people and body parts require no adjective. As another example, because the notion of self-reliant individualism is so prominent in Western culture, readers of the Bible (and artists) usually *assume* that Mary and Joseph traveled to Bethlehem alone. However, based on customs of the era, group travel would have been more likely, especially at a time when everyone was returning to their native cities.[5] This assumed virtue of rugged individualism also makes it particularly hard for many American Latter-day Saints to "submit to all things which the Lord seeth fit to inflict" (Mosiah 3:19) or to accept help from others.

Sometimes assumptions arise from artistic representations of history. For example, painters who depict the translation of the Book of Mormon have placed the plates on a table in view of the scribe, despite the fact that the plates were always hidden from the scribe. Some painters include a lamp or candle in the scene to symbolize the light of revelation, even though Joseph normally translated during daylight hours when there was so much light that he had to place the interpreters in a hat in order to see the message on the stones. Filmmakers who set Book of Mormon stories in the jaguar-filled jungles of Latin America lead people to assume where the Book of Mormon events occurred. Paintings of the mortal Jesus as anything other than a Middle Eastern–looking man do not depict reality but cultural assumptions. The image of handcarts—though used by only 5 percent of pioneers—has come to symbolize *all* pioneer experience. Errors presented visually can solidify into de facto interpretations of the past.

Another common assumption is that there are "lessons of history." Lessons are drawn out of the past by people living in the present; they are not objects to be found lying on the ground like arrowheads in a field. Lessons are interpretations we make. The Book of Mormon illustrates this process nicely. After the lengthy war chapters in the book of Alma, Mormon observes that "many had become hardened, because of the exceedingly great length of the war; and many were softened because of their afflictions" (Alma 62:41). The same lengthy war prompted participants to draw different lessons.

Because the past is gone, we should not make assumptions about it. We should not assume without asking for evidence. We cannot assume that we now know everything. And we cannot assume that our understanding of the past will never change.

Assumptions Cause Harm

So what's the harm with filling in the holes in our knowledge about the past with present assumptions? At the most basic level, assumptions contaminate our thinking. Terryl and Fiona Givens warned that our assumptions "get us off on the wrong foot, obscure our line of sight, or simply misdirect our focus. This is because, all too often, we don't realize the limiting assumptions with which we are working."[6] For example, if you *assume* that revelation comes only to prophets who kneel alone and ask for it, you'll miss the important shift *in the 1830s* to receiving revelation through the deliberations of councils. If you *assume* that the doctrine of the priesthood was solidified long ago, you'll miss the profound *recent* teachings about women, priesthood, and authority.[7]

Next, our incorrect assumptions can cause great personal stress. Speaking at the BYU Women's Conference in 1986, Francine Bennion illustrated how our assumptions can become immobilizing. If we assume that "suffering shouldn't exist, but it does" or that "prayer should cure the problem, but it hasn't— then it is not only the suffering that troubles us but also the great cracks in a universe that should make sense but doesn't." In these moments, "the pain of persons fumbling with their long-held assumptions" becomes so great that "the ancient questions rise afresh, though they had thought them already answered: Why is this happening? Can I stand it? What can I do? What am I? Is God real, or powerful, or good? What is life for? What does he want us to do with it?"[8]

One particularly harmful latter-day assumption imagines a future practice of plural marriage. This idea may cause some women to feel devalued. For men, the idea may condone a wandering eye of preparation, "just in case." Both might worry about the toll on intimacy, together time, or family finances. But there is not a single passage in the standard works that promises a return of plural marriage; its practice is not required for salvation. The most specific scriptural reference to the practice declares monogamy the rule and plural marriage an exception.[9] The pain caused by this assumption is unnecessary and can be avoided.

Finally, our assumptions—especially those woven invisibly into our cultures—can prevent us from accepting truth and change. Joseph Smith observed that the Saints of his day struggled to put off their own bad assumptions. "Even the Saints are slow to understand," he said. "I have tried for a number of years to get the minds of the saints prepared to receive the things of God, but we frequently see some of them, after suffering all they have for the work of God will fly to pieces like glass, as soon as anything comes that is contrary to their traditions."[10] Assumptions that carry cultures and viewpoints can be a source of individual and shared pain.

💬 Everyday Encounter: Believing in Teenagers

Many American adults *assume* that teenagers are rebellious, lazy, and shallow. However, in the past, humans between the ages of thirteen and nineteen accomplished marvelous things—Joan of Arc led her nation to victory at age thirteen, Louis Braille invented a way for blind people to read at age fifteen, Alexander the Great established his first colony at age sixteen, and Malala Yousafzai won the Nobel Peace Prize at age seventeen. In the scriptures we read of Mormon being asked to keep the plates at age ten, seeing Jesus at age fifteen, and becoming a general at age sixteen. Joseph Smith received an answer to his prayer at age fourteen.

What happened? How did young people change from being responsible to reckless? The current stereotypical assumption of teenagers was invented in the United States after World War II. In the early 1900s, large cities sprouted up in which youth experienced crime, child labor, and emotional stress. To protect children from these ills, reformers pushed for mandatory schooling, which pooled young people together for the first time. In the early 1940s, the word "teen-ager" was coined, and after the war an explosion of births produced the largest number of youths in history in the baby boomer generation. Economic stability after the war gave American families more disposable income, and to attract more of that money, advertisers began to market things directly to teenagers—cars, music, clothing, magazines, and movies.[11]

The idea of a "rebellious teenager" was thus invented in the 1950s and 1960s and sold (literally) to the baby boomer generation of youngsters, who grew up and passed this invented "tradition" down to their children, grandchildren, and now great-grandchildren in the twenty-first century. If we *assume* young men and women will act rebelliously, then when they do, they are simply meeting our expectations! In rebellion against my cultural surroundings and in support of the divine nature and potential of my children, I frequently tell them that "I don't believe in teenagers!"

Change Your Assumptions

Many of the myths we carry within us are linked to bad assumptions. To protect ourselves, we must develop the awareness to *see* our assumptions, such as the common ones identified in Appendix B, and the humility to *change* them. "Assuming is intellectually and spiritually lazy," observed Harper. "It is arrogant. It is easy."[12] By contrast, exposing the assumptions hidden in our culture, worldview, and subconscious requires hard, thoughtful work.

⚡ Thinking Habit:
Change Your Assumptions

Introspection	Humility
"Why do I think this?"	"I will stop thinking in this unhelpful way."

The best way to see our own assumptions is through introspective questioning. In teaching how to care for the poor, the Nephite King Benjamin warned against using an individualistic assumption—that "the man has brought upon himself his misery"—as a justification for withholding service. He urged his listeners to see beyond their assumptions by asking questions: "Are we not all beggars? Do we not all depend upon the same Being, even God, for all the substance which we have? . . . Has [God] suffered that ye have begged in vain?" (Mosiah 4:17, 19–20). We must pull unstated ideas out of our subconscious into our consciousness where they can be analyzed.

Ask why. To identify our assumptions, we might begin with a simple "Why?" Other helpful questions include "How do I know that?" or "Will you tell me more?" Each of these questions asks for evidence. Frequently the answer to the first "why" will lead to a restatement of the assumption or to a general viewpoint. Keep asking why if the responses are emotional or defensive. It may take three, or four, or five "whys" before you get to the root.

💬 Everyday Encounter: Good Parents Encourage Why Questions

Little children are good at asking questions . . . about everything. They ask the important *why* questions, sometimes to the point of exasperating the parents—"Why is it warm outside? Why is the sun warm? Why is it made of fire?" This ability to ask *why* questions is one of the blessed traits of children, and it is unfortunate that ineffective schooling and peer pressure often lead people to stop asking questions openly. The most effective parents will encourage their children to ask and will take the time to answer.

Look for the hidden "if." One way to find your assumptions is to ask where an "if" statement might be hiding. Often the *assumed* "if" statement is hiding beneath a *stated* "if." For example, the question "If the Church is true, then why do its members misbehave?" contains a hidden assumption that members of a true church cannot misbehave—*if* people misbehave, they are not true

Church members. This assumption bears no doctrinal or historical support. Another way to get at hidden ifs is by asking, "What has to be true about the world generally in order for this specific statement to be true?"

Be wary of exaggeration. Answers that use words such as *always* or *never* or *all of* or *none of* suggest that we need to keep asking questions to move beyond a generalized assumption.

Develop humility. When we find ourselves making an unwarranted assumption, we need the humility to change. I am inspired by the example of Joseph Fielding Smith. In 1958 he wrote, "It is doubtful that man will ever be permitted to make any instrument or ship to travel through space and visit the moon or any distant planet." Eleven years later, the Apollo 11 mission succeeded, and the following year Elder Smith became president of the Church. He was asked at a press conference about his previous statement, and he replied humbly, "Well, I was wrong, wasn't I?"[13] Admitting the errors in our own thinking is sometimes the most difficult part of understanding history.

Learn to feel empathy. Another antidote to making assumptions is to develop the capacity to feel empathy for others, both those around us and those in the past. Empathy means to understand "another person's feelings, thoughts, and condition from their perspective, rather than our own."[14] We often encourage empathy by saying something like "Put yourself in their shoes," but a more effective way to feel empathy is to observe and imagine how the person feels (rather than how you would feel if you were them). Empathy helps us care, mourn, and keep the commandments to love our neighbors and love our enemies (Matt. 5:44; 22:39). Empathy helps us see that a caricaturized mascot depicting a minority group is both inaccurate and harmful. It is selfish to consider that our thoughts, desires, pains, or hopes are more important than those of others. Empathy is a way to understand others (and ourselves) and leads to increased compassion.[15]

> **Everyday Encounter:**
> **Good Leaders Question Assumptions**
>
> The ability to question assumptions is "an increasingly desired skill in the job market."[16] In discussions of long-term strategy, you might ask *how* you know your business will increase, whether you know what your customers *actually* feel, or *why* you think the future will unfold the way you expect. You might consider alternatives when making choices about your customers, suppliers, or products. In problem-solving conversations, the ability to question assumptions can expose the root of a problem. The Toyota Motor Corporation pioneered a problem-solving method called the "5 Whys," which asks why five times in order to move beyond assumptions and identify the root causes of a problem, focusing on a failure of process rather than a failure of people.

You Try It

Rumor

I assumed . . .

Sniff Tests

1. *Exaggerated descriptions (hyperbole).* An unstated assumption lies beneath words such as *always, never, no one, nobody, everyone, everybody.*
2. *More emotion than evidence.* Our cultures inform our assumptions about the propriety of wealth, the reliability of the media, the importance of individuals and community, which

language(s) should be spoken, and which political party is best. Our religious culture informs how we think about dress standards, the appropriate number of children, the value of pioneer heritage, and the location of the "mission field." If any of these topics prompted feelings of emotion or defensiveness, you are likely overly influenced by cultural assumptions.

Real

Present assumptions distort the past.

Key Concepts

1. Assumptions are things we presuppose or take for granted or assert as true without offering any evidence. They are often based on personal viewpoints and values and may be hidden in our culture.

2. Erroneous assumptions can contaminate our thinking, cause personal stress, and prevent us from accepting the truth.

3. Identify your assumptions by asking why (repeatedly), by asking what unstated things must also be true for your assumption to be true, and by considering other options.

4. Develop the humility to change your assumptions when you discover they are incorrect.

Notes

1. Paul C. Richards, "The Salt Lake Temple Infrastructure: Studying It Out in Their Minds," *BYU Studies* 36, no. 2 (1996–97): 212–18.

2. Steven C. Harper, *Joseph Smith's First Vision: A Guide to the Historical Accounts* (Salt Lake City: Deseret Book, 2012), 7.

3. Richard Paul and Linda Elder, *Critical Thinking: Tools for Taking Charge of Your Learning and Your Life* (Upper Saddle River, NJ: Prentice Hall, 2001), 72.

4. Peter Kendall, "Answers Surface for Lake Enigma," *Chicago Tribune*, February 8, 1999, N1.

5. E. Randolph Richards and Brandon J. O'Brien, *Misreading*

Scripture with Western Eyes: Removing Cultural Blinders to Better Understand the Bible (Downers Grove, IL: InterVarsity Press, 2012), 100–101.

6. Terryl Givens and Fiona Givens, *The Crucible of Doubt: Reflections on the Quest for Faith* (Salt Lake City: Deseret Book, 2014), 2.

7. See Jean B. Bingham, "United in Accomplishing God's Work," *Ensign*, May 2020, 60–63; Russell M. Nelson, "A Plea to My Sisters," *Ensign*, November 2015, 95–98; Dallin H. Oaks, "The Keys and Authority of the Priesthood," *Ensign*, May 2014, 49–52.

8. Francine R. Bennion, in *At the Pulpit: 185 Years of Discourses by Latter-day Saint Women*, ed. Jennifer Reeder and Kate Holbrook (Salt Lake City: Church Historian's Press, 2017), 221.

9. See Jacob 2:27–30; D&C 49:15–17; Marcus B. Nash, "The New and Everlasting Covenant," *Ensign*, December 2015, 44–46; *Saints: The Story of the Church of Jesus Christ in the Latter Days*, 4 vols. (Salt Lake City: The Church of Jesus Christ of Latter-day Saints, 2018–), 1:121, 443.

10. Joseph Smith, January 21, 1844, in "History, 1838–1856, volume E-1 [1 July 1843–30 April 1844]," p. 1867, The Joseph Smith Papers, https://www.josephsmithpapers.org/paper-summary/history-1838-1856-volume-e-1-1-july-1843-30-april-1844/239.

11. See Grace Palladino, *Teenagers: An American History* (New York: Basic Books, 1996); Thomas Hine, *The Rise and Fall of the American Teenager* (New York: Perennial, 1999); Jon Savage, *Teenage: The Prehistory of Youth Culture, 1875–1945* (New York: Penguin Books, 2007).

12. Harper, *Joseph Smith's First Vision*, 7.

13. Joseph Fielding Smith, *Answers to Gospel Questions* (Salt Lake City: Deseret Book, 1957), 2:191; David Farnsworth, personal reminiscence of press conference, reported in Adam Kotter, "When Doubts and Questions Arise," *Ensign*, March 2015, 39.

14. "Developing the Empathy to Minister," *Ensign*, February 2019, 9.

15. "'Walking a Mile in Their Shoes' May Be Hazardous to Your Health: Researcher Says How We Arrive at Empathy Is as Important as Being Empathetic," ScienceDaily, May 11, 2017, https://www.sciencedaily.com/releases/2017/05/170511152133.htm.

16. Helen Lee Bouygues, "3 Simple Habits to Improve Your Critical Thinking," *Harvard Business Review*, May 6, 2019.

CHAPTER 4

Let the Facts
Speak for Themselves

Consider two facts about the late nineteenth-century Latter-day Saint Martha Hughes Cannon. Fact 1: Cannon was a physician. She earned four college degrees by age twenty-five in the fields of chemistry, medicine, pharmacy, and oratory. In 1882 she became the resident obstetric physician at Deseret Hospital in Salt Lake City, where she practiced medicine, lectured, and trained nurses. Fact 2: Cannon was the first woman elected as a state senator in the United States. In 1896 she ran as a Democrat in Utah and beat her husband, Angus M. Cannon, who ran as a Republican. She sponsored successful legislation to care for the deaf and blind, protect female employees, and create a state board of health.[1] Now, pay attention to the different ways I could present these two facts:

1. Cannon was a physician, but she was a state senator.
2. Though Cannon was a physician, she was a state senator.
3. While Cannon was a physician, she was a state senator.
4. Cannon was both a physician and a state senator.
5. Cannon, being a physician, was a state senator.

Each of these five presentations suggests a slightly different relationship between the two established facts. Did the two facts exist in some degree of opposition? (options 1 and 2). Did the two facts somehow complement each other? (options 3 and 4). Did one fact

cause the other? (option 5).[2] I hope you can see that the way I connect historical facts deeply influences their meaning!

Historical facts do not "speak for themselves." There are many
facts in history, but because the past is gone, the surviving facts need
to be explained in context to understand them. As a result there
is no history without interpretation. All facts must be interpreted.
This makes facts "squishy." If there are "cold, hard facts" in history,
they are mostly boring or useless unless someone can bring them
to life in a meaningful way. Facts don't speak, but storytellers do;
therefore, it is essential to understand how interpretation happens,
why storytellers speak the way they do, and how their stories work.

Interpretation Happens

Everyone must interpret history—no matter if the person is
a researcher, writer, speaker, painter, or film director. People make
interpretations as they select sources, assemble evidence, question
present assumptions, and tell stories. All history is interpreted.

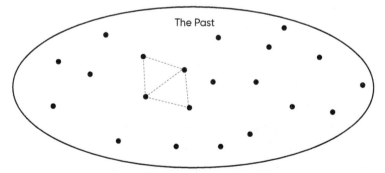

Imagine again that the past is represented by an oval, and dots
represent the pieces of the past that survive into the present. These
dots clearly do not tell a complete story, so we must look for more
pieces. With one piece in hand, we might declare of the large oval
that "the past was a dot." Finding a second piece, we connect the
two and say, "The past was a line." The discovery of a third piece

changes our understanding to see that "the past was a triangle." With the fourth piece, things get interesting. If the fourth piece lies within the boundary of our triangle, then we feel more confident that the past really was a triangle. But if it lies outside the boundary, we have to revise everything and conclude that "the past was a square" (or a rhombus or a diamond, depending on your perspective).

And so the process continues as we discover more pieces and determine how the new pieces fit with what we already know. Unlike assembling the pieces of a puzzle, we don't have all of the pieces—we don't even know how many there are—and we don't have a completed photograph to guide us. Sometimes, we must humbly confess that we don't really know how the pieces relate to each other or to the larger whole.

Because interpretation *always* happens, people may come away with new interpretations that differ from previous ones. History is erroneously presented to us as if it were complete, settled, done. But we must regularly revise our understanding of history. Sometimes, a new interpretation arises because a new piece of the past is discovered that sheds new light on an old topic. Other times we make new connections between previously known sources that yield new insights. Sometimes we examine old sources with new questions based on new needs that arise in the present. Sometimes we find that a cherished story has been told based on incomplete information. As a result, it is okay to revise what we know about history.

Some people get upset when new interpretations revise what we knew before. People are correct when they point out that the past has not changed since they were in school—it was gone then, and it remains gone now. But hopefully, the ongoing process of interpretation improves our entire understanding. No one would want to go to a dentist who worked only based on what was known about teeth in the 1950s, and no one should want only the stories of history they heard as a child. Latter-day Saint teachings include the provision that

"God . . . will yet reveal many great and important things" (A of F 1:9) and that humans learn things "line upon line, precept upon precept, here a little and there a little" (2 Ne. 28:30; see also Isa. 28:10).

The question is not whether to revise or not to revise but rather how to revise well. The process of evaluation allows for revelation and divine guidance to influence our careful thinking. The people who lived in the past belonged to their own times and places and circumstances. To have charity for their differences and empathy for their experiences, we must begin with humility about our own limitations. When new sources are discovered that provide new insight, it requires humility to revise our understanding.

Thus we see that the facts of history do not—cannot—"speak" for themselves. The facts originate as pieces of *the past* that must be recorded, saved, discovered, and used. In Lehi's language, facts are "things to be acted upon" (2 Ne. 2:14). The next question rightly follows: Who acts upon the facts? Or, who tells the *stories* about the past in the present? And why?

💬 Everyday Encounter:
Interpreting Flirtatious Facts

Perhaps no facts are subject to as many interpretations as those that occur in the course of flirting and dating. Did he wink at me or just blink? Did she dot her *i* with a circle or a heart? He didn't include an emoji in his text message—is he mad at me? Why is she taking so long to reply? How many romantic comedies are premised on the misinterpretation of the facts of interpersonal communication? Knowing that facts *don't* speak can help you turn your attention to the speaker's interpretation. Often the simplest way to improve your interpretation of the facts is to ask a follow-up question: "What do you mean by . . . ?" One of the ways to identify if you've found a compatible life partner is the ease with which you are willing to work to interpret one another's communication.

Facts Don't Speak—Storytellers Do

Stories about history have been told by people in the past and continue to be told by people living today. The earliest stories were told by those who participated in the events, and these accounts typically describe what the individuals experienced and why it was important to them. Some events prompt many participants to relate their experiences. Other events get forgotten until a later experience calls them to mind. Some participants tell their stories on multiple occasions to different audiences. But the participants have no say, as the musical *Hamilton* aptly notes, in "who lives, who dies, who tells your story." Stories get collected and retold by other people for many reasons—to entertain an audience, instill gratitude, sell a product, shape public opinion, inspire by example, or lobby for change. The stories are spoken, written down, or created in other forms by historians as well as by journalists, public figures, politicians, philosophers, theorists, scientists, advertisers, parents, and leaders. Each of these stories is an interpretation of the past—built on factual pieces and influenced by the teller's goals and perspective.

Every storyteller demonstrates a point of view or perspective about the past. Perspectives are influenced by multiple and complexly related factors including education, gender, age, ethnicity, social class, cultural upbringing, profession, political views, economic interest, life experience, peer group, faith, emotional state, and historical context. Eyewitnesses to the same event tell different stories because they bring different perspectives—different ideas, priorities, attitudes, beliefs, and motives. Sometimes these differences are so great that two people at the same event don't even have the same experience.

The combination of a person's perspective and goal is often called *bias*. Bias is typically described as a negative attribute, and weaker thinkers can identify bias only in others. However, every storyteller—including you and me—has bias. Your personal perspective and goals differ from those of people around you as well as from those of people in the past. We must also consider why an author expresses a view in a particular way. Interpretations of the past can range from a straightforward recitation of the content of sources to pure fiction that merely invokes historical people and places while inventing dialogue, details, and meanings. Because the past is gone, we can never really obtain an objective history. The best option is to evaluate the surviving pieces while recognizing that the full story can never be recovered.

Four Layers of Storytelling

One helpful way to discern the motives and methods of a storyteller is to pay attention to four layers of storytelling—storyline, structure, situation, and script.[3] For example, the Book of Mormon prophet Nephi wrote about his experiences in the wilderness and at sea (storyline) after he had arrived in the promised land (situation). He related episodes about traveling from and to Jerusalem (structure) and made comparisons to the people of Israel in the wilderness (script).

🔆 Thinking Habit:
Analyze the Four Layers of Storytelling

Storyline	The subject, characters, and plot
Structure	The story's ending and beginning, how it is organized
Situation	The time and place of the storyteller
Script	A general template, often hidden, for a specific story

The first layer of a story about the past is the stated *storyline*. The storyline is visible right on the surface and is what the story is about—the people and events in a specific time and place. In a work of fiction, this layer may be called "the plot." In a work of history, the storyline provides information about the past. We can evaluate a storyline by investigating the accuracy of the details and whether the information is presented coherently.

The storyline nestles within the second layer of the story—*structure*. The example of physician and senator Mattie Cannon demonstrates the impact of sentence-level structure, but larger structures are also at play. How does the story begin? How does it end? What are the turning points? Is the story told through words, pictures, or statues? In storytelling, the end is the most important part of the structure because all of the development moves toward that important outcome and the resolution of tension—the end of a war, the election of a president, the invention of a product. For example, the *Harry Potter* novels feature a clear structure that pulls Harry through escalating, annual confrontations that culminate in a live-or-die showdown with the villain Voldemort. The structure of a story provides important clues to the teller's perspective and motives. What vocabulary does the teller choose to use? How is the teller persuading the hearer? You'll also want to pay attention to the teller's tone and judge if you can trust the teller.

Closely related to the stated storyline and the structure is a third layer: the *situation* of the story's creation. When and where was the story told? How did the teller gather the information and decide what and how to share? Why was the story told? To whom was the teller speaking? Why, for example, did Joseph Smith prepare a history in the late 1830s? To respond to false reports "by evil-disposed and designing persons" (JS—H 1:1). Why were the first affidavits about plural marriage in 1840s Nauvoo not gathered until the 1860s? Because they were assembled to refute Joseph Smith's sons who had arrived in Salt Lake City and announced their father had never practiced it. Sometimes the teller leaves visible clues about the situation in the preface of a book or on a plaque on the backside of a monument. Frequently, however, this layer is hidden.

The situation comprises important context that helps us understand the meaning of history. The book *Revelations in Context* describes the situations of the revelations received by Joseph Smith. The authors recommend asking situational questions such as these: "What were the questions that prompted the revelations? What did the Lord's responses mean to those to whom they were addressed? How did those who heard the revelations respond to new teachings?"[4] In answering these questions themselves, the authors connect Joseph Smith's revelations with biblical ideas that permeated early nineteenth-century culture, political efforts to relocate Native Americans, activities of other Christian preachers, practices of hygiene and temperance, and so on.

🗨 Everyday Encounter:
Understanding the Situation of Scriptural Parables

Joseph Smith taught that one should survey the situation of the Savior's parables in order to understand them. He said, "I have [a] Key by which I understand the scripture—I inquire what was the question which drew out the answer."[5] This approach considers the contents of the parable within the situation of the conversations the Savior had with those around Him.

The deepest layer of a story exerts a powerful controlling influence on the storyline, the structure, and the situation. The *script* is a general template for the specific story being told by the storyteller.[6] Some scripts are helpful, and indeed we cannot really function without them; others, however, may inhibit our success and should be questioned. Scripts are often hidden in our culture and assumptions. Some scripts operate at a small scale, such as when we invoke a victim script ("it was not my fault") or a villain script ("it was all his fault") or a helpless script ("there is nothing we can do").[7] But scripts also operate at far larger and deeper levels. Examples include the progress script, the idea of ongoing progress throughout Western Civilization from past to present; the revolution script of sudden dramatic upheaval that changed everything; the American Dream script that all it takes is hard work to "pull yourself up by your bootstraps"; the culture war script of an evenly and unendingly divided partisan America, and the script of the common people versus the elites. Even the idea that history has no meaning and is just "one fact after another" forms a script that presents information as random, unconnected events.

Some of the more popular scripts rise to the level of myths, compelling stories that form part of our invisible culture. "Inherited ideas are a curious thing," said the inventor in Mark Twain's *A Connecticut Yankee in King Arthur's Court*. They flow "in ruts worn deep by time and habit, and the man who should have proposed to divert them by reason and argument would have had a long contract on his hands."[8] Most of the time, people don't know that they have accepted an underlying script, which gets handed down across time as part of culture and tradition.

We can illustrate how scripts work with Joseph Smith. There is a fixed body of facts that we know about his life, but applying different scripts produces different interpretations. The progress script can be used to illustrate how the world was gradually prepared for the Restoration; this interpretation often mentions the rise of printing, the Reformation, and the establishment of the United States as precursors to religious progress and eventually the full restoration of the gospel. Zeroing in on the Smith family, we could use the American Dream script to tell a story about a poor family of religious seekers who bounced around New England looking for economic stability and religious certainty before making their way to New York and eventually Illinois, where Joseph wielded religious and political power. We might adopt the people-versus-elites script to tell of Joseph sending Martin Harris to meet with the scholars in

New York City who refused to translate the characters, so Joseph, the poor unlearned farmer, had to do what the learned elites could not. We can easily apply these three different scripts with very little need for facts, filling in the details from cultural experience rather than specific historical information.[9]

Good stories are powerful, yet they also present a potential danger to our best understanding of the past. Information about the past is incomplete and sometimes contradictory, but our minds prefer completion and a lack of contradiction. "Historical narratives seduce you into thinking you really understand what's going on and why things happened, but most of it is guessing people's motives and their inner thoughts," observed philosopher Alex Rosenberg. When "you're satisfied psychologically by the narrative, and it connects the dots," then "it allays your curiosity" and it "has seduced you into a false account, and now you think you understand."[10] As a result, people easily *assume* that's the way it happened.

💬 Everyday Encounter: Using Scripts to Improve Your Teaching

A teacher who wants a gospel message to sink into the hearts of the students would be wise to call attention to the existing scripts. Instead of diving into the facts of a gospel story, a teacher might first give a brief big-picture outline to create a script for the specifics that will follow. President Boyd K. Packer encouraged seminary teachers to begin each year by teaching the plan of salvation as the framework for the class. The *Come, Follow Me* lesson on the book of Revelation introduces the plan of salvation as a script by which to make sense of the book's rich symbolism about premortal, mortal, and postmortal experiences.[11] If you don't provide a script for your students, your lessons will either get attached to whatever script they already have . . . or perhaps just be forgotten.

You Try It

Rumor

Let the facts speak for themselves.

Sniff Tests

1. *Hiding the interpretive process.* An author may claim to be objective or to present "just the facts" or to "let the documents speak for themselves." The author may say that "History teaches us . . ." or "History proves . . ." or "History predicts . . ." These phrases cover up the author's methods of selecting the facts and interpreting evidence; they hide the fact that the storyteller already made judgments to interpret the lessons of history.

2. *"We'll await the judgment of history."* History and time do not make judgments. People do.

Real

Facts don't speak—storytellers do.

Key Concepts

1. Every telling of history is an interpretation of the pieces of the past that remain.

2. Storytellers have different perspectives, motives, and skill.

3. Every story contains layers, including a surface storyline, a formal structure, an authorial situation, and an underlying script.

Notes

1. Jonathan A. Stapley and Constance L. Lieber, "'Do Some Little Good While We Live': Martha Hughes Cannon (1857–1932)," in *Women of Faith in the Latter Days,* 4 vols., ed. Richard E. Turley and Brittany A. Chapman (Salt Lake City: Deseret Book, 2014), 3:13–27. Martha was the fourth of Angus's six plural wives.

2. Adapted from Sam Wineburg, "The Cognitive Representation of Historical Texts," in *Teaching and Learning in History*, ed. Gaea Leinhardt, Isabel L. Beck, and Catherine Stainton (Hillsdale, N.J.: Lawrence Erlbaum Associates, 1994), 114.

3. Adapted from Jeretz Topolski, "The Structure of Historical Narratives and the Teaching of History," in *Learning and Reasoning in History*, ed. James F. Voss and Mario Carretero (London: Woburn Press, 1998), 9–22.

4. Matthew McBride and James Goldberg, eds., *Revelations in Context: The Stories behind the Sections of the Doctrine and Covenants* (Salt Lake City: The Church of Jesus Christ of Latter-day Saints, 2016), vii.

5. "Journal, December 1842–June 1844; Book 1, 21 December 1842–10 March 1843," p. [157] (January 29, 1843), The Joseph Smith Papers, https://www.josephsmithpapers.org/paper-summary/journal-december-1842-june-1844-book-1-21-december-1842-10-march-1843/165.

6. Other writers use the terms *schema* or *schematic narrative* for this layer. James V. Wertsch, "Specific Narratives and Schematic Narrative Templates," in *Theorizing Historical Consciousness*, ed. Peter Seixas (Toronto: University of Toronto Press, 2004), 49–62.

7. Kerry Patterson and others, *Crucial Conversations: Tools for Talking When Stakes Are High* (New York: McGraw-Hill, 2002), 93–118.

8. Mark Twain, *A Connecticut Yankee in King Arthur's Court* (New York: Oxford University Press, 1996), 98.

9. Margaret G. McKeown and Isabel L. Beck, "Making Sense of Accounts of History: Why Don't and How They Might," in *Teaching and Learning in History*, ed. Gaea Leinhardt, Isabel L. Beck, and Catherine Stainton (Hillsdale, N.J.: Lawrence Earlbaum Associates, 1994), 1–26.

10. Alex Rosenberg, in Angela Chen, "A Philosopher Explains How Our Addiction to Stories Keeps Us from Understanding History," *The Verge*, October 5, 2018, https://www.theverge.com/2018/10/5/17940650/how-history-gets-things-wrong-alex-rosenberg-interview-neuroscience-stories.

11. Boyd K. Packer, *Teach Ye Diligently* (Salt Lake City: Deseret Book, 1991), 141–43; *Come, Follow Me—For Individuals and Families, New Testament 2019: Living, Learning, and Teaching the Gospel of Jesus Christ* (Salt Lake City: The Church of Jesus Christ of Latter-day Saints, 2019), 191.

CHAPTER 5

There Are Two
Sides to Every Story

Somehow, no matter the topic, every Sunday School class ended up as a two-sided debate. One week, Reed praised his mission president for emphasizing "strict obedience," but William found success through "the spirit of the law." Another time, Catarina insisted everyone take sides on whether "happiness" was different than "joy." In October, near Columbus Day, Mario proudly boasted of his Italian ancestry, while Jared remembered that European "conquest" had meant suffering and displacement for his Native ancestors. At Christmas, Jedediah asserted Latter-day Saints should sing only those few "core" hymns that everyone knows, while Chris advocated the appreciation of all uplifting music.

Hiding beneath the details of each of these debates lies a common but harmful script—the myth that there are *only* two sides to every story and that we must give *equal* time to both sides in order to be fair, balanced, or truthful. This myth permeates our public culture as journalists report "both sides" of a story, politicians criticize the "other" party, and cable news hosts debate "for or against" the issue of the day. The biggest problem with this script is that the most important questions that we face usually can be approached in more than two useful ways. Many times, those who want to share misinformation will also invoke this false-balance script to demand airtime for ideas with little merit. We must actively work to resist this powerful myth. The antidote to oversimplifying into either/or options involves telling longer stories that embrace complexity and nuance.

More Than Either/Or

Either/or views of history often begin with an oversimplified or romanticized view of the past. People *assume* the past was a simpler and safer time, like the scenes in a Norman Rockwell painting. Frequently, oversimplification happens through *omission*. In a method I call the "missing middle," a story recounts the beginning of something and then jumps to the present day. For example, a commentator may link a political party of the 1860s with a party with the same name today, ignoring all of the significant changes that happened to that party in between then and now. The history of Relief Society is often told this way, opening with the founding of the Female Relief Society in Nauvoo before describing present conditions. This approach ignores everything that happened in between, including that the Relief Society was disbanded and then later reconstituted, that its leaders and members advocated for woman's suffrage, and that Relief Society women managed hospitals, silk production, and other local industries.[1]

In another method of oversimplification, the origins of a story are forgotten. Many Latter-day Saints do not know that modern Church humanitarian, welfare, and social service efforts trace their roots *all the way back* to the Relief Society's nineteenth-century grain storage program. Sometimes information is simply left out. There *were* women in the march of Zion's Camp—a fact omitted in many accounts of that historic march.[2]

The most common way that people oversimplify is by reducing an issue to a pair of opposites—good or evil, members or nonmembers, Democrats or Republicans, Black citizens or White police, faith or doubt. These binary pairings flatten the richness of human experience into two oversimplified either/or options. Bruce and Marie Hafen pointed out that "such polarizing dichotomies not only don't help us, they often interfere with genuine spiritual growth." Though we may be tempted to think in opposites, let's remember, as Lloyd D. Newell observed, "whenever two gospel truths seem to contradict each other, that's usually a sign that we lack complete understanding."[3]

Latter-day Saint scripture reveals that there is more to life than either/or. One of the most daring revelations taught by Joseph Smith rejected a binary view of heaven and hell in favor of a heaven with *three* kingdoms of glory (D&C 76). Jesus taught of wise and foolish men (Matt. 7:24–27), but He also taught of *six* different reactions to the word of God when sowed among varying soil types (Matt. 13:1–9). The Book of Mormon enters a debate about the truth or error of the Bible, declaring, "*Yes, and.*" Yes, the Bible has truth and errors, *and* there are additional scriptural records from the Nephites, the isles of the sea, and all other nations. The New Testament tells the story of a father who simultaneously professes belief *and* unbelief in Jesus while asking for a blessing for his son (Mark 9:24).

Even the oft-cited teachings about opposition from Lehi turn out, on closer inspection, to reveal more than simple opposites. Reading under the influence of dualistic thinking, we might try to stack up the binaries Lehi mentions to read like this:

For it must needs be, that there is an opposition in all things.
If not so, my firstborn in the wilderness,
righteousness could not be brought to pass,   neither wickedness,
               neither holiness   nor misery,
                  neither good   nor bad.
Wherefore, all things must needs be a compound in one; wherefore,

if it should be one body it must needs remain as dead,

having no life	neither death,
nor corruption	nor incorruption,
happiness	nor misery,
neither sense	nor insensibility. (2 Ne. 2:11)

This common reading forces the verse into two columns of opposites. But a closer look reveals that "misery" opposes both "holiness" *and* "happiness" and that the order of one of the pairs is reversed so that "corruption" lines up on the same side as "life" and "happiness." If we think about the passage again, we might look not for "opposites" but for "opposition"—the word that *actually* appears in the text and which does not reduce options to simple binaries. Accordingly, we might illustrate the concepts not as two columns but as a thirteen-sided object in which all of the elements can be connected to create "opposition in all things."

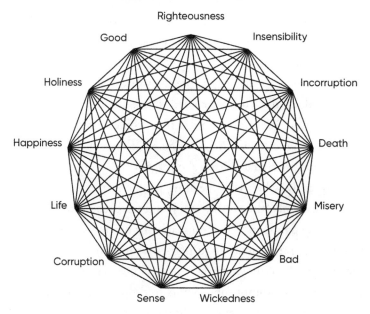

In this reading, "death" can link with "good" when it is time for a person to pass on, and "life" can link with "misery" and "bad" as we make sense of daily stresses and enduring trials. Our scriptures provide room for a complete view of past and present.

🗨 Everyday Encounter:
Seeing beyond "Us" and "the World"

An oversimplified view of scriptural teachings about "the world" can negatively influence our behavior. Talks, conversations, and social media posts commonly mention a dichotomy between "us" and "the world." This abbreviated usage omits the richness of scriptural teachings wherein the term *world* refers to our physical earth and other worlds created by God as well as to various geographical locations around the earth.

When referring to people, "the world" describes all persons who live on earth and all persons who are redeemed by "the Savior of the world." Sometimes the term simply differentiates what happens in private from what happens in public, or "before the world." Many scriptures use *world* not in reference to space but to time, speaking of our experiences "before the world was made," "in this world," and "in the world to come." There are, indeed, scriptural uses of the term "the world" to describe people who do not (or do not yet) belong to the Church, but many of these verses also identify more precise characteristics about them.[4]

Frequently, when well-meaning people implement a binary view of "us" and "the world," they end up causing unintended harm. Some Saints may raise unnecessary barriers against others when they use this binary to justify speaking disparagingly or less welcomingly about those of other faiths. Conversely, relying on this dichotomy may prompt some Saints to drop appropriate barriers against fellow Saints, thereby falling prey to scammers or sexual predators or apostates who appear in the sheep's clothing of membership (see Matt. 7:15; Acts 20:29–30).

It's a Long Story

One antidote for oversimplified opposites is to talk about the past as a "long story." The past was complicated and nuanced, but the complexities of the past are no excuse for not seeking clear understanding. After quoting thirteen chapters from Isaiah, Nephi states that his "soul delighteth in plainness" (2 Ne. 25:4) so he offers six chapters of his own, plainer commentary. Isaiah wrote "many things which were hard for many . . . people to understand" (2 Ne. 25:1), including complex prophecies rich with historical connections and multiple meanings. For Nephi, speaking plainly did not mean oversimplifying but rather clarity and completeness.

One concept that can help us make sense of the complexity of the past is *contingency*. A contingency is a possible event that cannot be predicted with certainty—the young college student might choose a path that leads to a quick job or she might go to graduate school. Looking forward, we find uncertainties, unknowns, and surprises lurking behind every corner. Looking backward, contingency represents decision points where some options were closed off while others opened up. There were always more "coulds" than "dids." Because we know the outcomes, we tend to ignore or forget the false starts, the experiments, the roads not taken, the many options considered before a decision was made. The sum total of events is not predetermined along a single line but clustered around decision points. It takes work to reconstruct past experiences that were open ended, with outcomes unknown. The best histories re-create all of the potential options and emotions.

A second concept essential to understanding a complete picture is *causation*. Many reasons, decisions, and factors contributed to what happened in the past. Some changes are caused by the choices of actors, whether individual humans or institutions. Decision makers and influencers far removed from the scene shape the laws and culture that infuse everyday life. There are many characters and many plot lines that converge in multiple ways on multiple occasions, resulting in both short- and long-term consequences. Frequently, changes in one area of experience spill over to others. The outcome may not be what the participants predicted or even intended. For example, the invention of the automobile changed transportation history, but its backseat also changed dating and courtship practices. In time, the room that had hosted courtship visits—the parlor—ceased to be included in home floorplans. At the intersection of individuals' choices and general conditions, there are many ways to see what caused events of the past.

One way to embrace the completeness of the past is by imagining not just a single timeline of events but several lines that converge like spokes on a pioneer wagon wheel. For example, an oversimplified story about the ending of the ban on priesthood and temple participation by Black Latter-day Saints would contain a single line that ends with President Spencer W. Kimball praying and receiving a revelation to end the ban (this oversimplified story frequently introduces an error that "no one had asked before," when in reality the Brethren had been studying and praying about changing the practice since at least the 1910s).

To the important spoke of President Kimball's humble determination, we can add many other lines of development—the civil rights movement and increasing racial integration changed views in the United States; African nations obtained independence from colonial powers; Church leaders gradually removed the priesthood restriction from Pacific Islanders and aboriginal peoples; the Church was growing across the earth, and people of many nations accepted the gospel, including Black converts in Africa and the Americas; internal studies of Church history, doctrine, and policy clarified uncertainties about the practice's origins and the potential for a reve-latory change; members of the Quorum of the Twelve came to una-nimity of agreement; and the Saints sustained the revelation by com-mon consent.[5] The quest to eliminate racism continues to this day.

The long complexity of the past is frequently one of the first victims of storytelling. Consider the last film version of a pioneer story that you watched. Chances are, the story focused on a family or two in a single pioneer company. Most likely, the story's pro-tagonists pulled a handcart alone across a barren landscape. You watched them struggle uphill, shiver in the blowing snow, ration their food, and weep at the graveside of their infant child. Perhaps you, too, shed a tear, before rejoicing at a scene of dramatic rescue.

The *complete* history of the pioneers turns out to be far richer and far more interesting. First, the scale was staggering—approxi-mately sixty thousand people made the journey, over the space of twenty years, as part of nearly four hundred companies. Handcarts were used by only about 5 percent of the pioneers; the rest came by wagon or horseback or on foot. But even among the ten handcart companies, eight made the journey without any significant issues. Viewed from a complete perspective, most of the pioneers didn't die; the mortality rate on the trail was only slightly higher than the national rate. One-third of the companies made the trek without a single death. And the pioneers also had fun during the journey! Their diaries, letters, and other records show that in addition to completing the tasks and chores of traveling, they formed friend-ships, helped one another, sang and danced, hunted game, gathered wild fruit, picked flowers, and climbed hills. Even the story of the rescue of the Martin and Willie handcart companies has been over-simplified: there were two wagon companies on the trail with them, at least six men (not three) helped them cross the Sweetwater River, and the rescue took more than two months and involved thou-sands of women and men from throughout the territory. Finally, the

Latter-day Saint pioneers were not alone; hundreds of thousands of Americans crossed the plains to California and Oregon. The Saints followed trails created by others and met people going both directions across a busy thoroughfare.[6]

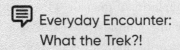

Everyday Encounter: What the Trek?!

Modern reenactments of the pioneer trek perpetuate many oversimplifications. The script simplifies time by combining the departure of the Mormon Battalion (summer 1846) with the Martin and Willie handcart experience (1856). The women whose husbands and sons left with the battalion did not pull handcarts alone. The trek experience also creates a false impression that the pioneers lived in some strange, technologically backward, suffering-prone existence—today's youth dress in different clothes, leave their family and electronic devices, eat strange food, and suffer the uncommon bodily ills of blisters and dehydration. But the youth who participated in the nineteenth-century trek wore the same clothes as their contemporaries, ate food cooked by the same open-fire methods as people who stayed home, and participated in largely the same types of daily activities as any frontier-dwelling American of the mid-nineteenth century.

What to do? You might begin by teaching the youth that there are oversimplifications and exaggerations in our pioneer stories, point them to better sources, and deputize them in the quest for completeness. In addition to talking about old clothing and habits, create times and places to talk openly about how the Holy Ghost actually works, what it feels like, and what counterfeits look like. While out in nature, design activities such as a night hike, star watch, or sunrise service that help youth encounter the great God of the cosmos—the Being who watched over and helped the pioneers can do the same for us today!

Change "Or" to "And"

We can improve our thinking by changing the "or" in the either/or script to "and." Life and history are not a simplistic decision between two opposites, such as whether to hang a roll of toilet paper so that the sheets come out over or under. Reality operates more like cell-phone coverage, which works a little with one bar and far better with four. We know a little bit more than those who lived in the past, but we also know a good deal less. We may never come to know the whole story, but we can do our best to make our stories as complete as possible. Moving beyond an either/or mindset makes us more steadfast in our thinking and faith.

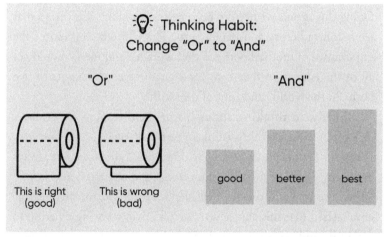

One way to change the script is to look for a more temperate *middle point* between the two apparent extremes. For example, the modern debate in the United States over abortion pits a "no, never" position against "yes, anytime." For its part, the Church has defined a position in the middle of these opposites that condemns abortion generally while also recognizing the merit of the choice in cases of rape, incest, and health complications for the mother or fetus.[7] Middle points need not be exactly in the center of the extremes.

A second way to dissolve a dualism is to accept *both* options.

Instead of seeing a tension between faith or reason, look to the scriptural charge to "seek learning, even by study and also by faith" (D&C 88:118). Instead of contrasting the mind to the heart, accept the Lord's explanation: "I will tell you in your mind *and* in your heart, by the Holy Ghost" (D&C 8:2; emphasis added). How did the Three Witnesses see the gold plates? In vision *and* with their eyes (see 2 Ne. 27:12; D&C 17:3). Can we find happiness in this life or in the life to come? Yes.[8]

Sometimes we can add to two opposing ideas to see *both/and.* We accept both and add other important concepts, including "I don't know (and that's okay)" and "the information is incomplete" and "there is conflicting information" and "things have changed." Doing this means we need to become comfortable with things that seem contradictory and paradoxical. The Church emphasizes the importance of motherhood *and* that women (and men) should get all of the education they can. Jesus encouraged the Saints to live both "in the world" and "not of the world."

Finally, in thinking about history and human experience, it is often most useful to think in terms of *good, better, and best.* President Dallin H. Oaks taught that life's choices are not always between "good" and "bad" but among "good, better, and best."[9] When the Holy Ghost directed Nephi to kill Laban, the message emphasized that this choice was "better" than allowing a nation to "dwindle and perish in unbelief" (1 Ne. 4:13). In the same way that our knowledge of technology, medicine, and hygiene improve over time, so too can our understanding of history go from good to better and from better to best.

💬 Everyday Encounter: Negotiating and Problem Solving

The ability to see beyond strict dichotomies will make you a better problem solver and negotiator in all aspects of your life.

If you view the world as having only two options of "mine" or "yours," and if you see any concession to another as a loss, then you will either "win" (and harm your neighbor), "lose" (and feel harmed), or quit negotiating (and gain nothing).

The best approach in difficult situations is to look for a both/and resolution. Are there ways for both parties to succeed? Business guru Stephen Covey offered two methods for thinking this way. One method is to "think win/win." You believe "that there is plenty for everybody, that one person's success is not achieved at the expense or exclusion of the success of others." You can also seek for a third alternative. "It's not your way, and it's not my way," says Covey. "It's a higher way. It's a better way than any of us have thought of before."[10] Is there a new or larger or otherwise different way to view the problem that offers a chance for all to achieve their goals?

You Try It

Rumor

There are two sides to every story.

Sniff Tests

1. *Only two options or sides.* Beware of histories (or politicians or news channels) that force you to choose between *only* two options—myth or reality, prophet or fraud, faith or reason, fact or fiction. Such false balances make for seductive clickbait, but they distort the past and the present.

2. *Omission.* Watch for stories with missing middles and forgotten origins. Beware of sources, stories, and studies that omit women or minorities.

3. *Oversimplification.* Just because something happened later does

not mean that it was caused by the thing that happened earlier. Just because two things happened together does not mean that one must have caused the other. In other words, "correlation is not causation." Both fallacies oversimplify the complexities of the past.

4. *"True facts are good and pure."* Beware of histories that assume or state that the only facts worth knowing are those that are good, moderate, or neutral.

5. *"True facts are dark and insidious."* Beware of growing but still immature thinkers who turn the corner on dichotomous thinking by simply flipping their binary—what once was true is now false. In this view, history is caused by scheming people, the true facts are dark and dirty, and there is always something sinister lurking below the surface. If Joseph Smith is *only* a fraud or if a restaurant *only* harms its guests or if the government *only* deceives its people, then the thinking is still *only* a dichotomy. If history happens only after midnight or in a darkened alley or in secret meetings of conspiratorial characters, then you've found a story that fails the sniff test.

Real

It's a long story.

Key Concepts

1. We must tell long stories about history because the past was complicated.

2. Any event or decision in the past involved the contingency of multiple options and outcomes.

3. We can understand causation by identifying the many decisions and factors that contributed to what happened in the past.

4. Latter-day Saint teachings embrace concepts far richer than

simple dichotomies. We can look to the middle of two extremes, accept both options, consider more than just two options, and differentiate between good, better, and best.

Notes

1. Jill Mulvay Derr and others, *The First Fifty Years of Relief Society: Key Documents in Latter-day Saint Women's History* (Salt Lake City: Church Historian's Press, 2016); Jill Mulvay Derr, Janath Russell Cannon, and Maureen Ursenbach Beecher, *Women of Covenant: The Story of Relief Society* (Salt Lake City: Deseret Book, 1992); *Daughters in My Kingdom: The History and Work of Relief Society* (Salt Lake City: The Church of Jesus Christ of Latter-day Saints, 2011).

2. Andrea G. Radke, "We Also Marched: The Women and Children of Zion's Camp, 1834," *BYU Studies* 39, no. 1 (2000): 147–65.

3. Bruce C. Hafen and Marie K. Hafen, *Faith Is Not Blind* (Salt Lake City: Deseret Book, 2018), 6; Lloyd D. Newell, "Instruments or Agents," *Ensign*, April 2019, 36.

4. See the entry for "World" in the Topical Guide.

5. "Race and the Priesthood," Gospel Topics Essays, The Church of Jesus Christ of Latter-day Saints, December 6, 2013, https://www.churchofjesuschrist.org/study/manual/gospel-topics-essays/race-and-the-priesthood.

6. Keith A. Erekson, "5 Things We Learn from Database of Mormon Pioneers," *Church News*, July 23, 2015; Melvin L. Bashore and H. Dennis Tolley, "Mortality on the Mormon Trail, 1847–1868," *BYU Studies Quarterly* 54, no. 3 (2014): 109–23; Chad M. Orton and Curtis Ashton, "Five Things You Might Not Know about the Handcart Rescue," Church History, The Church of Jesus Christ of Latter-day Saints, March 19, 2019, https://history.churchofjesuschrist.org/content/historic-sites/wyoming/five-things-you-might-not-know-about-the-handcart-rescue; Chad M. Orton, "The Martin Handcart Company at the Sweetwater: Another Look," *BYU Studies* 45, no. 3 (2006): 5–37; Chad M. Orton, "Francis Webster: The Unique Story of One Handcart Pioneer's Faith and Sacrifice," *BYU Studies* 45, no. 2 (2006): 117–40.

7. "Abortion," in *General Handbook: Serving in The Church of Jesus Christ of Latter-day Saints* (Salt Lake City: The Church of Jesus Christ of Latter-day Saints, 2020), 38.6.1.

8. Quentin L. Cook, "Shipshape and Bristol Fashion: Be Temple Worthy—in Good Times and Bad Times," *Ensign*, November 2015, 39.

9. Dallin H. Oaks, "Good, Better, Best," *Ensign*, November 2007, 107.

10. Stephen R. Covey, *The 7 Habits of Highly Effective People: Powerful Lessons in Personal Change* (New York: Simon & Schuster, 1989), 206, 207; Stephen R. Covey, *The 3rd Alternative: Solving Life's Most Difficult Problems* (New York: Free Press, 2011), 8.

CHAPTER 6

The Truth Is Enough

"Did you hear that Brigham Young did not like the tower of the St. George Temple?"

"No, what do you mean?"

"Well, when he was alive, he criticized its appearance, and he publicly told the local Saints to change it. But they refused. One year after his death, lightning struck the tower and it had to be replaced. I guess Brother Brigham got the last word after all!"

The first clue that this story is not entirely accurate is the fact that it ends with a punchline. Jokes need to be set up, so a joke teller will leave out details that don't lead to the desired end. What is true, and what was left out? It is true that although the architect's original sketch (1871) depicted a tall spire with straight edges culminating in a triangular peak, the temple was dedicated (1877) with a short, rounded dome on an eight-sided base. No record survives to explain the change, but Brigham Young publicly praised the rounded dome. He did criticize some of the *workmanship* inside the tower but not its design. It is also true that lightning struck the tower on August 16, 1878, shattering the dome and windows, melting nails, and shredding the roof's canvas cover. But instead of seeing a sign of divine disapproval, the Saints at the time found it miraculous that the whole building did not catch on fire and cited the protection of God in the "comparatively slight damage done." And, instead of restoring the rounded tower or building the original triangular peak, they installed a new squared tower with smaller rounded dome in 1882–83. The incomplete and distorted punchline version of the story was first told in a local newspaper in 1977 and continues to circulate online.[1]

The St. George Temple spire as sketched (1871), dedicated (1877), and repaired (1883). All images courtesy of the Church History Library.

Truth alone is not enough. Many deceptions operate by pairing a little bit of truth with other errors. A modern revelation teaches that "truth is knowledge of things as they are, and as they were, and as they are to come," with the added warning that "whatsoever is *more or less* than this is the spirit of that wicked one who was a liar from the beginning" (D&C 93:24–25; emphasis added). Our best understanding will come when we cherish the entire truth by working to recover all that we can and to remove the errors that creep in over time.

The Truth, the Whole Truth, and Nothing But

One useful way to think about the stories we hear is to invoke a phrase used in the courtrooms of many nations—we seek "the truth, the whole truth, and nothing but the truth." It is important to first acknowledge that many stories *do* contain true facts and meanings. I think this is one reason why people can feel internal confirmations of such stories—because there is truth in them.

Most stories do not contain the *whole* truth. True facts get omitted and forgotten over time as stories are retold. Stories that commemorate the pioneers largely forget that three members of Brigham Young's vanguard company were enslaved men—Green Flake, Hark Lay, and Oscar Crosby. While praying on a tower, Nephi the son of Helaman lamented, "Oh, that I could have had my days in the days when my father Nephi first came out of the land of Jerusalem," for "then were his people easy to be entreated, firm to keep the commandments of God, and slow to be led to do iniquity; and they were quick to hearken unto the words of the Lord" (Hel. 7:7). Yet, when we read about the earlier Nephi's actual experiences in 1 Nephi, we learn that his brothers were difficult to be entreated, reluctant in keeping the commandments, and quick to do iniquity.

Many stories also contain exaggerations or distortions that get added later. Snowbanks deepen, pathways run uphill (even both ways), fish grow longer, the ordinary gets romanticized. Over time, the glass and pottery shards used in the plaster of the Kirtland Temple transform into pieces of the women's fanciest china. Artist Del Parson's interactions with the employees in the Church's Curriculum Department who commissioned his painting *The Lord Jesus Christ* turn into meetings with General Authorities who gave Parson specific instructions about Christ's physical features until Parson "got it right."[2] Exaggeration is one reason why people can feel angered by such stories—because there are errors in them.

Because stories usually contain truth mingled with exaggeration, it is shortsighted to try simply to debunk them by turning them into myths. Instead, we should carefully analyze their contents. We should cherish what is correct (the truth), recover what has been omitted (the whole truth), and remove what was added later (nothing but the truth).

Take a Closer Look

We can use this approach to better understand the pioneer story of the crickets and gulls. This story has been told repeatedly from pulpits, in paintings, in curriculum materials, and even in a monument on Temple Square—and for good reason. The story contains many true facts supported by solid evidence. The Saints did settle in the Salt Lake Valley in the summer and fall of 1847, and they survived the first winter. Because warm weather came early in 1848, the 1,700 inhabitants had crops in the ground by April and anticipated a bountiful harvest by fall. During the last week of May, "crickets" appeared and began to eat the settlers' vegetables and grains. The wingless black katydids moved across the ground in swarms as large as a square mile. For weeks, the pioneers fought back against the insects with flooding, fires, beatings (with sticks, clubs, brooms, brushes, ropes, willows, and mallets), sonar (ringing bells and banging sticks on pans), and prayer. By the early days of June, with no response to prayer or relief in sight, some began to fear starvation; others considered moving on to California or Oregon. In this moment of growing fear and urgent despair, California gulls arrived and began to eat the crickets, even appearing to vomit them up before returning to eat more. "The sea gulls have come in large flocks from the Lake and sweep the crickets as they go," the stake presidency reported to Brigham Young on June 9. "It seems the hand of the Lord [is] in our favor."[3] Everything in this paragraph is true.

But there is also *more* to the story. The "whole truth" contains additional information that has been omitted and forgotten over time. First, the gulls stayed for several weeks, but the crickets remained in the area for two more months after the birds left. And in reality, the Saints had seen the tail end of the insects' pattern of seasonal visits the year before without realizing it. Trappers had noted gulls in the valley as early as 1825. In addition to insects, the growing season of 1848 also witnessed late frosts. Further, the Saints had not yet developed their irrigation methods, so the lack of water also proved problematic. Together, the triple threat of frost, drought, and insects caused significant damage to the crops, with the gulls providing relief for only one of the three. Despite the arrival of the gulls, the journals, letters, and reports of the Saints throughout the season continued to complain about their poor harvest.

While many diaries written in 1848 talk about the insects, few mention the gulls. Eliza R. Snow wrote in her journal on June 10 and June 15, worrying about the agricultural situation without referring to the gulls. Though he witnessed the suffering, Parley P. Pratt did not mention the gulls in his 1848 letters or his later autobiography. Most tellingly, a general epistle by the First Presidency written the following year notes frost, drought, crickets, and stampeding cattle but also does not mention the gulls. "The brethren were not sufficiently numerous to fight the crickets, irrigate the crops, and fence the farm of their extensive planning," Brigham and his counselors concluded.[4] Overall, gulls are noted (occasionally) in the records of the time as being helpful in a very rough year with many challenges and severe crop losses.[5]

There is also *less* to the story. Viewing the "truth" and "the whole truth" helps us peel away the additions and exaggerations that came later. The arrival of the gulls was not *unprecedented* (it had happened before and reoccurred after). The insects did not threaten *all* the food (primarily grain and vegetables), the birds did not come *immediately* after prayer (only after weeks of tiresome battling), and they did not eat *all* of the insects. Just as the Saints misidentified the katydids as crickets, they also did not seem to understand the biology of seagull digestion—the birds routinely swallow insects whole and then regurgitate the indigestible parts. And while the June 9 letter acknowledged the hand of the Lord in mitigating the effects of the insects, the gulls were not elevated to single-handed rescuers until later.

Where did the exaggerations come from? Orson Hyde seems to have been the first to tell an expanded version of the story, though he had been in Winter Quarters at the time and did not see the events firsthand. Drawing a contrast between scanty times when the Saints first arrived in the valley and their more general prosperity by 1854, he described the insects as being about to devour "everything" when the gulls came in a "rare" circumstance "that was never known to exist before, and never since to any extent." They left "just enough saved to feed the hungry with a scanty morsel."

Fifteen years after Hyde's remarks, George A. Smith, who had also been at Winter Quarters in 1848, added the vomiting element and said that the Saints did not pray until they had "contended with [the crickets] until they were utterly tired out." Like Hyde, he omitted the later infestations of 1849 and 1850 (and 1855) to observe, "I believe the crickets have never been a pest in this vicinity to any serious extent since." Thus, with the frost, drought, and stampeding cattle removed from the story, and with the biological facts and the large crop losses forgotten, the story of a rare and immediate rescue emerged. The event became a sign of chosenness that passed into local histories, curriculum materials, paintings, a 1913 monument, and the general collective consciousness. The particular katydid was renamed a "Mormon cricket," and the California gull became Utah's state bird in 1955.[6]

🔆 Thinking Habit: Seek for the Truth—Whole and Nothing But

The Truth	The Whole Truth	Nothing But the Truth
What facts, aspects, and meanings of the commonly told story are *true*?	What elements of the past have been *forgotten* or *omitted*? How has the story been *simplified*?	What has been *added* to the story over time? What has been *exaggerated*?

Looking for the truth, the whole truth, and nothing but the truth likewise sheds added light on the story of Thomas B. Marsh and the milk strippings, a tale often told to caution about taking small offenses. His wife, Elizabeth, got into a dispute with Lucinda Harris over the strippings, and Thomas defended his wife's character. Thomas left the Church the following month and testified against Church leaders in Missouri. He returned to the Church nearly twenty years later. But there is much more to Thomas's story that has been omitted over time. He and Elizabeth were among the first converts to the Church, and Thomas was appointed the first President of the Quorum of the Twelve in 1835. Two years later, he struggled with the fact that Joseph Smith called members of his quorum on missions to England, feeling it was his responsibility to make such assignments. Nevertheless, he remained loyal to Joseph as the Kirtland bank failed and other leaders were excommunicated. Having been already expelled from Jackson County in 1833, he grew worried by the increasing violence in Missouri in 1838, especially the violence committed *by* the Latter-day Saints. He swore an affidavit that the Saints intended to take over Missouri and the nation; it became one of the many pieces of evidence used to justify the expulsion or extermination of the Saints in Missouri.

The subsequent *exaggeration* of Marsh's story came in the form of extreme reduction—that the violence committed against the Saints in Missouri could all be traced to the squabble over milk. George A. Smith told the story this way in 1856 as a way of encouraging the Saints to take care of their fences. The following year, when Marsh reached out to Heber C. Kimball, and Kimball reported Marsh had reconciled with the Harris family and that "he has sinned before God and his brethren, and is pleading for mercy." Marsh was mocked publicly by Church leaders upon his return, but he confessed to the congregation that he had been blinded by anger and jealousy, and he settled in the territory and remained to the end of his life.[7]

Rewrite the Underlying Script

Frequently, recovering all of the truth and removing the exaggerations are not enough. The distortion of stories over time often aligns with a deeper script (see chapter 4). The underlying script matters because the details of the story hang on it like clothing on a hanger. The meaning of the script exists independently of the facts, making the story feel "timeless." Scripts are simultaneously hidden from our immediate consciousness yet easily visualized and remembered. Often, the underlying script is also true—"God protects people" or "small things make a big difference"—so people *really want* the details of a story to be true, even the parts that have become exaggerated. When the same script is used repeatedly by many—the participants, their hearers, leaders, and artists—we forget who originally told the story because "everyone knows it." Tellers and listeners thus become emotionally and personally attached to the stories. If we simply provide more details without changing the hanger, the additional facts will not stay and quickly become forgotten once again.

The story of the gulls operates on a *third-party rescue*

script—the pioneer victims of crickets were rescued by the sending of a third party: the gulls. Latter-day Saints can easily imagine a family praying in a field of crickets with birds visible on the horizon. But if we want to include all of the truth about drought, frost, crickets, seasonal-migration patterns, and a generally poor harvest, then we need to find another script.

The Book of Mormon tells of the people of Alma, who prayed for deliverance from bondage but received instead strengthened backs, lightened burdens, and cheerful patience (see Mosiah 24:12–15). The gulls did not solve all of the pioneers' problems—they did not even eat all of the katydids—but the appearance of the birds did provide respite from the constant fighting against insects, emotional rejuvenation, and some tangible crop relief (more crops would have been lost without the gulls). President Russell M. Nelson took this broader view in a BYU devotional in 1997, reframing the miracle not as the narrow arrival of birds but as the entire success of the Saints: "It was also miraculous that a permanent settlement survived in the valley of the Great Salt Lake. Seagulls that saved the crops were part of that miracle."[8] Hopefully visual artists will depict drought and frost—more of the truth—on the next monument.

Perhaps no underlying script causes as much angst for Latter-day Saints as does the *assumption* that prophets are infallible. At the surface level, we happily state that Jesus lived the only perfect life, and we contrast our view of prophets against the Catholic idea of papal infallibility. And yet, at some deeper level, we have elevated Wilford Woodruff's observation that the Lord will not permit a prophet to lead the people astray (see OD 1) into a hidden belief that prophets cannot make mistakes. We hold this script despite scriptural stories about prophets who denied knowing Jesus or betrayed Him, resisted the Lord's calls, disagreed publicly with each other, failed and brought suffering on their followers, fell into follies and errors (repeatedly), and were chastised or punished by God.[9] Many Church leaders have acknowledged that prophets are not perfect, don't know everything, and make mistakes.[10]

We solve this problem neither by denying that prophets make mistakes nor by charging the Church with deception, but by rewriting the underlying script. Prophets *can* (and *do*) make mistakes, yet God can still use them to accomplish His work. Elder Jeffrey R. Holland observed that "imperfect people are all God has ever had to work with. That must be terribly frustrating to Him, but He deals with it. So should we."[11] When introducing the Church's new four-volume history, *Saints*, Elder Quentin L. Cook advocated replacing the script of "perfect people in the past" with something more helpful: "We will find examples of imperfect people who went forward with faith and allowed God to work through them to accomplish His work. In doing so, we will see better how He can work through imperfect people like you and me."[12]

💬 **Everyday Encounter:**
Placing Our Trust in God Instead of Individual Prophets

What are we to do when we encounter instances in the past or present when the fallibility of prophets appears to be prominent? First, this is not an either/or question (see chapter 5). God can and does use prophets who are imperfect. We must shift the question from "When is the prophet right or wrong?" to "How can I know that God is speaking through this prophet?" God (not the prophet) is the source of true revelation, and fortunately He has provided a guide. The way we know if a prophet has "preached by the Spirit of truth" is to listen with the Spirit. "Wherefore, he that preacheth and he that receiveth, understand one another, and both are edified and rejoice together" (D&C 50:21–22).

This approach changes our focus to things in our control: Do we know how the Holy Ghost communicates with us? Are we worthy to receive that communication? Do we feel edified and rejoice as we receive the communication? Brigham Young worried that Latter-day Saints would "have so much confidence in their leaders that they [would] not inquire for themselves of God whether they are led by Him." The end result would be that the Saints would "settle down in a state of blind self-security trusting their eternal destiny in the hands of their leaders with a reckless confidence that in itself would thwart the purpose of God."[13] This perspective helps us shift from placing our trust in individual prophets to placing our trust in God.

You Try It

Rumor

The truth is enough.

Sniff Tests

1. *True but incomplete.* Beware of histories that present true information but only some of it. Consider the phrases "Franklin Roosevelt: Man who is pictured on the dime" or "Titanic: One of the largest ocean liners ever built; only used once."[14] The facts in these sentences are true, but when presented in isolation, the entire picture is incomplete.

2. *Reduction.* Reduction is a form of oversimplification that attributes dramatic, sweeping outcomes to a tiny event. This is illustrated by the old proverb "for want of a nail," which suggests that for want of a nail, a horseshoe fell off; for want of a shoe, a horse was stopped; for want of a horse, a messenger was stranded; for want of a messenger, a battle was lost and a nation lost and a people conquered and on and on. It is true that small things make a difference, but it typically is an exaggeration to attribute enormous changes to tiny details.

3. *Debunking.* Beware of an author who seeks only to "debunk" errors. All sources, stories, and studies contain a mixture of truth and error; it is an oversimplification to reduce an event to either a fact or a myth.

Real

We seek the truth, the whole truth, and nothing but the truth.

Key Concepts

1. To find the entire truth, we must accept what is accurate (the truth) while working to recover information that has been lost or forgotten (the whole truth) and to remove information that has been exaggerated or added (nothing but the truth).

2. We need to adjust our stories—especially the underlying scripts—to include the entire truth.

Notes

1. Darrell E. Jones, "The St. George Temple Tower: Evolution of a Design," *Journal of Mormon History* 34, no. 2 (Spring 2008): 113–29.
2. Noel A. Carmack, "Images of Christ in Latter-day Saint Visual Culture, 1900–1999," *BYU Studies* 39, no. 3 (2000): 59–65.
3. John Smith, Charles C. Rich, and John Young to Brigham Young, June 9, 1848, Brigham Young Office Files, 1832–1878, box 42, folder 9, Church History Library, Salt Lake City.
4. "First General Epistle of the First Presidency," *Latter-Day Saints' Millennial Star* 11 (1849): 228.
5. *Saints: The Story of the Church of Jesus Christ in the Latter Days,* 4 vols. (Salt Lake City: The Church of Jesus Christ of Latter-day Saints, 2018–) 2:100–101, 103–5; William Hartley, "Mormons, Crickets, and Gulls: A New Look at an Old Story," *Utah Historical Quarterly* 38, no. 3 (Summer 1970): 224–39; Richard W. Sadler, "Seagulls, Miracle Of," in *Encyclopedia of Mormonism,* ed. Daniel H. Ludlow (New York: Macmillan, 1992), 1287–88; Claire Margaret Haynie, "Savior Seagulls: The Evolution of a Mormon Myth" (master's thesis, University of Oxford, 2018); "Crickets and Seagulls," Church History Topics, The Church of Jesus Christ of

Latter-day Saints, 2020, https://www.churchofjesuschrist.org/study/history/topics/crickets-and-seagulls?

6. Orson Hyde, September 24, 1853 [1854], in *Journal of Discourses*, 26 vols. (Liverpool: F. D. Richards, 1855–86), 2:114; George A. Smith, June 20, 1869, in *Journal of Discourses*, 13:83.

7. Heber C. Kimball, July 12, 1857, in *Journal of Discourses*, 5:29. See also Kay Darowski, "The Faith and Fall of Thomas Marsh," in *Revelations in Context: The Stories behind the Sections of the Doctrine and Covenants* (Salt Lake City: The Church of Jesus Christ of Latter-day Saints, 2016), 54–60; George A. Smith, April 6, 1856, in *Journal of Discourses*, 3:280–91; Brigham Young, September 6, 1857, in *Journal of Discourses*, 5:206–13.

8. Russell M. Nelson, "The Exodus Repeated: Pioneers" (devotional, Brigham Young University, Provo, UT, September 7, 1997), https://speeches.byu.edu/talks/russell-m-nelson_exodus-repeated/.

9. Peter denied knowing Jesus (Matt. 26: 69–74), and Jesus compared him to Satan (Matt. 16:22–23); Jesus was betrayed by His apostle Judas (John 13:21–27); calls were resisted by Moses (Ex. 4:1–14), Enoch (Moses 6:31–32), and Jonah (Jonah 1:1–3); Paul publicly disagreed with Peter (Gal. 2:11–14); Nephi failed twice to obtain the brass plates and had to flee with his brothers for their lives (1 Ne. 3:10–13, 23–27); Joseph Smith published accounts of his repeated follies and subsequent chastisements (JS—H 1:28; D&C 3:6–10; 5:21–22; 64:5–7; 90:1; 93:47–49); God punished Moses by not allowing him to enter the promised land (Num. 20:7–13; Deut. 32:48–52).

10. Joseph Smith, May 12, 1844, in *Teachings of Presidents of the Church: Joseph Smith* (Salt Lake City: The Church of Jesus Christ of Latter-day Saints, 2007), 522; Gordon B. Hinckley, "'Charity Never Faileth,'" *Ensign*, November 1981, 97; Russell M. Nelson, "Honoring the Priesthood," *Ensign*, May 1993, 39; M. Russell Ballard, "God Is at the Helm," *Ensign*, November 2015, 24–25; Dieter F. Uchtdorf, "Come, Join with Us," *Ensign*, November 2013, 22.

11. Jeffrey R. Holland, "Lord, I Believe," *Ensign*, May 2013, 94.

12. Quentin L. Cook, "Out of Obscurity: How Merciful the Lord Has Been" (devotional, BYU–Idaho, Rexburg, June 12, 2018), https://www.byui.edu/devotionals/elder-quentin-l-cook-spring-2018.

13. Brigham Young, "Remarks," *Deseret News*, February 12, 1862, 257.

14. Carol Kammen, *On Doing Local History*, 2nd ed. (Walnut Creek, CA: AltaMira Press, 2003), 119.

CHAPTER 7

They Were Just Like Us

The images on the screen surprised Noelle. Sitting in her school's computer lab, she had listened closely as the librarian taught about researching on the internet. When instructed to "type something in the search bar that you know about," she typed "Book of Mormon." Her family read the book each day, and she had recently begun to read it on her own.

After she typed the words and hit Enter, she expected to see something about Nephi or the golden plates, but instead pictures of rocks filled the screen. She had not heard about seer stones, and she had never seen a picture of one! Noelle's mind began to fill with questions. What is a seer stone? What does it have to do with the Book of Mormon? How come I've never heard about this?

Noelle's experience reveals a couple of common problems. First, she encountered something she didn't know before and doesn't know how to make sense of it. This is a relatively minor problem since all good learning should introduce us to new things. Her second problem is that what she learned about the past—that the Book of Mormon was translated using a seer stone—was different than what she thought it would be. Further, the use of a seer stone is unfamiliar to her present experience. That past experience is different from our present experience is often surprising because we frequently *assume* that our understanding of the past is both correct and complete and that the people in the past were "just like us" when, in reality, almost everything was different for them.

A good starting point for making sense of rumors, myths, and history is to expect that everything in the past was different. We may find some similarities along the way, but attending to the differences is our first priority. Thinking about change, continuity, and distance helps us place people and events from the past into their proper contexts.

Everything Was Different

As we seek to make sense of history, we discover people, places, experiences, and traditions different from our own. Differences in science and technology gave people different experiences with travel and home construction, birth and medicine, eating and hygiene, race and prejudices, friendship and dating, love and marriage, and aging and death. Different political and economic systems provided people in the past different experiences with education, choice, freedom, and opportunity. As a result, they most likely had different perspectives than we do today on work, family, public service, or the role and status of women and minorities. Though speaking our same language, they may have used different words or words that exist with different meanings today. They likely celebrated different holidays or perhaps the same holidays in different ways. The past was different than the present, and that's okay.

The profound differentness of the past can be illustrated by looking at the United States in the 1830s, the decade in which the Church was organized. During this period slavery was legal and debated, abolitionists were considered troublemakers, women did not vote, federal government was small, and there was

no electricity. The experience of the Church was also very different: meetings were held less frequently, women would not have
spoken in meetings of mixed-gender audiences, fasting was not a
structured monthly practice, and men and women used alcohol
and tobacco products.[1] If transported back in time to an 1830s
Church meeting, we would instantly see and sense social and cultural differences.

Differences also appear within short timeframes. Someone
might see a date in the 1840s and another in the 1880s and think
that, since both dates are in the nineteenth century, they must be
similar. But those two decades are forty years apart. Think about
everything that was different just forty years ago—people prepared
food differently (home microwaves were just catching on), they
communicated differently (no personal cell phones), they learned
about the news differently (no online or social media sources), and
they dressed differently (it was the early 1980s).

Difference can exist even within a single word. Today, when
we speak of *translation*, we commonly think of a person who converts one language to another by using their knowledge of both
languages, as well as a dictionary, lexicon, or electronic tools. So
what did Joseph Smith mean when he said he "translated" the Book
of Mormon "by the gift and power of God" (Book of Mormon title
page)? He clearly did not mean that he was fluent in the Nephite
language, nor could he have used a dictionary or lexicon, so "translate" meant something different to him. Elder Ulisses Soares suggested, "We ought to look at the process more like a 'revelation'
with the aid of physical instruments provided by the Lord, as
opposed to a 'translation' by one with knowledge of languages."[2]
In a further twist, the word also meant different things in each of
Joseph's three translation projects. For the Book of Mormon, he
used the Nephite interpreters and seer stone; for the King James
Bible translation, he referred to published commentary and offered

inspired additions; for the Book of Abraham, he copied Egyptian characters into a study notebook, though he never became fluent in the language. In each case, the different mechanics of translation served as means for channeling revelation.

📺 Best Resources: Sources on the Changing Meanings of Words

Within the comparably brief history of the Church, the meanings of commonly used words have changed over time. These resources help understand what words meant in the past.

1. Noah Webster's first dictionary was published in 1828, two years before the Church was organized, and provides a good understanding of how the first generation of Latter-day Saints would have heard and understood words, such as *translate* or *keystone* (it also meant "binding" or "sealing"). The dictionary can be found online and in apps.

2. The glossary on the Joseph Smith Papers website documents the use of words in Joseph Smith's revelations and writings, such as *keys*, *anoint*, and *ordain*. These and many other words were used differently in the 1830s and 1840s than they are today.

Change, Continuity, and Distance

Three concepts help us make sense of the differentness of the past—change, continuity, and distance. The temporal aspects of human experience *change* over time in ways both small and great. Some changes appear sudden, such as a surprise military attack or a natural disaster or Saul's conversion after a miraculous experience on the road to Tarsus. Other changes occur gradually, as when people grow and develop, or when ideas emerge and expand, or when social movements begin and then coalesce. Some changes occur over centuries, and no individual person or generation witnesses the shift, such as the gradual acceptance of left-handedness (formerly viewed as a sign of evil), the adoption of polyphonic music (singing different notes or words at the same time) in religious services, or the shift from using the Bible to support slavery to citing the Bible in support of racial equality.[3]

The concept of *continuity* goes hand-in-hand with change because everything does not change at the same rate or at the same time. A law may be passed that reverses a definition of legal behavior, but previous perceptions of the behavior may linger for generations. Technological development may leap ahead in providing new ways to interact, but social norms that govern the use of technology may be slower to evolve. An individual who has a profound emotional or spiritual experience may continue to be perceived as the same person, even though their inner perspective has changed.

Consider the changes and continuities discernible from two photographs of Church leaders. In 1895, women's rights activist Susan B. Anthony visited Salt Lake City because Latter-day Saint women had participated in national suffrage meetings and international women's congresses for decades. In 2017, Relief Society General President Jean B. Bingham spoke to the United Nations about humanitarian efforts to support refugees.[4] Among the changes captured by the photos, the issue changed from woman's suffrage to refugee resettlement, and the setting changed to embrace the new international body created in the mid-twentieth century. Technological changes are evident (the second image was published in color), and the style of portrait composition changed from posing persons after an event to capturing a speaker in the moment. Yet these images also show continuity—Church leaders continue to collaborate with national and international leaders to accomplish shared goals that strengthen communities and nations.

Because of the interplay between continuity and change, even the things that stay the same can begin to appear different because

*Susan B. Anthony (seated center) with Relief Society General
President Zina D. H. Young (seated left of Anthony, second row) in
Salt Lake City in 1895. Courtesy of the Church History Library.*

*Relief Society General President Jean B. Bingham addresses
the United Nations in New York City in 2017. Courtesy of
The Church of Jesus Christ of Latter-day Saints.*

so much of the context around them has changed. For example,
take the well-documented anatomical fact that humans have grown
taller over the past two hundred years. Now imagine a family in the
United States in which every man in every generation was five feet,
eight inches tall (173 cm). During the 1880s, the men of this family would have been one to two inches *taller* than their peers, by the

1920s they would have been of average height, and by the 1960s they would have been one to two inches *shorter* than the average man.[5] Even though the men's height remained constant over time, the perception of the men's height would change.

Latter-day Saint teachings and practices support the interplay of change and continuity. President Russell M. Nelson taught that the constants amid change include the reality and love of the Godhead, Their plan for our happiness and salvation, the promises of the priesthood, the consequences of transgressing or obeying moral law, a future final judgment for all, and the potential for forever families. "Even though one's understanding of the truth may be fragmentary," he observed, "truth itself does not change."[6] Latter-day Saint scripture teaches that learning of truth increases "line upon line, precept upon precept, here a little and there a little" (2 Ne. 28:30). Nephi reported that God spoke to people on many continents to "prove unto many that I am the same yesterday, today, and forever," while adding in the very same verse the caveat "because that I have spoken one word ye need not suppose that I cannot speak another; for my work is not yet finished" (2 Ne. 29:9)—continuity and change. In 1831, the Lord told the Saints, "I, the Lord, was angry with you yesterday, but today mine anger is turned away" (D&C 61:20). We believe in a church that is "true and living" (D&C 1:30); living things grow and develop.

Changes in Church practices are signs that God lives, He is communicating with us, and we are growing. Over the years, Latter-day Saint practices have transitioned in many ways. We've added new revelations to our canonized standard works, aligned the text of scripture with historical sources, updated the language in temple instruction, consolidated our meetings into a three-hour block and then shortened it to two hours. Whereas the first generation of Church members anticipated the Second Coming during their lifetimes, we have seen several generations pass. Whereas early Saints sealed themselves horizontally, to their living nonrelative peers, we are now sealed vertically, up and down generational family lines. Whereas Latter-day Saints (like many other Christians) advocated communal and communitarian principles in the nineteenth century, we distanced ourselves in the twentieth century from those words (but not all of the practices) during the Cold War struggle against Soviet communism.[7] Change is part of our doctrine and our history, and so we must look to the past with the understanding that previous people's standards, customs, attitudes, cultures, languages, and behaviors can and will be different from our own.

💬 Everyday Encounter:
Reasons for Marriage Are Different

Today, many people hold ideas about marriage that are relatively new—we find a soul mate, fall in love, choose to marry, and live happily ever after. These ideas about romantic love emerged slowly in Western culture over the last 250 years. Before that, people arranged marriages for different reasons, including to perpetuate the family, transfer property through inheritance, and form economic and political alliances. Plural marriages among nineteenth-century Latter-day Saints added additional reasons, such as to obey God or "raise up seed" (Jacob 2:30). One reason that polygamy seems so different today is that our cultural expectations of romantic love and marriage have changed. Today's idealized vision of romantic love does not always prepare us for the realities that marriage involves self-discipline, mutual respect, hard work, and the choice to love and care for one another.

The final concept that helps us make sense of the differentness of the past is the idea that our *distance* from the past is something that we imagine or construct. There is temporal distance between us and the past—World War II ended in 1945 and gets farther away with each passing year—but there is also an emotional component to how we imagine the people who lived during the war. As humans, we have the creative ability to imagine that someone in the past was "just like us" (close in distance) or radically different from ourselves (far in distance).

The concepts of change, continuity, and distance help address the question of seer stones. Clearly, their use in translation is very different from today. No modern Church leader claims to use stones to translate between languages or to communicate with God in the twenty-first century. During Joseph's time, however, many people believed that physical objects could be used to receive divine messages. These beliefs were based, in part, on biblical stories in which objects such as clay and Moses's staff were used for divine purposes (see Num. 17:1–10; 2 Kings 5; John 9:6). A revelation Joseph received for the organization of the Church explained both the change and continuity in that God "gave [Joseph] power from on high, by the means which were before prepared, to translate the Book of Mormon" (D&C 20:8). Though the "means" included a seer stone, we can still discern the doctrinal message "that God does inspire men and call them to his holy work in this age . . . ; thereby showing that he is the same God yesterday, today, and forever" (D&C 20:11–12).

While the means of the communication has clearly *changed* over time, God's inspiring of people is a *continuity*. One might construct a great *distance* between today and the past, asserting that the use of a stone is very strange or even evil. On the other hand, one might construct a closer distance between today and the past, as when Elder Uchtdorf observed that his cell phone is "like a seer stone" in that he can use it to communicate across the world and translate languages. "If it is possible for me to access the knowledge of the world through my phone," he asked, "who can question that seer stones are impossible for God?"[8]

Failure to acknowledge that the past was different is called presentism. When we make present-minded *assumptions* about history—inserting our present goals, values, and ways of thinking into the past—we harm our ability to understand the real story. We should not assume that people in the past thought, believed, or acted just like us. We must seek to understand them in the context of their own times and places and cultures.

Putting Things into Contexts

The best way to avoid presentism is to strive to see things in proper contexts. Nephi admitted that he understood Isaiah's prophecies better than his children because he knew "the things of the Jews," "the manner of prophesying among the Jews," and "the regions round about" Jerusalem (2 Ne. 25:5, 1, 6). A thing may also have different meanings in multiple contexts. For example, the contexts of the interpersonal relationship changed as King Lamoni went from viewing Ammon as a prisoner to viewing him as a potential marriage partner for his daughter, a servant, a powerful warrior, and an inspired teacher (see Alma 17–18). Our understanding of history, scripture, and the world around us improves as we learn to discern multiple contexts.

Historical context includes everything that was going on in a particular time and place. An example of placing an event into historical context can be found in the Gospel Topics Essay on "Peace and Violence among 19th-Century Latter-day Saints." The essay describes the tragic murder of 120 immigrants in Utah in September 1857 that has come to be known as the Mountain Meadows Massacre. The essay sees the event within the local contexts of the ongoing "Reformation" among the Saints, the Utah War of the mid-1850s, and the Latter-day Saints' relationship with

American Indians. The violence can also be viewed in relation to other acts of violence in the Utah Territory, acts of violence during the Mormon-Missouri War of the 1830s, and vigilantism in the nineteenth-century United States. Additionally, the essay connects the massacre of the 1850s with religious persecution in the 1830s and 1840s.[9] All of these contexts help as we try to understand why this horrific event occurred.

There may also be a *literary context* for what you encounter. For example, the Gospel Topics Essay on "Becoming Like God" situates Latter-day Saint views of the relationship between God and humankind within the context of views recorded by biblical authors and early Christian writers. What you read may also have a *biographical context*, which considers the life of the author, or an *eternal context*, which situates something within the plan of salvation. The immediate *situation* of an event forms part of the context, as do the *material* characteristics of a source and the *ethical* choices faced by historical actors.

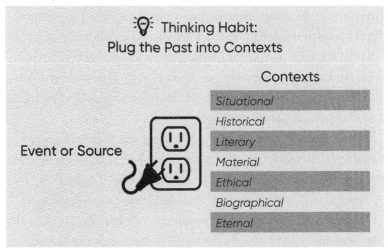

**Thinking Habit:
Plug the Past into Contexts**

To see things in their proper contexts, imagine a toaster or other home appliance that does not work unless it is plugged into an outlet and connected with power. By a similar process, we must plug pieces of the past into multiple contexts to gain the fullest understanding. Do this by imagining each type of context as a timeline. Timelines record events and dates in chronological order so that we can see sequence (which came first), simultaneity (what happened at the same time), and changes and continuities over time. Some changes began and ended in the past, such as between the 1840s and 1860s. Other changes began in the past and continue to unfold today. Be precise in knowing when things happened on the timeline. Look for changes in technology, economics, politics, culture, religion, race, gender, and mass media. From these basics, we can infer or deduce causes and contexts.

Consider the 1960 experience of surgeon Russell M. Nelson in receiving inspiration for how to perform a previously unknown surgical technique. Looking at the biographical contexts, we see the patient, a Latter-day Saint patriarch with nowhere else to turn, and a surgeon with prior medical training and an openness to inspiration. The historical contexts for the event include aspects of medical history—open-heart surgery was less than a decade old, and knowledge of heart physiology and functions were rapidly expanding. Dr. Nelson did not publish a report of his findings, so the procedure did not find its way into the medical literature of the time, but Elder Nelson's telling of the story at general conference in April 2003, with lessons about the power of prayer, placed the experience within the literary context of Latter-day Saint teachings.[10]

Plug into Context: A Revelatory Surgery

Event	Contexts
1960 surgery by Russell M. Nelson	*Situational:* Latter-day Saint patriarch requests surgery by Dr. Nelson *Historical:* recent invention of open-heart surgery

> *Literary:* not published in medical journals
>
> *Biographical:* the patient's faith and Dr. Nelson's training
>
> *Eternal:* an example of the power of prayer

You Try It

Rumor

They were just like us.

Sniff Tests

1. *"The past was just like the present" (presentism).* Beware of histories that assume no difference over time and that project present feelings, thoughts, and values onto people in the past. There are not any unchanging primordial archetypes of "teenager" or "hero." The concepts of "democracy" or "civilization" have meant different things in different times.

2. *"The past was nothing like the present."* Beware of approaches to history that cut it off entirely from the present. Yes, the past was different and distant, but it should not be alienated from the present as a lifeless curiosity in a small glass case with no relevance or connection to today.

3. *Taking history out of context.* Beware of histories that present true information out of context. Critics of Joseph Smith will cite his use of a seer stone to hunt treasure but not his prophetic use of the seer stone in translation. Joseph readily acknowledged *both* facts. In another example, President Russell M. Nelson reported that his photograph was once taken while he was sitting on a lawn waiting for a taxi after completing work on a government

contract. The photo was given the caption "Governmental Consultant at the National Center," suggesting that all he did as a consultant was lounge around. He noted, "The picture was true, the caption was true, but the truth was used to promote a false impression."[11]

4. *Taking scriptures out of context.* Beware of writers who cite just a few words or a verse of scripture in order to prove their own (modern) point.

Real

The past was different.

Key Concepts

1. Everything was different (and that's okay).
2. We can understand the differentness of the past with the concepts of change, continuity, distance, and context.
3. Change over time is part of Latter-day Saint doctrine that includes a "living church" (D&C 1:30) and the promise that God will "yet reveal many great and important things" (A of F 1:9).
4. We can understand pieces of the past by plugging them into multiple contexts—situational, historical, literary, material, ethical, biographical, and eternal.

Notes

1. See Patrick Q. Mason, *Planted: Belief and Belonging in an Age of Doubt* (Salt Lake City: Deseret Book, 2015), 88–90.
2. Ulisses Soares, "The Coming Forth of the Book of Mormon," *Ensign*, May 2020, 33.
3. Craig Harline, "What Happened to My Bell-Bottoms? How Things That Were Never Going to Change Have Sometimes Changed Anyway, and How Studying History Can Help Us Make Sense of It All," *BYU Studies Quarterly* 52, no. 4 (2013): 49–76.
4. Barbara Jones Brown, "Susan B. Anthony and Her Strong Utah Ties," *Better Days 2020* (blog), December 15, 2017, https://www.

betterdays2020.com/blog/2017/12/15/susan-b-anthony-and-her
-strong-utah-ties; "New Mormon Relief Society President Speaks
at the UN," Newsroom, The Church of Jesus Christ of Latter-day
Saints, April 13, 2017, http://newsroom.churchofjesuschrist.org/
article/new-mormon-relief-society-president-speaks-un.

5. Max Roser, Cameron Appel, and Hannah Ritchie, "Human
Height," Our World in Data, 2019, https://ourworldindata.org/
human-height.

6. Russell M. Nelson, "Constancy amid Change," *Ensign*, November
1993, 35.

7. See David A. Bednar, "Gather Together in One All Things in
Christ," *Ensign*, November 2018, 21–24; James B. Allen, "Line
upon Line," *Ensign*, July 1979, 32–39.

8. Dieter F. Uchtdorf (@churchofjesuschrist), "Not long ago, the
Church published photos and background information on seer
stones," Instagram photo, June 21, 2016, https://www.instagram.
com/p/BG7QoiWDyB6/.

9. Sarah Barringer Gordon and Jan Shipps, "Fatal Convergence in the
Kingdom of God: The Mountain Meadows Massacre in American
History," *Journal of the Early Republic* 37, no. 2 (2017): 307–47.

10. Russell M. Nelson, "Sweet Power of Prayer," *Ensign*, May 2003,
7–9; Austin A. Robinson and Curtis T. Hunter, "Discovering a Surgical First: Russell M. Nelson and Tricuspid Valve Annuloplasty,"
BYU Studies Quarterly 54, no. 1 (2015): 6–28.

11. Russell M. Nelson, "Truth—and More," *Ensign*, January 1986, 71.

CHAPTER 8

What a Coincidence!

"Look at these remarkable parallels!" The speaker's voice trembled as he listed similar information about Joseph Smith and Abraham Lincoln. "Both men were born in the first decade of the 1800s. They both read the Bible—both were, in fact, named after biblical prophets. They both moved to the state of Illinois. Both men witnessed times of sorrow and war. They both ran for president, both were murdered, and today both are revered."

I could almost feel the stirring music rise in the background . . . until I realized that the speaker had actually said almost nothing of significance. Joseph and Abraham were joined by hundreds of thousands of men who were born in the United States during first decade of the 1800s. Millions of Americans read the Bible and named their children after its characters—Josephs and Abrahams lived among an uncountable number of Adams, Isaacs, Jacobs, Matthews, Marks, Lukes, Johns, and Pauls. In the nineteenth century, most Americans were on the move as westward expansion pulled migration into Illinois, the Midwest, and beyond. Everyone who lived in the nineteenth (or any other) century witnessed sorrow. The number of men who ran for president is smaller but still runs in the hundreds during the two men's lifetimes, as does the number of Americans who were murdered.

———————————— Q ————————————

Coincidences do not demonstrate that something is important. So how do we determine what actually matters? Because history is incomplete, different than we often assume, and open to interpretation, we must review all of the surviving evidence with careful discrimination. We must also "put [our] trust in that Spirit which leadeth . . . to judge righteously" (D&C 11:12).

Coincidences Don't Cut It

Let's begin by declaring unequivocally that coincidences don't cut it! Coincidences or parallels are created through selective, imprecise, and misrepresentative details. Historian Margaret MacMillan pointed out that "it is easy to pick and choose what you want. The past can be used for almost anything you want to do in the present."[1]

The coincidences between Abraham Lincoln and Joseph Smith display a lack of precision. The comparisons are loose and vague and could be made between hundreds or thousands of people. Sometimes, the comparisons may also be inconsequential: two people have similar names, their names begin with the same letter, or two events happened in the same calendar year.

Most of the time, coincidences are generated by misrepresenting some of the details, sometimes by mixing little errors with larger facts. The most prominent of the facts may be accurate, such as a person's birth year or the date of election to office. But the list of facts may also present smaller errors, such as a date that is off by one year or the outright invention of details so small that nobody usually checks their accuracy. Occasionally, all of the details are wrong. For example, a story circulates of a Farmer Fleming who saved the son of a nobleman, so the nobleman paid to educate the farmer's son Alexander, who went on to discover penicillin, which was used to save once again the life of the nobleman's son, sick with pneumonia—the nobleman was Lord Randolph Churchill and his son, Sir Winston Churchill. What a wonderful coincidence! But it never happened. Alexander Fleming did invent penicillin, but Churchill never suffered from pneumonia. He did suffer from a different illness, but he was treated by a different doctor with a different drug.[2]

Whether inconsequential, vague, or erroneous, coincidences prey on our psychology, the way our brains try to make sense of the world. Surrounded by too much information, we seek for patterns, causes, and actors. We have faulty memories that do not recall everything, so we tend to remember only things that are recent, unusual, or dramatic or that confirm our beliefs. We're generally bad at understanding the mathematical probabilities of occurrences.[3]

Coincidences are often used by those seeking to deceive. One of the frauds of fortune-telling is to make dozens of predictions, thus increasing the odds of getting one right while expecting the victim to forget the others that were not true. In history, storytellers emphasize coincidence to hide a lack of evidence. They often do this by presenting a long list of coincidences. Unlike tiny threads that grow stronger when braided into a larger rope, heaping up errors only creates a longer list of errors.

Significance Is Better

How can we tell what is actually important? Which sources and stories are the most meaningful? Which studies yield the best answers? Instead of piling up coincidences, we should evaluate significances. Significance is not an objective quality—something is not significant in the same way that it is tall or blue. Rather, significance is a judgment made by different people at different times who bear different relationships to the event or source in question. Thus, significance implies an audience—something is not significant in and of itself; it is significant *to* someone (or to a group of people) at a specific point in time for specific reasons. Although the term *significance* is typically used only in the singular, I occasionally use it in the plural to emphasize that there can be many reasons why people, events, and sources may be considered significant.

Historical significances. In its own time, an event or source may be considered significant because of its impact on other events and sources. It may have created immediate consequences or caused new developments. It may connect to larger trends and stories. The event or source may have produced long-term impacts that were widely felt. It may have set a precedent for future actions or interpretations. It may have been the first of its kind or something that changed the way people looked at things. People in the past could have recognized an event or document was important, or the importance may have become apparent more slowly over time.

Usable significances. An event or source may be considered significant because it helps us today. Though an event may not have been considered significant in the past, it could gain significance later. A source may document past conditions, illuminating history for us today. It might allow us to make claims about life at the time the event occurred and about the history's creator or its preserver. The question of potential future usability is frequently part of the decision to save a document or artifact in a library or archive.

Personal significances. Finally, a source or event may be considered significant because of a personal connection. The source may be relevant to *you* in the present. Perhaps the author or creator of a source is your ancestor. Or you may be able to draw out personal lessons from a source to guide your decisions.

We may be able to discern all three kinds of significance in an event or source. For example, we know the First Vision was historically significant because it was the starting point for the

Restoration of the gospel. The First Vision also has usable significance since we can look at it again and again to find lessons about the nature of God or the process of seeking personal revelation.[4] And the event bears personal significance for individual people who are inspired by the story to seek and bear a testimony of their own. The same three categories of significance can be found for many other events and sources. The Declaration of Independence became historically significant in 1776 as a statement of rebellion that inspired a war for independence. The document's usable significance was demonstrated in 1848 when the women's rights convention at Seneca Falls used it as a model for a new "Declaration of Rights and Sentiments." And an individual might find personal significance in being a descendant of one of the signers.

To claim something as significant requires a statement supported by evidence. You must make a judgment about the past, evaluate the sources and their possible meanings, and discern the important from the unimportant. Declaring something significant does not change the past, but it does change how we view things from the present.

Finally, significance is different than truth. Something may be true but not significant—it is true that there are rocks in the flower bed in front of my home, but that fact is hardly significant. On the other hand, something may be significant but not true—a false rumor may prompt real fear or other consequences. Claims of significance reveal how individuals judge the impacts, consequences, or merits of an event or source. As with all acts of judgment, discussions of significance do not automatically bring consensus. We might agree that the Civil War was significant—it profoundly shaped the history of the nation—while disagreeing on its causes or meanings. Some eternal truths that can save us in the kingdom of God may not be perceived as significant by those who have not felt a witness of the Spirit.

💬 Everyday Encounter:
Communicating Significance in Testimony Meeting

It is important to match the right kinds of significance to the right settings. For example, consider a testimony borne in fast and testimony meeting that recounts minute details about the speaker's ancestors. While the information clearly holds *personal significance* to the speaker, odds are the ancestor was not *historically significant*. Thus, it is essential to explain some *usable significance* to the audience—a lesson learned or relevance beyond the family circle. In this way, both the speaker and the hearers can "understand one another, and both are edified and rejoice together" (D&C 50:22).

So You Think You Can Liken?

The single most common method for drawing significant lessons from history is to make an analogy or comparison. The practice is very common in public life—a current president is compared to past presidents, current wars are compared to previous wars, or current economic downturns are examined against the Great Depression. Latter-day Saints often use the terms *apply* or *liken* to describe the process of analogizing from a scripture passage or historical story to our present experience.

Despite being a common practice, the art and craft of making analogies is frequently muddled. Analogies must be built carefully. We should first define the categories in the past and present that we want to compare. This step is frequently forgotten and actually requires the most thinking. Next, we need to identify correct information from the past and present for each category. Then we compare the information from past to present, testing to be sure that the comparisons are valid. If the comparisons are all valid, then the analogy is sound. The comparisons identify points of alignment between past and present and can be used to frame the present.[5]

:💡: Thinking Habit:
Build a Sound Analogy

1. Define categories for comparing things in the past and present.
2. Identify correct information from the past and present to compare.
3. Ensure that each comparison of the past to the present is valid.
4. Use the comparisons to frame the present.

Categories for Comparing	Information from the Past	Information from the Present

Bad analogies omit the categories and the information. To simply declare that one's opponent "is like Hitler" provides no reason for the comparison. To say that the Holy Ghost works like "the force" in *Star Wars* requires one to ignore the actual details of both scripture and science fiction. Mounting a list of Latter-day Saint persecutions, without even comparing them to things suffered by Black Americans, is not an analogy but a defensive reflex. Because the past is gone and it was different and complicated, beware also of analogies that present a "perfect fit." Analogies are only ever rough approximations. If every fact and detail lines up perfectly, then you can be sure something has been omitted. Analogies may also be taken too far—while it is true that a ball and an apple can be both round and red, the ball is not also delicious or nutritious.[6]

While analogies can sometimes be used irresponsibly, simple analogies may be helpful in making connections or improving clarity. Sister Chieko Okazaki compared bottles of peaches from the mainland with baskets of fruit from the Hawaiian Islands to observe, "The basket and the bottle are different containers, but the content is the same: fruit for a family."[7] President Boyd K. Packer encouraged teaching through analogies and outlined a template: something difficult to comprehend "is like unto" something already known and understood. This is the theory behind object lessons.[8] The Book of Mormon prophet Lehi used this technique in hoping that his wayward sons would be "like unto this river, continually running into the fountain of all righteousness" or "like unto this valley, firm and steadfast, and immovable in keeping the commandments of the Lord" (1 Ne. 2:9, 10). Every analogy demonstrates the thinking of its creator; someone in a different time or place, for instance, might have judged different geological features to be firm and steadfast.

More complex analogies can be made, but they require more careful discipline and structure. For example, Nephi made a historical analogy to persuade his brothers to keep striving to obtain the brass plates. After two failed attempts and a visit from an angel, his brothers complained: "How is it possible that the Lord will deliver Laban into our hands? Behold, he is a mighty man, and he can command fifty, yea, even he can slay fifty; then why not us?" (1 Ne. 3:31). Nephi then presented an analogy to persuade them to return for the plates. After the analogy, his brothers "were yet wroth, and did still continue to murmur," but they returned with him to Jerusalem (1 Ne. 4:4). How did Nephi's successful analogy work?

Nephi compared their hoped-for deliverance from Laban to the past deliverance of the Israelites from Egypt (1 Ne. 4:1–3). In this case, the comparisons connected known aspects of Moses's past deliverance with unknown elements of Nephi's immediate future, thereby helping his brothers understand the precedent for divine support and having trust in the Lord.

Build an Analogy: Deliverance

Categories for Comparing	Information from the Past	Information from the Present
Protagonists	Moses and "our fathers" (v. 2)	Nephi and his brothers
Antagonists	Armies of Pharaoh	Laban and his fifty
Strength of God	God is "mightier than all the earth" (v. 1).	"Then why not mightier than Laban and his fifty, yea, or even than his tens of thousands?" (v. 1).
Means of Deliverance	Waters of Red Sea parted, fathers escaped, armies drowned (v. 2).	"The Lord is able to deliver us, even as our fathers, and to destroy Laban, even as the Egyptians" (v. 3).
Witnesses	"Ye know that this is true" (v. 3).	"Ye also know that an angel hath spoken unto you; wherefore can ye doubt?" (v. 3).
Call to Action	"Let us be strong like unto Moses" (v. 2).	"Ye also know that an angel hath spoken unto you; wherefore can ye doubt?" (v. 3).

Many successful analogies might inform our teaching. Francine Bennion compared the Old Testament story of Jephthah to modern theological questions about suffering, noting, "We do not all read the same things into Jephthah's story, or into sacrifice." President Russell M. Nelson drew a sophisticated parallel between the Israelites and the pioneers, comparing geography, leadership, miracles, and spiritual strength to exhort covenant keeping and the modern gathering of Israel. President M. Russell Ballard drew a rich and compelling comparison between the parents of Helaman's stripling warriors and modern parents seeking to "raise the bar" for missionaries who must first improve themselves. And Elder Dieter F. Uchtdorf drew an extended literary analogy to frame the journey of our lives within the adventure of *The Hobbit*.[9]

> ### 🗩 Everyday Encounter: Turning Scripture Application Inside Out
>
> Frequently in our classrooms or scripture study, we begin with a scripture passage and then ask, "How does this apply to you?" A more personal and helpful way of building an analogy might begin by asking a question before turning to the scriptures: "What is an issue in my life, and where in the scriptures can I find a story that relates to it?" For example, rather than looking for facts to fit a story in the assigned reading block, we can begin with our present needs and then search the scriptures for a story with elements that can be compared to our needs and help frame our next steps. We may have to search all of the standard works, but when we find the right "fit," it will provide guidance, strength, and motivation.

You Try It

Rumor

What a coincidence!

Sniff Tests

1. *Coincidences.* Coincidences are chance occurrences or loose parallels created through selectivity, imprecision, and misrepresentation of details.

2. *More coincidences.* A long list of selective, imprecise, or misrepresented details is still only a list of errors. Beware any story that turns on "remarkable parallels."

3. *Incomplete analogies.* Beware of analogies that simply assert equivalence (without evidence), confuse the categories for the information, or present inaccurate or incomplete information from the past or present.

4. *Superlatives.* Simply calling a person or event "the greatest" or "most important" or "most documented" is not the same as providing evidence to support that claim. It is not enough to claim to be first, or most, or least. Using superlatives without evidence is a lazy way to assert importance.

Real

Significance is best.

Key Concepts

1. We judge the significance of past events by paying attention to historical significances (important in its time), usable significances (helpful to us today), and personal significances (relevant to me or my family).

2. Analogies are built by defining *categories* for comparing the past and present, identifying correct *information* from the past and present, ensuring that each *comparison* between the past and present is valid, and using the comparisons to *frame* the present.

3. One of the fruits of the Holy Ghost is to judge righteously as we liken past events to our present circumstances.

Notes

1. Margaret MacMillan, *Dangerous Games: The Uses and Abuses of History* (New York: The Modern Library, 2009), xi; see also Douglas F.

Salmon, "Parallelomania and the Study of Latter-day Scripture: Confirmation, Coincidence, or Collective Unconscious?" *Dialogue: A Journal of Mormon Thought* 33, no. 2 (Summer 2000): 129–55.

2. Kevin Brown, *Penicillin Man: Alexander Fleming and the Antibiotic Revolution* (Stroud, Gloucestershire: The History Press, 2005), 25, 155–56.

3. Steven Novell, *The Skeptic's Guide to the Universe: How to Know What's Really Real in a World Increasingly Full of Fake* (New York: Grand Central Publishing, 2019), 9–18, 28–32, 94–105, 134–36.

4. James B. Allen, "Emergence of a Fundamental: The Expanding Role of Joseph Smith's First Vision in Mormon Religious Thought," *Journal of Mormon History* 7 (1980): 43–61; Carlos E. Asay, "Oh, How Lovely Was the Morning!" *Ensign*, April 1995, 44–49.

5. Adapted from Barry Schwartz, *Abraham Lincoln in the Post-Heroic Era: History and Memory in Late Twentieth-Century America* (Chicago: University of Chicago Press, 2008), 60–90.

6. David Hackett Fischer, *Historians' Fallacies: Toward a Logic of Historical Thought* (New York: Harper & Row, 1970), 244–58.

7. Chieko N. Okazaki, "Baskets and Bottles," *Ensign*, May 1996, 13.

8. Boyd K. Packer, *Teach Ye Diligently* (Salt Lake City: Deseret Book, 1991), 34, 268–81.

9. Francine R. Bennion, in *At the Pulpit: 185 Years of Discourses by Latter-day Saint Women*, ed. Jennifer Reeder and Kate Holbrook (Salt Lake City: Church Historian's Press, 2017), 219; Russell M. Nelson, "The Exodus Repeated: Pioneers" (devotional, Brigham Young University, Provo, UT, September 7, 1997), https://speeches. byu.edu/talks/russell-m-nelson_exodus-repeated/; M. Russell Ballard, "The Greatest Generation of Missionaries," *Ensign*, November 2002, 46–49; Dieter F. Uchtdorf, "Your Great Adventure," *Ensign*, November 2019, 86–90.

PART II
HOW TO INVESTIGATE

CHAPTER 9

Which Sources Can I Trust?

"That hearse carried Brigham Young's dead body!"

Standing in line for the Haunted Mansion ride at Disneyland was the last place I expected to hear a rumor about Church history. Painted a gleaming white and mounted on large wagon wheels, the hearse looked like a marble sarcophagus, accented by sculpted columns. An empty horse harness attached to the front swayed side to side in ghostly fashion. Surely this noble vehicle was fit to carry the corpse of a powerful leader. Why not Brigham Young?

President Young died in 1877. A closer look at the hearse reveals craftsmanship that was more common after the 1890s, and there is no record of the hearse's existence before the 1970s! But the most important piece of evidence is Brigham Young's will—it specified that his body be *hand carried* from the place of his death to the site of his grave. Brigham's body never entered a hearse![1]

We encounter pieces of the past like this hearse every day. Maybe you've found an old journal or a set of letters in your grandmother's attic. You might read a talk by a Church leader from the early days or see a newspaper clipping about a past event. Every piece of the past needs to be investigated by asking questions to evaluate whether we can trust what we have found. This chapter introduces a model for discerning what is real and what is rumor that draws on the concepts introduced in part 1.

Discerning Real and Rumor

Combined together, the concepts and thinking habits from part 1 become tools to help you investigate sources, stories, and studies. Before you even begin examining a source, you can survey its *situation* (chapter 4). An example of this kind of anticipatory thinking is found in the Book of Mormon. King Limhi sent forty-three people to find the land of Zarahemla. The searchers returned after discovering the ruins of a large settlement and records engraved in an unknown language on metal plates. Despite not being able to read the records, they wondered, in Limhi's words, "Perhaps, they will give us a knowledge of a remnant of the people who have been destroyed, from whence these records came; or, perhaps, they will give us a knowledge of this very people who have been destroyed" (Mosiah 8:12). Before you read a source or story, you can prepare your mind by posing similar questions about when and where it was created, its author and the author's purpose in writing to the audience, and the type of source or story it is. Keeping these thoughts in your mind as you read will help you evaluate the strengths and limitations of what you encounter.

As you read, analyze the *contents* by paying attention to the topics and ideas that are both included and omitted (chapter 6), the evidence and assumptions (chapters 2–3), and its structure and form (chapters 4–5). You should also connect sources, stories, and studies to relevant *contexts* (chapter 7). As you finish your investigation, attempt to evaluate how the source, story, or study is *significant* (chapter 8).

🔅 Thinking Habit:
Investigate Real and Rumor

Situation
Before you read, survey . . .

- Time and place
- Author
- Audience
- Purpose
- Type of history

Contents 🔍	Contexts
While you read, analyze . . .	While you read, connect . . .
• Storyline and structure	• Historical
• Argument	• Literary
• Assumptions and values	• Material
• Script and form	• Ethical
	• Biographical
	• Eternal

Significances ⚖️
After you read, evaluate . . .

- Historical
- Usable
- Personal

Look for . . . ACCURACY, AUTHENTICITY, RELIABILITY, FAIRNESS,
AND COMPREHENSIVENESS

Because we live in a world awash with rumors, myths, hoaxes, misinformation, and lies, we must learn to investigate what we encounter. We must learn to discern, as President Russell M. Nelson taught, "between schemes that are flashy and fleeting and those refinements that are uplifting and enduring." Elder David A. Bednar explained that discernment "helps us to distinguish the relevant from the irrelevant, the important from the unimportant, and the necessary from that which is merely nice." The Holy Ghost helps us discern truth and error, as well as things that are cunningly crafted or just silly. Discernment is a gift of the Spirit as well as a thinking skill that we can improve. Through practice and inspiration, we can develop a discerning eye, an analytical mind, and good judgment.[2] This chapter and those that follow will introduce criteria for evaluating the trustworthiness of sources, stories, and studies. These criteria are accuracy (chapter 9), authenticity (chapter 10), reliability (chapter 11), fairness (chapter 12), and comprehensiveness (chapter 13).

We investigate by asking questions. Elder Dieter F. Uchtdorf reminded that "we are a question-asking people. We have always been, because we know that inquiry leads to truth."[3] What happened in the past? What pieces remain? What do they mean? Which interpretation is better? How did the past shape the present? What lessons can I draw? The disposition to ask questions may be called "a healthy skepticism," a sense of awareness, or an attribute of discipleship. The best questions, like the samples in Appendix A, are open ended (not answered by a simple "yes" or "no") and produce more than one useful answer. They seek to understand how and why things happened (not just to learn a specific date or fact). They ask about what has been omitted. They invite deep thought and seek for all relevant evidence. They draw comparisons and seek for connections. The best questions originate in your own heart and mind as you take responsibility for your learning and growth.[4]

Investigating an Old Journal

Let's begin with a source from the past—Wilford Woodruff's journal. An old journal is one of the most interesting and useful kinds of sources to discover. Journals or diaries or daybooks— whatever the authors call them—usually contain strong evidence about the past. In a journal, an author records firsthand testimony of things experienced, thought, or felt. Journal writers often record their thoughts each day or every few days, meaning they describe events close to when they occurred.

Before opening Wilford's journal, we can survey the *situation* of his writing. He joined the Church in Kirtland, Ohio, when he was twenty-six years old. In the same month that he was baptized, December 1833, he began to keep a journal, and he kept the record for more than sixty years until his death in 1898. He produced nearly three dozen volumes containing more than seven thousand pages that detail his daily activities as well as some extraordinary events. He wrote summaries, drew sketches, and recorded tallies of routine activities. The journals remained in his possession during his lifetime and have been kept by the Church ever since.[5]

🖥️ Best Resources: Wilford Woodruff's Journals

You can view Wilford Woodruff's journal for yourself at ChurchHistoryLibrary.org by searching for "Wilford Woodruff Journals and Papers." His handwriting is beautiful, and his doodles are charming. Don't miss his account of driving Brigham Young into the Salt Lake Valley (July 24, 1847) or his painful visit to a dentist (December 1857).

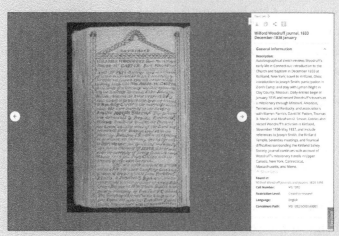

Wilford Woodruff's April 13, 1837, journal entry about his marriage to Phoebe Carter. Courtesy of the Church History Library.

Let's look more closely at the *contents* of the first volume. The book is bound in a leather cover that has become worn with time. The first of 194 pages contains a table listing the names and birthdates of Wilford's parents and siblings. The second page bears the inscription "Wilford Woodruff's Journal Containing an Account Of my life and travels from the time of my first connection with the Church of the Latter-day Saints." After a blank page, there are two pages of testimony, titled "The first Book of Wilford," that begin with a question: "When in the course of human events has there ever been a more important period than at the present day and age of the world"? He presents a one-page summary of his life before making his first daily entry on December 29, 1833. Entries in 1834 recount his first meeting with Joseph Smith and his participation in the Camp of Israel (Zion's Camp). He makes nearly daily entries during 1835, 1836, and 1837 that describe his missionary travels and meetings in Kirtland. The final entry in this volume was made on January 3, 1838.

If we step back from the immediate entries, we can connect Wilford's journal to many *contexts*. It fits within the historical context of early Church activities in the 1830s. He participated in well-known events, such as Zion's Camp, and the journal also provides wonderful firsthand information about missionary service in the era. If we think about the book in the context of Wilford's life, we see a young man, an enthusiastic convert, and a hard-working missionary. He won't be called as an apostle until volume 2 (April 1839), but he marries Phoebe Carter in this volume and celebrates the occasion with a two-page journal entry framed in an ornamental border (April 13, 1837).

Wilford Woodruff's journal provides a *significant* window into events and daily life during the earliest decades of Church history. In later volumes Wilford records Joseph Smith's sermons, his personal experiences crossing the plains, and his service in leading

Church councils and working with the temples in St. George and Salt Lake City.

Accuracy Matters

As we investigate the journal, we should wonder about the trustworthiness of the information reported. To establish *accuracy*—the first of five important criteria for investigating what is real and what is rumor—historians follow a process called corroboration to demonstrate that facts in one source can be found and verified in another. Sometimes we verify information by piecing together details from multiple sources in a process called triangulation. Often the gaps in one source are filled in by another, but it takes work to find them all. Ideally, we'd like to corroborate all facts—"the mouth of two or three witnesses" is better (2 Cor. 13:1)—but it doesn't always work out.

Can we corroborate Wilford's information? He recorded his first meeting with "our beloved Brother Joseph Smith the prophet & Seer," which took place on April 25, 1834. Joseph Smith's journal contains entries on April 23 and 30, but it makes no mention of meeting Wilford.[6] In other places, Wilford provides the only piece of the past that has survived to document an event, such as a revelation received by Joseph Smith (January 5, 1837) or minutes of a Church conference (April 1843).

Wilford was the only person to record teachings from forty-seven of Joseph Smith's discourses, but there are many other sermons where multiple accounts survive. For example, four people recorded notes about Joseph's "King Follett Sermon." Wilford recorded 2,400 words, about half as many as Thomas Bullock but more than twice as many as Willard Richards.[7] In these instances, we can compare Wilford's records to those made by others, and we see that Wilford was an accurate record keeper. The best approach to corroborating historical sources is to gather and analyze every existing account, whether they be accounts with the same author (e.g., Joseph Smith and the First Vision) or accounts from many people who participated in the same event (e.g., the several people who heard Joseph deliver a sermon).

Sometimes, the search for corroboration requires extensive contextual work. Consider the nineteenth-century Latter-day Saint convert, pioneer, and spiritual leader Jane Manning James. Instead of compiling a daily journal, she left only an eight-page autobiographical summary, which she dictated to a scribe near the end of her life. In this reminiscence made many years after the events, she recounts her baptism and walking to Nauvoo because the river boat would not allow free Blacks to ride; she relates her experiences with the gift of tongues, healings, and revelation, and with handling a seer stone; she describes working in the homes of Joseph Smith and Brigham Young as well as learning about plural marriage, crossing the plains, raising children with one of her husbands, and performing baptisms for the dead in the temple. No records survive in her hand, and she is mentioned in only a few other places and appears in a few photographs. Jane's modern biographer confesses, "Much of this story, then, is conjectural: I have combined the few documents that do exist with evidence about the lives of Jane's peers—African Americans, women, Latter-day Saints—to flesh out the possibilities and follow the suggestions of the evidence. Where the sources are inconclusive, I imagine the possibilities and discuss the most plausible scenarios."[8] Often that is the best we can do.

Other times, the search for corroboration reveals inaccuracy. For many years, published statements attributed section 135 of the Doctrine and Covenants to John Taylor, an apostle who was in the jail at Carthage and later became Church President. The headnote to the section in the 1981 edition of the Doctrine and Covenants stated that Taylor was the author, but its cited source—*History of the*

Church—did not name an author of the section. The first edition of the Doctrine and Covenants to publish the section (in 1844) did not list Taylor as its author.[9] Published commentaries attributed the section to Taylor without citing evidence or citing sources that did not exist.[10] In October 1922, Heber J. Grant mentioned, "I have understood that this splendid account of the martyrdom of Joseph and Hyrum Smith was written by President John Taylor."[11]

However, because the search for corroboration could not verify the fact, in the 2013 edition of the Doctrine and Covenants, the attribution of the section to John Taylor was removed. Because the section was published in September 1844, it was likely written in July or August and must have drawn on the eyewitness testimonies of John Taylor and Willard Richards, who were both in the jail and worked closely with the printing office in Nauvoo. The section also quotes from earlier newspaper editorials and notices that Taylor and Richards helped to write.[12] But the section in its final form was never attributed to John Taylor during his own lifetime, and no evidence has survived to corroborate this conclusion.

Sometimes corroboration comes only after a very long time. Take, for example, the ability of the Nephites to verify that Jerusalem had been destroyed. Before Lehi left Jerusalem, he and other prophets predicted that the city would be destroyed in the future (see 1 Ne. 1:4, 18). Nephi later added that his people would "know at some future period that the word of the Lord shall be fulfilled concerning the destruction of Jerusalem" (1 Ne. 7:13). Since Lehi's family crossed the ocean, the first references came through additional prophecy when Jacob and Nephi later testified that the destruction had occurred (see 2 Ne. 6:8; 25:10). Hundreds of years later the Nephites stumbled upon the Mulekites, who corroborated the city's captivity from their own traditions (see Omni 1:14–16). The quest for corroboration requires patience and perseverance.

> 💬 **Everyday Encounter:**
> **Corroborating Personal Revelation**
>
> People often ask, "How do I know if I'm receiving revelation?" The Holy Ghost uses a method of corroboration by communicating with our minds *and* our hearts: "I will tell you in your mind *and* in your heart, by the Holy Ghost" (D&C 8:2; emphasis added). Alma's metaphor of planting a seed notes that a good word will "enlighten my understanding" *and* "enlarge my soul" (Alma 32:28). Joseph Smith described baptism for the dead as a topic that "seems to occupy my *mind*, and press itself upon my *feelings* the strongest" (D&C 128:1; emphasis added). Therefore, if you wonder if a thought comes from God, you can pray and ask for a confirming feeling in your heart. If you don't know how to make sense of an unsettling feeling, you can pray for mental enlightenment. Your mind and heart corroborate inspiration from the Holy Ghost.

You Try It

Rumor

That sounds like a nice story.

Sniff Tests

1. *No attempt at analysis.* Information doesn't just exist—it comes from somewhere. Before sharing information, we must investigate it.
2. *No attempt at corroboration.* We should attempt to corroborate all information. We should not share information that cannot be corroborated.

Real

Accuracy matters.

Key Concepts

1. We discern real and rumor by investigating the situation, contents, contexts, and significances of sources, stories, and studies.
2. The best criteria for discerning trustworthiness include accuracy, authenticity, reliability, fairness, and comprehensiveness.
3. We establish accuracy through corroboration, by finding the same information in multiple sources.

Notes

1. Lynn Arave, "Disney Hearse Has No Link to Brigham Young," *Deseret News*, February 23, 2001, C01.
2. Russell M. Nelson, "Ask, Seek, Knock," *Ensign*, November 2009, 83; David A. Bednar, "Quick to Observe: The Gift of Discernment" (devotional, Brigham Young University, Provo, UT, May 10, 2005); Joe Nickell, *Real or Fake: Studies in Authentication* (Lexington: University Press of Kentucky, 2009), 12.
3. Dieter F. Uchtdorf, "The Reflection in the Water" (address, Worldwide Devotional for Young Adults, November 1, 2009), video, https://www.churchofjesuschrist.org/media/video/2009-11-0050-the-reflection-in-the-water?
4. David A. Bednar, *Increase in Learning: Spiritual Patterns for Obtaining Your Own Answers* (Salt Lake City: Deseret Book, 2011), 102–14; David Hackett Fischer, *Historians' Fallacies: Toward a Logic of Historical Thought* (New York: Harper & Row, 1970), 4–38.
5. Wilford Woodruff Journals and Papers, 1828–1898, Church History Library, Salt Lake City.
6. Joseph Smith, journal, April 23, 30, 1834, The Joseph Smith Papers, https://www.josephsmithpapers.org/paper-summary/journal-1832-1834/83.
7. "Accounts of the King Follett Sermon," The Joseph Smith Papers, https://www.josephsmithpapers.org/site/accounts-of-the-king-follett-sermon.

8. Quincy D. Newell, *Your Sister in the Gospel: The Life of Jane Manning James, a Nineteenth-Century Black Mormon* (New York: Oxford University Press, 2019), 5; Jane Manning James, autobiography, circa 1902, Church History Library.

9. Joseph Smith, *History of the Church of Jesus Christ of Latter-day Saints*, 7 vols., ed. B. H. Roberts, (Salt Lake City: Deseret Book: 1902–12), 6:629–31; Doctrine and Covenants (1844), section 135, The Joseph Smith Papers, http://www.josephsmithpapers.org/paper-summary/doctrine-and-covenants-1844/446; B. H. Roberts, *A Comprehensive History of The Church of Jesus Christ of Latter-day Saints*, 6 vols. (Salt Lake City: The Church of Jesus Christ of Latter-day Saints, 1930), 2:334–37.

10. Hyrum M. Smith and Janne M. Sjodahl, *The Doctrine and Covenants, Containing Revelations Given to Joseph Smith, Jr.*, rev. ed. (Salt Lake City: Deseret Book, 1958), 855 (no citation); Roy W. Doxey, *The Latter-day Prophets and the Doctrine and Covenants*, 4 vols. (Salt Lake City: Deseret Book, 1965), 4:503 (cited Heber J. Grant's general conference address in October 1933; should have been 1922).

11. Heber J. Grant, in Conference Report, October 1922, 7; *Improvement Era* 26, no. 2 (December 1922): 102.

12. Jeffrey Mahas, "Remembering the Martyrdom," in *Revelations in Context: The Stories behind the Sections of the Doctrine and Covenants*, ed. Matthew McBride and James Goldberg (Salt Lake City: The Church of Jesus Christ of Latter-day Saints, 2016), 299–306.

CHAPTER 10

You Sure It Ain't Fake?

"There is a photograph of Joseph Smith for sale on Etsy!"

I clicked the link in the email to see that the seller "Pictures2die4" was indeed offering a "PROPHET JOSEPH SMITH Death Photo & Portrait Daguerreotype ca. 1844." The year was correct: Joseph was murdered in 1844. The technology was correct: daguerreotypes were the first viable method of photography, invented in 1839. But the image was clearly a fake. The "Joseph" looked more like a Dracula, lying in a coffin dressed in a luxurious tuxedo. The Etsy "Rare Find" icon alerted me that there was only one item in stock, and the asking price of $50,000 qualified for free shipping.

We live in a golden age of fakery. Photoshopped images and deep-faked videos go viral on social media, cable channels air documentaries about mermaids and monsters, rumors spread through our congregations. Such counterfeits are nothing new. Amalickiah's propagandists preached from towers, just as King Benjamin had done (see Mosiah 2:8; Alma 48:1). In the earliest days of the Church, the Saints faced fake spirits and counterfeit revelation to the point that multiple revelations provide warnings about "false spirits," "deceivers and hypocrites," and even "the devil as an angel of light" (D&C 50:2, 6; 129:8).

Because appearances can be deceiving, in this chapter we apply our investigation skills to fakes and forgeries. Examining the situation, contents, and contexts help establish *authenticity*, the second important criteria for knowing what to trust.

Authenticity Matters

In addition to being accurate, the best sources are also authentic. Long before *authenticity* meant a carefully staged photo on Instagram, it described important qualities of historical sources. An authentic document was created in the past, by the person who claimed to have created it, and at the time and place it purports to have been created. Additionally, we have the most confidence in a source's authenticity when we know where it has been from the time of its creation until now. A historic site is authentic if it has the original structures at the original location with the original content. Mount Vernon is the original building, located in the place where George Washington built it, and his possessions are on display there. By contrast, at Disneyland the "historic" buildings are invented structures (not original), in a convenient public location (not original), with fabricated content (not original). The Plimoth settlement in Massachusetts features original structures that have been moved to a non-original site with an effort to find or create replicas of original content.[1] Sometimes a good-faith effort with the few pieces of the past that remain is the best we can do.

Creators of fake or forged documents stretch the limits of authenticity. It is most difficult to manufacture an entirely new work—to create a total forgery. More often, perpetrators create fakes by altering or adding to an authentic work, such as by forging a signature onto a historical piece of paper. Additionally, someone has to invent a story to connect the fake item to a person or event in the past and to describe how the item survived to the present.

Perpetrators exploit the weaknesses of human thinking. To

begin with, we seem to have an innate sense of trust; we *assume* that what we experience is true. Frankly, it is not possible or feasible to verify everything. As a result, our minds create shortcuts for evaluating the world around us—we are likely to trust a source if we are familiar with it, if it is easy to understand, if there is a memorable story or pattern, if it contains scientific formulas or graphs, if we feel pleasant emotions, or if it aligns with what we already think or believe.[2] It turns out we're naturally quite bad at identifying fakes. One recent study revealed that people could identify fake images only 60 percent of the time; and when they *knew* the image was false, they could spot the error only 45 percent of the time.[3]

💡 Thinking Habit:
Think the Second Thought

Knowing that our first tendency is to trust, we should cultivate a habit of *thinking the second thought*. Imagine that we have two systems for thinking: a first that works quickly and reflexively and a second that concentrates and makes choices.[4] To activate the second, we must pause and consciously ask, "Is this real?" (see Alma 32:35). This process is the old adage to "trust but verify." An angel taught the prophet Nephi to "look" again and again when Nephi was responding to the angel's questions and taking in new information (see 1 Ne. 11–14). One reason that fakes spread so quickly on the internet is the online environment conditions us to scroll quickly and react with emotion while liking and sharing, without pausing for the second, cautionary thought. Develop the habit of reconsidering, of *thinking the second thought*.

Consider the story of Joseph Smith's murder as told by William M. Daniels, a non–Latter-day Saint who happened to pass through the town of Carthage, Illinois, on that fateful day. Daniels was outraged by the mob violence and signed a simple affidavit denouncing the actions for the authorities within the week. The ire of locals combined with a dream Daniels had led him to join the Church, and the following year he published a pamphlet, titled *A Correct Account of the Murder of Generals Joseph and Hyrum Smith*. The pamphlet caused a stir, in part because Daniels provided many details of "danger, excitement and wickedness." However, it was his account of what happened after the murder that would leave a lasting impression. He told of a "ruffian" who approached Joseph's dead body with a desire to cut off its head. The man "raised the knife and was in the attitude of striking, when a light, so sudden and powerful, burst from the heavens upon the bloody scene." The light, Daniels observed, "baffles all powers of description," and "the arm of the ruffian, that held the knife, fell powerless." Joseph's body had been rescued from defilement.[5] The pamphlet includes a rough woodcut of the scene, depicting the jail, the people, and the light from heaven.

Daniels was called to testify at the trial of the alleged murderers. Pressed about the story under oath, he retracted details, admitted he might have been a little careless with the facts, and then blamed the pamphlet's typesetter for adding the story about the light. "I did not write that," he declared of the story, "neither did I authorize it to be written."[6] But his testimony, eked out in the trial, did nothing to stop the previous circulation of the pamphlet.

This story took another dramatic twist when a letter that "corroborated" the pamphlet was published. See if this letter passes your sniff tests. It was supposedly written by a William Webb to an *unnamed* newspaper that never published it. The newspaper was later acquired by a new, *unnamed* owner, who found the letter in the newspaper's files and handed it to an *unnamed* friend. That friend happened to show it to two missionaries, Elders McEwen and Wareham, who made a certified copy. If all of the unnamed links didn't raise your suspicions, I can add that no missionaries by those names appear in the Church's missionary database during the relevant period.[7]

Artist C. C. A. Christensen depicted the fabricated story of a ray of light stopping the desecration of Joseph Smith's body. C. C. A. Christensen (1831–1912), Exterior of Carthage Jail, ca. 1878, tempera on muslin, 78 x 114¹/₂ inches. Brigham Young University Museum of Art, gift of the grandchildren of C. C. A. Christensen, 1970.

But the deed was done, and the letter found its way into the hands of a young convert named C. C. A. Christensen, who presented the scene in bold colors as part of his *Mormon Panorama*, twenty-three paintings that chronicle the history of the Church from the First Vision to the Saints' arrival in the Salt Lake Valley. Elder B. H. Roberts lamented that "this whole fabric of myth and legend" had "unfortunately, found its way into some of our otherwise acceptable church works, and still more unfortunately has entered into the beliefs of many Latter-day Saints."[8] A fabricated story, denied under oath, had been re-created by one of the Church's most influential artists.

Every fake involves six related components: (1) a perpetrator with (2) a motive, (3) a target constituency with (4) a desire, and (5) a fabrication with (6) a provenance. In this case, the *perpetrator* Daniels sought notoriety and influence, though his *motive* quickly dissipated under legal cross-examination. The *targeted* Saints who believed the story—the earliest hearers, the painter, and earnest re-tellers—*desired* stories that confirmed their faith in a God who calls and protects prophets. This example involves two *fabrications*—the pamphlet and the "corroborating" letter. In both instances, the fabrications were stories, though sometimes they take more sophisticated forms, such as materials created to pass for historical documents. *Provenance* is the term historians use to describe how an item was created in the past and handed down to the present. Daniels told one version of provenance (he saw the events occur) before changing his story under oath (the typesetter inserted it). The letter had a shadowy provenance to begin with. Ironically, even though this story has every component of a fake, some less-alert victims grow more excited by a string of amazing coincidences.

Not all perpetrators and retellers of fakes or myths possess nefarious motives. Some seek to honor an ancestor, defend the Church, or inspire faith. Others just want to teach a lesson or make themselves look important or informed. Some myths arise out of ignorance or from a well-meaning intention to fill in the gaps. And even when a story is a fabrication, the underlying desires of the perpetrator and target constituency might reveal truths about the community.

Book of Mormon writers paid particular attention to prov-enance, frequently writing about where their records came from and how the records were passed from one person to the next.[9] Provenance was essential in identifying which seer stone Joseph Smith used to translate the Book of Mormon. When the Church published a photograph of the stone in the *Ensign* and in a Joseph Smith Papers volume, the accompanying explanation provided sources from the past documenting that Joseph used this particu-lar stone. These sources describe it as oval, rounded, egg-shaped, brown, striped, and chocolate colored. The explanation also cited sources showing that this stone had been passed from Joseph to

Oliver Cowdery, to Oliver's wife Elizabeth, to Brigham Young's brother Phineas, to Brigham, to his wife Zina, to their daughter Zina, and finally into the Church's custody.[10]

It Ain't Nothin' but a Forgery

Your investigation skills are necessary in a world where forgers deliberately fabricate sources about the past. Forgeries date back to the earliest days of Church history when three men from Kinderhook, Illinois, manufactured six brass plates, covered them with inscriptions, and staged a "discovery" in an Indian mound. After Joseph Smith's death, recent convert James Strang forged a letter stating that Smith appointed Strang as his successor. In the first case, Joseph Smith looked at the plates, announced he would investigate them more fully, and then never got around to completing a thorough analysis.[11] The Strang forgery led many early Saints away from the Church, some of whom never returned.[12] Forgeries bring serious consequences, and Joseph learned early that he and we "cannot always tell the wicked from the righteous" (D&C 10:37).

When the *Church News* announced that, based on my analysis, the notes presumably written by Elvis Presley in a Book of Mormon were actually forged, I was flooded with messages of disbelief and criticism. Some left comments online or sent emails; others telephoned or traveled to Salt Lake City to confront me in person. With your skills, you can now appreciate the complete investigation I published in *BYU Studies Quarterly*. The annotations in the Book of Mormon—a signature and handwritten notes on thirty-six pages—do not match Elvis's authentic signature, do not match his handwriting, and do not align with his method of annotating. He underlined and wrote brief words in book margins using rough, block-print letters, whereas the forged annotations were in smooth, cursive lettering that carried on a dialogue with the text;

the signature bore signs similar to other forgeries of his signature that have surfaced in auction houses.

Further, the alleged context of his writing placed the book in his hands during the last two weeks of his life, which meant he would have read and marked hundreds of pages of scripture while hosting his nine-year-old daughter, preparing to go on tour, and reeling from the publication of a damaging exposé. And multiple stories of provenance told by the donor of the book competed with each other—Elvis's father wanted the book destroyed, Elvis's father wanted the book given to the Osmond family, or the book was sent to an auction house that decided not to sell it. The first time I examined the book, the strained context did not pass the sniff tests. Then I easily discovered the noncorroboration of the signature since numerous authentic signatures exist. Finally, a little bit of research turned up samples of Elvis's annotations in other books and multiple competing versions of the provenance story. Five independent experts in Elvis Presley's handwriting and writing habits corroborated my conclusion that the annotations were forged.[13]

This kind of investigation helps the staff of the Joseph Smith Papers identify authentic Joseph Smith documents. A letter from David R. Atchison to Joseph Smith dated September 1, 1838, ultimately failed the tests of contents, contexts, and provenance. The letter mentions historical events that actually occurred on different dates, and the handwriting in the letter did not match known samples of Atchison's writing. The provenance of the document was likewise suspect—only a photocopy survived, the photocopy was donated in 1981, and nothing is known about where the letter had been between 1838 and 1981. Then, another photocopy of the same letter turned up at the University of Utah, and this copy had been given to the donor by convicted forger and murderer Mark Hofmann.[14] The Joseph Smith Papers staff did not publish this letter because it was a forgery.

To detect more sophisticated forgeries, forensic methods are necessary to study a document's material composition and microscopic qualities. Examiners can see the thickness and ingredients of the paper. Methods used to make paper appear old or dirty to the natural eye leave some microscopic cracks or residues on the document. Ultraviolet light can reveal unnatural color patterns or hazing.[15] But advanced technologies aside, your investigative skills, coupled with a keen nose for sniff tests, can help you develop a discerning eye and good judgment.

💬 Everyday Encounter:
Tears Are Not Necessarily a Testimony

President Howard W. Hunter offered a "word of caution" to those who "may begin to try to counterfeit the true influence of the Spirit of the Lord by unworthy and manipulative means." He explained, "I get concerned when it appears that strong emotion or free-flowing tears are equated with the presence of the Spirit. Certainly the Spirit of the Lord can bring strong emotional feelings, including tears, but that outward manifestation ought not to be confused with the presence of the Spirit itself."[16]

Worth a Thousand . . . Questions

Photographs are more difficult to authenticate than written documents. This runs counter to the conventional saying that "a picture is worth a thousand words." But *think* about it. Unless someone has written notes on the back, when you find a photograph in an attic, you often don't know who took the photograph, who is in the photograph, or when or where or why it was taken. Photographs often reveal a lot about the *contents* of history—physical appearances, clothing styles, locations and settings—but not always as much about *situations*, *contexts*, or *significances*.

I always have "a thousand questions" when someone shows me

what they believe to be a photograph of Joseph Smith. No known photograph of Joseph Smith survives, though it's possible he sat for a photograph—the daguerreotype technology was invented in 1839 in France and brought to the United States the following year.[17] No journals or letters record Joseph sitting for a photograph, but two daguerreotypists set up shop in Nauvoo, the first in the summer of 1844 (the year of Joseph's death), and others traveled or operated in nearby cities where Joseph traveled. At least once a year someone brings a supposed photograph of Joseph Smith into the Church History Library. We've turned away photographs of an elderly gray-haired "Joseph" with a cane (Joseph was *thirty-eight* when he was murdered) and photos of a young raven-haired "Joseph" (locks of his *light brown* hair have survived).

We can attempt to corroborate a potential photograph of Joseph from a few imperfect reference points. A death-mask cast was made of his face after he was murdered, and while the cast is helpful for determining his bone structure, we're not totally sure how it was influenced by injuries and swelling (Joseph fell from a second-story window).[18] While he was alive, Joseph sat for two portrait paintings and was sketched by one courtroom reporter.[19] However, people who knew Joseph emphatically declared that the paintings did not capture his appearance. Bathsheba Smith, who knew Joseph, called all artistic attempts "little better than caricatures."[20]

The most common mistake made by modern people is to assume that an old photograph of one of the oil paintings is actually a photograph. In order to definitively identify an actual photograph of Joseph Smith, we'd need an image that corroborates surviving physical descriptions plus a well-documented story about how he sat for the photograph (historical context) and a really clear story about where the photograph has been hiding for more than 175 years (provenance). *Every* claim of a photograph of Joseph Smith should be investigated very carefully.

💻 Best Resources:
Websites to Authenticate
Photos and Videos on the Internet

Photographs have long been doctored, sometimes to make a model look more beautiful or to remove a former-political-ally-turned-foe. But the advent of digital photography and video, cheap editing tools, and instant distribution through social media has turned our day into a golden age of fakery and hoaxes. The internet is "a maze filled with trap doors and blind alleys, where things are not always what they seem."[21] Authentic pieces of the distant past do not begin online; someone had to scan and upload them, often without attribution. Elder Neil L. Andersen lamented that "internet information does not have a 'truth' filter."[22] Without that, what can we do?

When analyzing the websites that host images and videos, pay more attention to the *situation* and *contexts*. This means that instead of reading "vertically" down the contents of a site, look "laterally" at other sites and online information. Don't be fooled by a site's domain name, an official-looking logo, a nice layout, or the presence of citations. Find out who hosts the site and why. Search for information about the creator or owner of a site in the internet's official registry (**whois.icann.org**). Find out what kinds of (reputable or disreputable) sites link to the site you are analyzing with a "backlink" checker, such as Majestic (**majestic.com**) or Ahrefs (**ahrefs.com**).

Several tools can help authenticate an image. Google offers a reverse image search that lets you see where else an image appears online (**images.google.com**). Tin Eye searches the web for images and offers a "Compare" feature that highlights any differences caused by cropping, resizing, skewing, or other manipulation (**www.tineye.com**). FotoForensics reveals if an image has been modified (**fotoforensics.com**), and Jeffrey's Image Metadata

Viewer reveals information about the creation of specific digital images (**exif.regex.info/exif.cgi**). For videos, the YouTube Data Viewer reveals when a video was originally posted and extracts image thumbnails that can themselves be searched in reverse (**citizen-evidence.amnestyusa.org**).

You Try It

Rumor

What I found on the internet must be true.

Sniff Tests

1. *Too good to be true.* If it seems too good to be true, it probably is.
2. *No provenance.* A source that surfaces without any account of where it's been since it was created should raise questions.

Real

Authenticity matters.

Key Concepts

1. Fakes exist because perpetrators with motives act upon target constituencies who have desires and human limitations.
2. We establish authenticity by verifying that a source was created in the time, place, and way that it purports and accounting for its whereabouts since creation—the provenance.
3. Fakes can be identified by investigating an item's situation, contents, contexts, and material characteristics.

Notes

1. Diane Barthel, *Historic Preservation: Collective Memory and Historical Identity* (New Brunswick, NJ: Rutgers University Press, 1996), 2–10.

2. Elizabeth J. Marsh and Brenda W. Yang, "Believing Things That Are Not True: A Cognitive Science Approach to Misinformation," in *Misinformation and Mass Audiences*, ed. Brian G. Southwell, Emily A. Thorson, and Laura Sheble (Austin: University of Texas Press, 2018), 15–34; Loren Collins, *Bullspotting: Finding Facts in the Age of Misinformation* (Amherst, NY: Prometheus Books, 2012), 18–28.

3. Kendra Pierre-Louis, "You're Probably Terrible at Spotting Faked Photos," Popular Science, July 18, 2017, https://www.popsci.com/fake-news-manipulated-photo/.

4. Daniel Kahneman, *Thinking, Fast and Slow* (New York: Farrar, Straus and Giroux, 2011), 20–21.

5. William M. Daniels, *A Correct Account of the Murder of Generals Joseph and Hyrum Smith* (Nauvoo, IL: John Taylor, 1845), 23, 15.

6. Dallin H. Oaks and Marvin S. Hill, *Carthage Conspiracy: The Trial of the Accused Assassins of Joseph Smith* (Urbana: University of Illinois Press, 1975), 88–90, 127–34; Davis Bitton, *The Martyrdom Remembered: A One-Hundred-Fifty-Year Perspective on the Assassination of Joseph Smith* (Salt Lake City: Aspen Books, 1994), 63–66, 94–95.

7. B. H. Roberts, *A Comprehensive History of The Church of Jesus Christ of Latter-day Saints*, 6 vols. (Salt Lake City: The Church of Jesus Christ of Latter-day Saints, 1930), 2:333–34; "Church Publications for the Period," in *History of the Church of Jesus Christ of Latter-day Saints*, 7 vols., ed. B. H. Roberts, (Salt Lake City: Deseret Book: 1902–12), 7:558–59; Missionary Database, The Church of Jesus Christ of Latter-day Saints, https://history.churchofjesuschrist.org/missionary.

8. Roberts, *Comprehensive History*, 2:332–33.

9. Anita Wells, "Bare Record: The Nephite Archivist, The Record of Records, and the Book of Mormon Provenance," *Interpreter: A Journal of Latter-day Saint Faith and Scholarship* 24 (2017): 99–122.

10. Richard E. Turley, Mark Ashurst-McGee, and Robin Scott Jensen, "Joseph the Seer," *Ensign*, October 2015, 49–55.

11. "Kinderhook Plates," Church History Topics, The Church of Jesus Christ of Latter-day Saints, https://www.churchofjesuschrist.org/study/history/topics/kinderhook-plates?; Don Bradley and Mark Ashurst-McGee, "'President Joseph Has Translated a Portion': Joseph Smith and the Mistranslation of the Kinderhook Plates," in *Producing Ancient Scripture: Joseph Smith's Translation Projects in the Development of Mormon Christianity*, ed. Michael Hubbard MacKay, Mark Ashurst-McGee, and Brian M. Hauglid (Salt Lake City: University of Utah Press, 2020), 452–524.

12. William D. Russell, "King James Strang: Joseph Smith's Successor?" in *Mormon Mavericks: Essays on Dissenters*, ed. John Sillito and Susan Staker (Salt Lake City: Signature, 2002), 131–58. The letter is preserved at Yale University. Charles Eberstadt, "A Letter That Founded a Kingdom," *Autograph Collector's Journal* 3 (October 1950): 2–5, 32.

13. Keith A. Erekson, "Elvis Presley's Copy of the Book of Mormon Ain't Nothin' but a Forgery, Church History Experts Say," *Church News*, November 14, 2018; Keith A. Erekson, "Elvis Has Left the Library: Identifying Forged Annotations in a Book of Mormon," *BYU Studies Quarterly* 57, no. 4 (2018): 51–77.

14. See Robin Scott Jensen, "The Joseph Smith Papers and Questions of Authentic Documents," The Joseph Smith Papers, November 22, 2017, https://www.josephsmithpapers.org/articles/november-2017-questions-of-authentic-documents; Richard E. Turley, *Victims: The LDS Church and the Mark Hofmann Case* (Urbana: University of Illinois Press, 1992).

15. Michael Hubbard MacKay, Katie Smith, and Katie Anderson, "Faked: Identifying a New Hofmann Forgery," *Mormon Historical Studies* 16, no. 2 (Fall 2015): 35–67.

16. Clyde J. Williams, ed., *The Teachings of Howard W. Hunter: Fourteenth President of The Church of Jesus Christ of Latter-day Saints* (Salt Lake City: Bookcraft, 1997), 184.

17. Ronald E. Romig and Lachlan Mackay, "What Did Joseph Look Like?" *Saints Herald* 141, no. 12 (December 1994): 8–10, 12.

18. The best study of Joseph's appearance is Ephraim Hatch, *Joseph Smith Portraits: A Search for the Prophet's Likeness* (Provo, UT: Religious Studies Center, Brigham Young University, 1998).

19. Andrew H. Hedges, Alex D. Smith, and Richard Lloyd Anderson, eds., *Journals, Volume 2: December 1841–April 1843*, The Joseph Smith Papers (Salt Lake City: Church Historian's Press, 2011), 221.

20. Bathsheba W. Smith, Angus M. Cannon, John Smith, in *Collected Discourses Delivered by President Wilford Woodruff, His Two Counselors, the Twelve Apostles, and Others*, 5 vols., ed. Brian H. Stuy (Sandy, UT: B.H.S. Publishing, 1987), 5:33.

21. Sam Wineburg and Sarah McGrew, "Lateral Reading: Reading Less and Learning More When Evaluating Digital Information," Stanford History Education Group Working Paper (Rochester, NY: Social Science Research Network, October 6, 2017), 15, https://papers.ssrn.com/abstract=3048994.

22. Neil L. Andersen, "Joseph Smith," *Ensign*, November 2014, 29.

CHAPTER 11

You Got a Source
for That Story?

"The saying went abroad in the church . . ." What is a person to do with such a story? The only fact is straightforward and verifiable. Alma had "departed out of the land" and he was "never heard of more." After that fact came "the saying" that Alma had been "taken up by the Spirit, or buried by the hand of the Lord, even as Moses." Such an event might be plausible, Mormon noted. After all, Alma "was a righteous man," but that is still not sufficient proof of his being taken up like Moses. Without a source to document Alma's final activities, Mormon concluded simply, "we know nothing concerning his death and burial" (Alma 45:18–19).

Modern variations of Alma's story begin with "My seminary teacher said . . ." or "I can't remember which General Authority told this story, but . . ." or "I was reading online . . ." Latter-day Saints hear hundreds of stories throughout the course of weekly Church attendance and participation in conferences, classes, firesides, workshops, and pageants. Some speakers tell stories of their personal experiences, others make more generic attempts at crafting "parables," but most stories told by Latter-day Saints are about the past.

No story should be allowed to float freely in our midst. We must submit stories to a process of investigation. Often, the first question to ask is whether the story has a source beneath it. In the twenty-first century, the internet can be a powerful resource for tracing stories to a source.

Trace a Story to a Source

The first step in analyzing any story is to trace it to a source. Sometimes, stories come with clear attributions, but most of the time stories are vague or heard secondhand. In these cases, we must ask questions to identify specific details, follow those details to specific sources, and then evaluate the accuracy and authenticity of the sources in order to determine the reliability of the story.

⚡ Thinking Habit:
Trace a Story to a Source

1. Identify *specific* details.
2. Follow the details to *specific* sources.
3. Evaluate the *accuracy* and *authenticity* of the sources.
4. Determine the *reliability* of the story.

Let's begin with an example of a work that includes a citation. In her influential 1945 biography of Joseph Smith, *No Man Knows My History*, Fawn Brodie alleged that David Whitmer, one of the Three Witnesses, changed his testimony about the gold plates over time. According to Brodie, shortly after the Book of Mormon was published, Whitmer explained that "Joseph had led him to an open field, where they found the plates lying on the ground"—a very different story than Moroni showing the plates to the Three Witnesses. In her text, Brodie says of the story that "David Whitmer told the editor of the *Reflector*" and at the bottom of the page the footnote reads "Palmyra *Reflector*, March 19, 1831." As it turns out, there is a copy of this newspaper in the Church

History Library, and sure enough there is a story on that date titled "Gold Bible No. 6." When we get to the part of the story about Whitmer, the source is not David but an unnamed "informant," and as it happens, the "informant did not recollect precisely" the details that the author goes on to describe. Browsing through other articles in the paper, it quickly becomes evident that many of the pieces in the *Reflector* were satirical—a common literary device in satire is to attribute fuzzy stories to a shadowy informant.

At minimum, we should distrust this story because it is reported at least thirdhand—Whitmer to an unnamed informant to the newspaper editor. In contrast, there are more than two hundred *firsthand* statements by the witnesses. And, seeing this story in the context of other satirical stories, we can conclude that this story is not accurate.[1]

Let's look at a story without a citation but one that's still relatively easy to investigate. A friend made a comment that the Church is planning to remove the restriction on drinking cola drinks because the Church recently purchased a controlling stake in the Coca-Cola Company. Because the heart of this story involves a large, publicly traded corporation, I'd start with one of the websites that evaluates facts and hoaxes. Typing "Mormon Coca-Cola" in the search box at Snopes.com yields a single result that declares this hoax to be categorically false. The author checked the public list of Coca-Cola shareholders and did not find the Church on the list. I also like that the explanation points out that the company is too large for any one person or group to control. The largest shareholder at the time of writing was Berkshire Hathaway, whose 400 million shares were valued at $31 billion but represented only 9 percent of the company.[2] Since the most important fact in this story is not accurate, the rest of it falls.

Now another. A classroom teacher fervently explains that a Catholic priest prophesied of the Restoration in 1739. Writing in an old book that ended up in a library in Basel, Switzerland, the

Catholic wrote that the true gospel was lost, false doctrine filled the earth, and an angel would come to the earth within one hundred years to restore the truth to believers who would build a great city before being driven to the shores of a great lake. The teacher relates that he served in the Swiss mission many years ago, and though he did not see the book, other missionaries had seen it before it mysteriously disappeared.

Thankfully, the teacher shared a lot of specific details that can become your internet search terms—Catholic priest; 1739; Basel, Switzerland; and prophecy. Hopefully in your internet search, you were able find an article in *BYU Studies* in which medieval historian Paul Pixton reported his thorough study of this story. He traced the story back to spurious origins among Latter-day Saint missionaries. The story was told (and proven false) in Church periodicals by 1908, but it continues to circulate. Pixton's entire article is an entertaining read into the process of how false stories grow and morph over time.[3]

Let's try one a little more difficult. Someone in your Sunday School class tells a story about Joseph Smith publicly criticizing Brigham Young for something he did not do. Rather than defending himself, Brigham humbly arose and asked what Joseph wanted him to do. Then Joseph revealed his criticism was only a test and Brigham had passed! My go-to source for odd little stories about Joseph Smith is Truman Madsen's *Joseph Smith the Prophet* for two reasons: First, the book and the lectures on which it is based received very wide circulation (so there's a good chance someone in your ward read or heard it); and second, Madsen told a lot of unique stories about Joseph Smith, so it's a great place to start.

Opening the book to the index, we find "Young, Brigham, rebuked by JS" that points to pages 87–88, where the story is told. Footnote 16 takes us to page 166, which lists an article Madsen wrote for the *New Era* in 1976 that tells the same story with no sources. But the footnote in the book also adds that Madsen heard this story from Hugh B. Brown, who heard it from his wife, Zina Card Brown, Brigham Young's granddaughter, who never knew him and told the story approximately a century after he died.[4]

So what should we do? This source comes a very long time after the fact and is at least fourth hand. But it also comes from within a family who is the most likely to have heard and passed along the story. Our next thought might be to try to corroborate the story. It does not appear in any of the records on the searchable Joseph Smith Papers website. The diary of Apostle Abraham H. Cannon relates a story of Brigham presiding over a trial at which Joseph expressed objection and Brigham withdrew the charge. Not quite the same as Joseph publicly testing Brigham, and the dates for Cannon's story don't quite match up.[5] If we decide to retell this story, the best we can do is to preface it with an explanation that it is known only in family lore and the facts and wording may not be exactly accurate, but it probably illustrates the spirit of Brigham's humility and devotion to Joseph Smith.[6]

🖥 Best Resources: Websites That Help Trace Stories to Sources

Several websites monitor hoaxes, urban legends, and scams, including Snopes (**snopes.com**) and Hoax Slayer (**hoax-slayer.com**). If the information is politicized, use political fact-checking sites, such as the Annenberg Public Policy Center's FactCheck (**factcheck.org**), Politifact (**politifact.com**), or the *Washington Post*'s Fact Checker (**washingtonpost.com/news/fact-checker**). Watchdog sites are generally suspicious of the thing they watch. Quack Watch (**quackwatch.org**) debunks health-related frauds, myths, and misconduct. Source Watch (**sourcewatch.org**) tracks public-relations firms, think tanks, and industry-funded organizations that seek to influence public opinion and policy.

Reliability Matters

Once we find a source for stories, we must evaluate their *reliability*, our third investigative criterion. How do we know about Joseph Smith's family and early life? Did men really wait in the woods to ambush Joseph after he got the plates? Lucy Mack Smith was Joseph Smith's mother, she was an eyewitness to his early life and the beginnings of the Church's history, and she dictated a lifetime of memories to a scribe in the months following the deaths of her sons. She is the sole source for many of the personal and colorful details that we know about Joseph Smith and the earliest days of Church history. Her memoir has been published multiple times on different continents in original, "corrected," and "enhanced" versions. Her history was banned by one prophet and cited by others; its reliability has been challenged and its details corroborated.

Before you even open Lucy Smith's history, you can survey the *situation* by asking questions about her and her work. You may start by noting that she was Joseph Smith's mother, meaning she knew him well during his early life, but she would not have been present at all of the events of his adult life. Thus, some things she can report firsthand and others she can report hearing from him or others in the community. She dictated this memoir late in life, so the events and details are remembered rather than recorded in the moment. The dictation process also means that the scribe, Martha Jane Knowlton Coray, had an influence on how the stories were told and the memoir was structured. Lucy began the project in 1844, months after her sons Joseph and Hyrum were murdered and her son Samuel passed away.

The *contents* of Lucy's memoir are rich and fascinating. She opens with several chapters on her family's ancestry, relating her and her husband's spiritual experiences. She introduces all of her children and says little about Joseph's childhood. She describes

Joseph Smith's leg surgery and how the family responded to his visionary experiences and accepted the gospel.

We can connect Lucy's history to several different *contexts*. First, it was written at a time of personal grief and community crisis. She notes that upon seeing the bodies of her martyred sons, she cried out, "My God, my God, why hast thou forsaken this family?" A month later Samuel died of an illness and she reported feeling "left desolate in my distress."[7] The Smith family's misfortunes were compounded by questions over who should succeed Joseph as Church President and rising tensions with Illinois neighbors. Lucy proclaimed loyalty to the westward-moving group of Saints, but her sole surviving son, William, was persuaded for a time to follow James J. Strang and later established his own church before joining with the Reorganized Church under the direction of his nephew. Lucy stayed in Nauvoo until her death in 1856, living near her daughters and her daughter-in-law Emma.

A second relevant context involves the publication and reception of Lucy's memoir. Two identical copies of the finished manuscript (known as the "fair copy") were made; one was given to Brigham Young, and the other was kept by Lucy. Apostle Orson Pratt obtained Lucy's copy and published it in England in the fall of 1853. Brigham Young called the book a "tissue of falsehoods" and, citing "a written copy of those sketches in my possession for several years," he demanded corrections made. In 1865, he ordered Church members to destroy their copies of the memoir.[8] A "corrected" edition was published by the Church in 1901 and 1902, under the direction of Lucy's grandson President Joseph F. Smith. This version was created by comparing the published 1853 edition against the Church's "fair copy," and only 2 percent of the text was changed. Subsequent historical analysis has confirmed that Lucy's memory of events proves very accurate.[9] Brigham's objections may have had less to do with the contents of the book and more with its contexts. In the context of community crisis, Lucy wrote lovingly and approvingly of all of her children, including William, whom Brigham viewed as an apostate and a competitor. And in the publishing context, Brigham had an ongoing series of disagreements with Orson Pratt that may have influenced his impression of the work.

Lucy Smith's history of her son and family is *significant* for many reasons. In her own day, her announcement at the October 1845 general conference that she was preparing the history inspired the Saints during a difficult time, and the book's publication prompted controversy. Looking back from the twenty-first century, we see that Lucy's facts and timelines have stood up well against challenges of inaccuracy. Accordingly, her history is significant because it provides unique details about Joseph Smith's life.

When a source is consistently accurate, we extend more trust to it and consider it reliable. The Church review changed only a very small portion of the text, and subsequent analysis corroborated her facts "in every case where there is some vital or legal record that permits verification of the story."[10] This means that we can be more confident in accepting other stories in the memoir that cannot be verified, such as her stirring account of exhorting and praying to crack open the winter ice that impeded the Saints' migration to Ohio.[11] To ask about reliability is not to defame or demean but to identify and embrace what is true.

🖥 Best Resources: Versions of Lucy's History

I'm frequently asked which version of Lucy's history a person should read, to which I answer with a question of my own: what would you like to know about Lucy?

Manuscript sources. When Lucy dictated her memories, Martha Coray recorded them in eighteen notebooks, then rearranged them into five "rough" manuscripts before polishing them off into two "fair" copies. Of these, only the following have survived: one of the notebooks, two of the rough manuscripts, and one fair copy. The Joseph Smith Papers website published the two rough manuscripts as Lucy Smith's "History, 1844–45" and the fair copy as Lucy Smith's "History, 1845." All of the manuscripts were prepared by Martha Coray; none are in the handwriting of Lucy Mack Smith.[12]

First edition. The first edition was published in England in 1853 under the title *Biographical Sketches of Joseph Smith the Prophet, and His Progenitors for Many Generations.* Its text is now in the public domain, and it has been reprinted at least six times.[13]

"Corrected" edition. The corrected edition was published serially in the *Improvement Era* between 1901 and 1903. All chapters were published in a single volume in 1902 as *History of Joseph Smith by His Mother Lucy Smith as Revised by George A. Smith and Elias Smith.* Later editions dropped the "as revised by" part of the title.[14]

Critical text edition. Lavina Fielding Anderson compared the entire first edition (1853) with the rough manuscripts (1844–45) and produced a volume that presents both versions side by side.[15]

"Blended" editions. A few editors have assumed incorrectly that Martha's earlier manuscripts contain Lucy's more authentic voice and therefore blend the text of the first edition with quotes and snatches from the manuscripts. Along the way, they often modernize spelling, change words and structure, and otherwise "enhance" the text. They do not tell readers which words come from Martha's manuscripts, the first edition, or their own creativity.[16]

Recommendation? If you'd like the best sense of what Lucy dictated, listened to, corrected, and approved for publication, read the first edition. *Saints* cites the first edition as well as both the rough manuscript and the fair copy. I would avoid a blended version.

You Try It

Rumor

It's okay to share stories without sources.

Sniff Tests

1. *No source.* A story without a source might be interesting and entertaining, but it may not be accurate and reliable.
2. *Vague attribution.* If the story comes from an unnamed person, or thirdhand from a friend of a friend or from a shadowy informant, that's a good sign that the story may be unreliable.
3. *Vague or conflicting details.* If the story's details are loose or contradictory, then it will be hard to pin them all down. Chances are, the story's unreliable.

Real

Reliability matters.

Key Concepts

1. Stories often circulate with missing or vague attribution and must be traced to their original sources to evaluate reliability.
2. You can trace a story to a source by identifying specific details, following the details to specific sources, evaluating the accuracy and authenticity of the sources, and then determining the reliability of the story.

Notes

1. Fawn M. Brodie, *No Man Knows My History: The Life of Joseph Smith*, 2nd ed. (New York: Vintage Books, 1995), 78; "Gold Bible No. 6," *The [Palmyra, NY] Reflector*, March 19, 1831, 126; Richard Lloyd Anderson, *Investigating the Book of Mormon Witnesses* (Salt Lake City: Deseret Book, 1981); John W. Welch, ed., *Opening the*

Heavens: Accounts of Divine Manifestations, 1820–1844, 2nd ed.
(Provo, UT: Brigham Young University Press, 2017), 79–227.

2. David Mikkelson, "Mormon Ownership of Coca-Cola," Snopes,
   August 27, 2012, https://www.snopes.com/fact-check/lds-sense/.

3. Paul B. Pixton, "Play It Again, Sam: The Remarkable 'Prophecy' of
   Samuel Lutz, Alias Christophilus Gratianus, Reconsidered," *BYU
   Studies* 25, no. 3 (1985): 27–46.

4. Truman G. Madsen, *Joseph Smith the Prophet* (Salt Lake City:
   Bookcraft, 1989), 87–88; Truman G. Madsen, "Hugh B. Brown—
   Youthful Veteran," *The New Era*, April 1976, 16.

5. Abraham H. Cannon, *The Apostle's Record: The Journals of Abraham
   H. Cannon*, ed. Dennis B. Horne (Clearfield, UT: Gnolaum Books,
   2004), April 9, 1890.

6. Madsen noted that the story was "never recorded" and told in "family lore" and that the nature of the criticism was "unclear." However,
   Madsen then went on to describe Joseph's motives and the thoughts
   running through Brigham's mind, attributing it with the phrase
   "the story says"—a way of telling the story that adds more life and
   detail than warranted from the source. Madsen, *Joseph Smith the
   Prophet*, 87–88.

7. Lavina Fielding Anderson, ed., *Lucy's Book: A Critical Edition of
   Lucy Mack Smith's Family Memoir* (Salt Lake City: Signature Books,
   2001), 749, 751.

8. Brigham Young, in 1855 and 1868, as cited in Anderson, *Lucy's
   Book*, 101, 105.

9. Richard Lloyd Anderson, "The Reliability of the Early History of
   Lucy and Joseph Smith," *Dialogue: A Journal of Mormon Thought* 4,
   no. 2 (Summer 1969): 13–28; Jan Shipps, *Mormonism: The Story
   of a New Religious Tradition* (Urbana, University of Illinois Press,
   1985), 86–107.

10. Anderson, "Reliability of the Early History of Lucy and Joseph
    Smith," 13–28.

11. Lucy Mack Smith, "Where Is Your Confidence in God?" in *At the
    Pulpit: 185 Years of Discourses by Latter-day Saint Women*, ed. Jenni-
    fer Reeder and Kate Holbrook (Salt Lake City: Church Historian's
    Press, 2017), 3–5.

12. The "rough" copy is Lucy Mack Smith, "Lucy Mack Smith, History,
    1844–1845," The Joseph Smith Papers, https://www.josephsmith-
    papers.org/paper-summary/lucy-mack-smith-history-1844-1845/1;
    the "fair" copy is Lucy Mack Smith, "Lucy Mack Smith, History,

1845," The Joseph Smith Papers, https://www.josephsmithpapers. org/paper-summary/lucy-mack-smith-history-1845/1. The original manuscripts are located in the Church History Library in Salt Lake City. See Sharalyn D. Howcroft, "A Textual and Archival Reexamination of Lucy Mack Smith's History," in *Foundational Texts of Mormonism: Examining Major Early Sources*, ed. Mark Ashurst-McGee, Robin Scott Jensen, and Sharalyn D. Howcroft (New York: Oxford University Press, 2018), 298–335.

13. Lucy Smith, *Biographical Sketches of Joseph Smith the Prophet, and His Progenitors for Many Generations* (Liverpool: S. W. Richards, 1853), available at http://contentdm.lib.byu.edu/cdm/compoundobject/collection/NCMP1820-1846/id/17401/rec/1. Three "facsimile" editions have been produced by Jerald and Sandra Tanner (1965), Arno Press (1969), and Grandin Press (1995). The RLDS Church (now the Community of Christ) reset the type and published editions in 1880 (1908 reprint) and 1912 (1969 reprint).

14. *History of Joseph Smith by His Mother Lucy Smith as Revised by George A. Smith and Elias Smith* (Salt Lake City: Improvement Era, 1902); *History of Joseph Smith by His Mother, Lucy Mack Smith, with Notes and Comments by Preston Nibley* (Salt Lake City: Stevens and Wallis, 1945).

15. Lavina Fielding Anderson, ed., *Lucy's Book: A Critical Edition of Lucy Mack Smith's Family Memoir* (Salt Lake City: Signature Books, 2001).

16. Scott Facer Proctor and Marine Jensen Proctor "blend" the first edition (1853) with the rough manuscripts (1844–45) in *The Revised and Enhanced History of Joseph Smith by His Mother* (Salt Lake City: Bookcraft, 1996); Susan Evans McCloud blends the Proctor version with the 1945 Nibley reprint of the corrected edition.

CHAPTER 12

What If It's Antagonistic?

"Does anyone even run into that faith-challenging, anti-Mormon stuff?" an older woman asked.

"The only people who do are the ones hanging out in bars and places like that," said a man of her same generation.

I was surprised how prevalent this assumption is, so I began to gather evidence. During the summer of 2019, I spoke to hundreds of Latter-day Saint youth at conferences and firesides. Using an anonymous polling system that operated through their phones, they responded to this question: "Have you ever encountered something that challenged your testimony?" The "yes" results were usually in the 90 percent range and never less than 80 percent. The most surprised people in the room were the adults!

As we consider the stories told about history, we should remember that we live in an era of antagonists and deception. The Book of Mormon tells of Antichrists whose perverted thinking deceived many. Today we might wonder, How could anyone be so gullible, so easily misled? A former con artist explained our condition succinctly: "If you think you can't be conned, you're just the person I want to meet!" We cannot tuck deceivers away into "some corner of ancient history and go about our unguarded ways."[1] If we want to strengthen ourselves and our children, we must prepare for *when* not *if* we encounter antagonistic information.

All of the thinking skills introduced so far can be applied to defend against deception. A magician writing in a Cold War–era manual for international spies explained that "practically every popularly held opinion on how to deceive, as well as how to safeguard one's self from being deceived, is wrong in fact as well as premise." The hand is not quicker than the eye. Rather, "a trick does not fool the eye but fools the brain."[2] Your understanding of the nature of the past, how evidence is used, and how to investigate sources and stories are useful guards against the deceptions of antagonistic writers.

A New Story in an Old Pamphlet

One of my favorite stories about handling antagonistic authors occurred around Philadelphia in 1849. This story was misunderstood for more than 150 years, until a closer reading of a source—a pamphlet—helped revise it. The pamphlet opens with a blisteringly caustic letter to a new Church convert from a Maryland pastor, leading booksellers to list the pamphlet among anti-Mormon materials.[3] But the pastor did not compile the pamphlet. His letter was presented at the beginning so that the real compiler, the young convert he attacked, could demolish his claims.

The story begins with twenty-three-year-old Sarah Stageman. Born in England in 1826, Sarah immigrated to Maryland with her family when she was fourteen years old. While in her early twenties, Sarah met and listened to Latter-day Saint missionaries, grew excited about their message, and shared it with her family and the wife of the pastor of her local congregation. Rev. Abraham De Witt, pastor of Rock Creek Presbyterian Church, authored a scorn-filled letter that chastised Sarah for considering the Church, declaring that she possessed an "excitable and unstable mind" and warning her to "escape as for your life from this vortex of fanaticism."

Sarah responded by publishing his 3½-page letter with her 8½-page response in a small pamphlet. Sarah began with the evidence, pointing out that De Witt had not cited any scripture in his letter. Accordingly, her response is a virtual tour de force of the Bible that cites more than forty passages to testify of the truth of the Restoration in the last days.

Sarah also skillfully refuted De Witt's major claims. She had a ready answer for De Witt's criticism of Joseph Smith. "You say if Joseph Smith was inspired, why did he locate that temple where it would be begun, but never finished: If he had, you would believe." She pegged De Witt as being like one of the unbelievers of an earlier scriptural age: "I say thus it is now, as it was in the days of Christ. In Mark, Chap. 15, 'They said, let the king of Israel descend from the Cross, that we may see and believe.'"[4]

Sarah's story reveals the marvelous testimony of a young woman whose mind and heart were filled with light and wisdom as she embraced the truths of the restored gospel. Her story demonstrates that misleading and antagonistic voices have long been heard—and that there are powerful answers to all their claims.

Fairness Matters

The presence of critics has been an enduring constant in Church history, from Joseph's first telling of his First Vision to the latest blog post in the twenty-first century. After the Saints were expelled from Missouri, they were instructed to "gather up the libelous publications that are afloat; and all that are in the magazines, and in the encyclopedias, and all the libelous histories that are published" (D&C 123:4–5)—this practice continues in the Church History Library today. Encountering a criticism about the Church for the first time in the twenty-first century does not make it new. In fact, one of the most interesting things to me about today's antagonistic criticism is how largely unoriginal it is.

Joseph Smith has ever been the subject of ridicule and fear—people have attacked his visions and revelations, his claims of prophecy and leadership, his ability to command the blind obedience of his followers, his institution of secret temple rituals, and the practice of plural marriage. As time passed, the critics updated their topics to include race-based restrictions, violent actions at Mountain Meadows, the oppression of women, or secret Church influence on business or government. Each generation of critics reuses the same well-worn tactics that Sarah Stageman confronted—attack, ridicule, exaggerated stereotypes, and plucking quotations out of context.[5]

Though the content has remained relatively constant, the media that carries the message has changed dramatically. Everywhere that early missionaries preached, local ministers responded to the perceived threats to their congregations and livelihoods. The magazines and encyclopedias of the 1830s became pamphlets and broadsides (hand-painted posters) by midcentury before transforming into public lectures illustrated by lantern slides by the end of the century. In the twentieth century, criticism circulated in mass-produced books, silent films, or videocassettes, and today it has moved onto social media, streaming video, and crowd-funded websites.[6] With the change in media has come an accompanying expansion of reach—the number of people who passed a broadside tacked to a pole in nineteenth-century England is dwarfed by the number of people connected worldwide by the internet today. But most of the criticisms discoverable on the internet today have already been made *and* refuted in the past.

In the twenty-first century, authors of antagonistic websites, books, pamphlets, and letters to Church leaders frequently present themselves as people who have discovered something new. They fancy themselves as asking brilliant new questions about the Church's deepest secrets. They see themselves as more intelligent or more "woke" than their benighted brothers and sisters who are, by implication, naïve, blind, brainwashed, or gaslighted. Elder Dieter F. Uchtdorf noted that such persons may offer patronizing comments, such as "I wish I could believe the way you do." He declared, "Let me be clear: there is nothing noble or impressive about being cynical. Skepticism is easy—anyone can do it. It is the faithful life that requires moral strength, dedication, and courage."[7]

These writers, speakers, and podcast hosts fail to meet another one of our criteria for trustworthiness—*fairness*. Weak thinkers learn to see only the mistakes in others. "Sophistry is the art of winning arguments regardless of whether there are obvious problems in the thinking being used," explain the authors of a well-regarded book on critical thinking.[8] Striving for fairness involves holding yourself to the same standard as you hold others, recognizing when you have a vested interest in an issue, and sympathetically representing the viewpoints of others.

🖥 Best Resources:
Church Sources on Current and Historical Topics

1. The Church Newsroom publishes official statements and news releases and provides current information about topics, leaders, facts, and statistics. It is part of the Church's official website. (**newsroom.ChurchofJesusChrist.org**)

2. Thirteen "Gospel Topics Essays" were published by the Church between 2013 and 2015 about the tough topics of Church history, including multiple accounts of the First Vision, scripture translations, polygamy, racism, and violence.[9]

3. Hundreds of "Church History Topics" have been published in conjunction with *Saints*, the four-volume history of the Church. In addition to providing more information to supplement the volumes, they also address topics such as Joseph Smith's wives, early forgery, and masonry in Nauvoo.[10] The essays and topics are accessible in the "Church History" section of the Gospel Library app.

Just Cut Off Their Arms

Antagonists frequently use methods that are the inverse of those I'm sharing in this book. Either the antagonists foolishly do not know how history works *or* they realize that many Latter-day Saints don't know how history works. The authors of antagonistic materials hope people will abandon their faith and leave the Church. Antagonists are also generally pleased when defenders try to respond to every criticism raised. Beyond departure or rebuttal, I prefer a third approach, drawn from the Book of Mormon. When thieves scattered King Lamoni's flock, Ammon did not join them, nor did he attempt to engage each bandit in a series of gentlemanly duels. No—he just cut off their arms (see Alma 17:35–37). By extension, we need not read and respond to every online criticism; once we perceive the author's intent and distortions, we can simply close the browser. Other scriptures teach that our faith can "quench . . . the fiery darts" (Eph. 6:16) of the adversary. The critics' darts don't find a target, nor are they dodged; they are simply extinguished.

🔆 Thinking Habit:
See it. Quench It.

1. Perceive when information is being taken out of context, piled up, twisted into a conspiracy, or forced into a false dilemma.

2. Talk to someone.

3. Take your concerns to the Lord.

4. Make peace with your concerns soon.

"*What a weird thing!*" Probably the most common tactic in antagonistic writing is to pluck a single fact or quote out of the past and serve it up to modern readers out of context as something strange: a comment from a nineteenth-century Church leader about race or violence, a marriage between an old man and a younger woman, a different account of the First Vision. Cue the creepy background music. The intent is to shock you. It is easy to present the past as "weird" by imposing present assumptions and ignoring that the past was different. Usually, the authors do not acknowledge that a fact is part of a long story or that the past is gone and only pieces remain. Often, an antagonist presents a fact or quote as if it fell from the sky, hoping that you won't ask why the author selected only this portion. But you know facts don't speak; storytellers do. In this way, antagonistic authors try to distract you and redefine our sacred history.

This technique is not unique to authors antagonistic to the Church. Internet trolls, political partisans, Holocaust deniers, and conspiracy theorists all use this method, which is called "anomaly hunting." An anomaly is something that is different from what is standard, normal, expected, or *assumed* to be common sense. The objective in hunting for anomalies is not to find truth. Rather an author merely tries to point out contradictions or raise questions. Typically, the author presents a tone of openness or curiosity. "I'm not trying to be critical," he says, "but have you noticed this weird thing?" But the author is not usually interested in making sense of the past, only in wreaking havoc in the present.

"*A lot of weird things!*" Most anomaly hunters don't stop at finding one or two weird things. Rather, they dump an indiscriminate mountain of weird things on you—"indiscriminate" because the individual pieces are often unrelated beyond a loose connection to Church history, and a "mountain" because the author simply dumps the pieces on the reader in an attempt to overwhelm by sheer volume. A good thinker who knows to ask for evidence is able to summarize and condense. Anomaly hunters, on the other hand, substitute quantity for quality, piling up a lot of weak evidence. This strategy leads, in the end, to an assertion that if you won't or can't refute every single claim and anomaly, then you are admitting that they are right![11]

Make no mistake, every fact about the Church's history that has been ripped from its contexts so as to seem weird can be placed back into context and understood with good thinking skills. But good historical thinking requires a lot of work, and the antagonist hopes you will choose to be lazy. Often you *feel* this approach before you can put your finger on it. It is as if the author begins by flicking a grain of sand in your eye, but before you can wash it out, he flicks another grain and another, until you're staring into a howling sandstorm. The "grains" could be statements by Church leaders taken out of context or facts that the author claims speak for themselves. The criticism may be packaged as "a letter" to a teacher or Church leader or spouse with a list of questions the recipient supposedly cannot or refuses to answer. Another approach is to package the pile of anomalies as a list of scriptures. Either way, the work seeks not to examine and understand evidence but rather to dump and overwhelm.

"*Something dark connects them!*" Having buried the victim in a deep pile of seeming contradictions, the next step is to suggest or state outright there is a deep, dark conspiracy that both connects the weird things and has kept them hidden from you for so long. In national and world histories, the alleged conspirators are secret brotherhoods, wealthy elite, or unnamed government agencies. In Church history the alleged conspirators might be the secret Council of Fifty, the Danites, a big sugar trust, or the Correlation Department. The conspiracy may involve covering up a single event or it may extend to an entire organization or system. Conspiracy theories appeal to the hearer's own pride: "You studied the gospel every day as a missionary and never heard this; they must be hiding it from you."

Conspiracy theories are intellectually lazy because they require no structure to the evidence, just a list of stuff. Any logical evidence presented to counter the conspiracy is twisted into "part of the plot to make people think they are not covering it up." For example, conspiracists charged the Church with hiding its history, until the Gospel Topics Essays were published with open acknowledgment of tough issues. Then conspiracists moved the target, wondering why the essays were simply published and not announced. But the finished essays were announced by the Church Newsroom, so then conspiracists warned that the essays sat isolated on the Church's website without connection to official curriculum. In time (because curriculum writing takes time), the essays were integrated into the Church's instructional materials. That's all fine and good, countered conspiracists, but will members even read the curriculum? The claims of conspiracy never end.

"*You can go on being duped or choose the truth.*" The end goal of most antagonistic material is to create a simple either/or binary, a false dilemma, that places its message on one side and the Church's message on the other. "You thought Joseph was a pure and perfect prophet, but he is really a fake and fraudulent charlatan." What once was white, now is black; everything you thought was true is now a lie. You can either be true to yourself or to what you once thought—there's no middle ground.

You need not be troubled by this flipped binary because you now know that the best thinking about history accepts complexity and is suspicious of either/or. If you find a video with shadowy graphics and spooky music on YouTube, or a web page listing dark secrets of the Church, or a letter presenting a series of supposedly unanswerable questions, you now have the skills to recognize poor thinking and poor evidence. You may not have the answer to every random factoid presented, but you can recognize what the antagonist is doing. You will find information presented with no citation or with abbreviated citations that obscure original sources. You'll find weak historical evidence and no spiritual evidence. You will find present assumptions being projected onto past experience. You will find a major, forced either/or position in which the creator demands that you choose one side or the other.

You *can* quench the influence of antagonistic writing. When you encounter something that troubles you, don't put it on a shelf. Resolve it now by talking with someone. Long before she became a popular author and multimedia personality, a teenaged Tamu Smith heard criticism of the Church from a friend, so she talked to her father, who explained "that ultimately I would have to seek the truth for myself and decide how I would respond."[12] Take it to the Lord, and He will give you peace to move forward.

You Try It

Rumor

Don't talk about tough topics because they spread doubt.

Sniff Tests

1. *"What a weird thing!"* Antagonists take accurate information out of context to make it seem weird. They also look for coincidences, contradictions, and strange items in a practice known as anomaly hunting.

2. *"A lot of weird things!"* Critics pile up strange facts in order to overwhelm, a fallacy known as proof by verbosity. If you cannot or will not respond to every item, they will declare victory.

3. *"Something dark connects them!"* Conspiracy thinking lazily avoids the use of evidence, telling stories that appeal instead to fear or pride. They give the illusion of thinking without demonstrating any analysis. Those least likely to believe conspiracy theories understand how thinking and evidence work.[13]

4. *"You can go on being duped or choose the truth."* Antagonists aim to force readers into an either/or choice between their position and everything else, in a fallacy known as a false dilemma.

5. *"Put your concerns 'on a shelf.'"* This advice usually means to "just stop worrying about it," and it is unhelpful. Instead, we can actively seek peace by talking with others and the Lord. The Holy Ghost will speak peace to our minds and hearts, sometimes in

the form of answers and clarity, other times by reinforcing our patience and trust as we "wait upon the Lord" (Isa. 40:31).

Real

Just cut off their arms.

Key Concepts

1. In our information age, the question is not what to do *if* we encounter antagonistic material but *when*.
2. Critics have challenged the Church since its earliest days, and the Church collects their materials. Much of today's criticism is recycled from the past.
3. Even the newest converts can counter false claims; your testimony and good thinking skills can help you disarm antagonistic material.

Notes

1. R. Paul Wilson, *The Art of the Con: How to Think Like a Real Hustler and Avoid Being Scammed* (Guilford, CT: Lyons Press, 2014), 345; Carlos E. Asay, "Opposition to the Work of God," *Ensign*, November 1981, 67.
2. H. Keith Melton and Robert Wallace, *The Official C.I.A. Manual of Trickery and Deception* (New York: William Morrow, 2009), 69, 76, 77.
3. Peter Crawley, *A Descriptive Bibliography of the Mormon Church*, 3 vols. (Provo, UT: Religious Studies Center, Brigham Young University, 2005), 2:68–112; Chad J. Flake and Larry W. Draper, eds., *A Mormon Bibliography, 1830–1930: Books, Pamphlets, Periodicals, and Broadsides Relating to the First Century of Mormonism*, 2nd ed., 2 vols. (Provo, UT: Religious Studies Center, Brigham Young University, 2004), 1:331, 343; 2:324–5.
4. *Correspondence between Rev. Abraham De Witt, Pastor of Rock Church, Cecil Co., Md. and Miss Sarah Stageman, One of His Flock, Regarding the Principles and Faith of the Church of Jesus Christ of Latter-day Saints* (Philadelphia: Bicking & Guilbert, 1849).
5. Donald Bruce Center, "A Study of the Rhetorical Strategy of Maligning as Exemplified in Anti-Mormon Rhetoric, 1847–1890"

(master's thesis, University of Houston, 1975); Brian C. Hales, "Naturalistic Explanations of the Origin of the Book of Mormon," *BYU Studies Quarterly* 48, no. 3 (2019): 105–48.

6. See Craig L. Foster, *Penny Tracts and Polemics: A Critical Analysis of Anti-Mormon Pamphleteering in Great Britain (1837–1860)* (Salt Lake City: Greg Kofford Books, 2002); Terryl L. Givens, *The Viper on the Hearth: Mormons, Myths, and the Construction of Heresy* (New York: Oxford University Press, 1997); J. Spencer Fluhman, *"A Peculiar People": Anti-Mormonism and the Making of Religion in Nineteenth-Century America* (Chapel Hill: University of North Carolina Press, 2012).

7. Dieter F. Uchtdorf, "Be Not Afraid, Only Believe," *Ensign*, November 2015, 78–79.

8. Richard Paul and Linda Elder, *Critical Thinking: Tools for Taking Charge of Your Learning and Your Life* (Upper Saddle River, NJ: Prentice Hall, 2001), 2.

9. "Gospel Topics Essays," https://www.churchofjesuschrist.org/study/manual/gospel-topics-essays/essays. There is also a Gospel Topics entry on "Book of Mormon Geography" (2019).

10. "Church History Topics," https://www.churchofjesuschrist.org/study/history/topics. Topics include "Fanny Alger," "Kinderhook Plates," and "Masonry."

11. Loren Collins, *Bullspotting: Finding Facts in the Age of Misinformation* (Amherst, NY: Prometheus Books, 2012), 24–27; Steven Novell, *The Skeptic's Guide to the Universe: How to Know What's Really Real in a World Increasingly Full of Fake* (New York: Grand Central Publishing, 2019), 118–28.

12. Zandra Vranes and Tamu Smith, *Can I Get an Amen? Celebrating the Lord in Everyday Life* (Salt Lake City: Deseret Book, 2019), 61.

13. See Brian Resnick, "The Dark Allure of Conspiracy Theories, Explained by a Psychologist," *Vox*, May 25, 2017, https://www.vox.com/science-and-health/2017/4/25/15408610/conspiracy-theories-psychologist-explained; Jan-Willem van Prooijen and Michele Acker, "The Influence of Control on Belief in Conspiracy Theories: Conceptual and Applied Extensions," *Applied Cognitive Psychology* 29, no. 5 (September/October 2015): 753–61; Jeffrey Kluger, "Why So Many People Believe Conspiracy Theories," *Time*, October 15, 2017; Mandy Oaklander, "Here's Why People Believe in Conspiracy Theories," *Time*, August 14, 2015; "Conspiracy Thinking Less Likely with Greater News Media Literacy, Study Suggests," *Science Daily*, November 30, 2017.

CHAPTER 13

How Good Is That Book?

"What's wrong with Wikipedia?"

This common question is asked by nearly every student. The free, online encyclopedia contains more than forty million articles in more than three hundred languages. Content studies by historians and scientists reveal that its facts are generally correct, and its accuracy approaches that of the *Encyclopedia Britannica.*[1]

But accurate facts are not the only things that matter. Historian and biographer Richard Bushman spent decades of his life reading the sources and pondering questions related to Joseph Smith. When he reviewed the Wikipedia entry on the Prophet, he noted that it does contain accurate facts that can be traced to nineteenth-century documents. "What I think is the real failing of this piece is that it lacks scope," he observed. "It just picks its way along from one little fact to another little fact. . . . It . . . isn't inaccurate, but it sort of lacks depth. It ends up being shallow."[2]

In addition to sources and stories, we can also encounter in-depth studies. Studies of history seek to understand the past by examining the pieces that survive as well as previous interpretations. Studies are shaped by the sources and stories available but also by the researcher's own assumptions, values, and needs. The best studies are comprehensive, accurate, and documented; they check every source, quote accurately and in proper context, and show the reader where the information came from. Most often, the findings of a research study are reported in the form of an article or book. In the end, we hope that the process of study and research helps us understand the sources better and tell better stories.

Comprehensive Arguments Are Best

The best way to present clear information about the past is with an argument. An argument is not a "fight" between the author and others, nor is it simply an author's opinion. An argument is a reasoned way of presenting and evaluating information—a way of assembling the pieces of the past, using them as evidence in order to draw conclusions. Peter reminds us that a statement of belief is not enough since we should "be ready always to give an answer to every man that asketh you a *reason* of the hope that is in you" (1 Pet. 3:15; emphasis added). Arguments help sort facts from opinions, something most Americans do not do well.[3] And they allow us to see things in their proper scope and depth. The strongest arguments come after studying all of the sources and stories. The goal of an argument is not to "win" but to increase in understanding.

The best arguments are *comprehensive*, our final criterion for establishing trustworthiness. They seek out all of the accurate facts, authentic sources, and reliable stories. It is not enough to find an entry in Wikipedia or select one medical study in an online data-base. Arguments dive deeply into the complexities of the past and the relevant contexts. They consider a breadth of perspectives and interpretations. They select, connect, and interpret information in fairness. The best arguments strive to present the truth, recover the whole truth, and strip away anything that has been added or exaggerated over time. They present information logically in a way that makes sense, always recognizing our limitations in understanding the past from the standpoint of the present.

I like to envision an argument in the form of a pyramid. At the pinnacle of the pyramid is the main point, or major claim, or thesis. This peak rests on a middle layer of supporting claims that form subcomponents of the major claim. All of these claims then sit on a broad base of assembled evidence. Valid evidence includes sources from the past as well as stories told by others, including contemporary analysts, public figures, historians, as well as philosophers, theorists, or scientists. And our present conditions also find their way into the evidence in the form of newly discovered sources, new social problems to solve, or new values and ways of thinking. Finally, the evidence and the claims are held together by the mortars of logic and creativity. Logic is used to compare pieces of evidence, to link evidence with claims, and to relate all of the claims to the main point. Thinking is a creative activity because we can imagine what evidence might exist, how it might have been lost, or where it might be found.

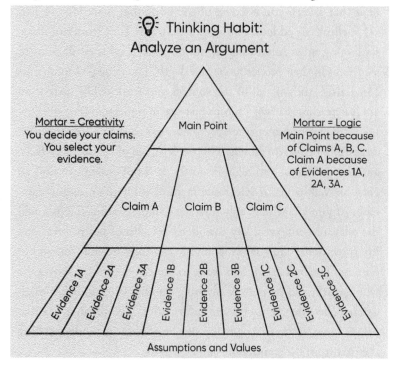

Thinking Habit:
Analyze an Argument

Mortar = Creativity
You decide your claims.
You select your
evidence.

Main Point

Mortar = Logic
Main Point because
of Claims A, B, C.
Claim A because
of Evidences 1A,
2A, 3A.

Claim A Claim B Claim C

Evidence 1A Evidence 2A Evidence 3A Evidence 1B Evidence 2B Evidence 3B Evidence 1C Evidence 2C Evidence 3C

Assumptions and Values

An argument, with its claims and evidence, also sits on a foundation of assumptions and values that are not always visible. Often, you'll need to read between the lines to discern them. President Dallin H. Oaks observed of Latter-day Saints that "on many important subjects our assumptions—our starting points or major premises—are different from many of our friends and associates." As an example, he said that "because Latter-day Saints know our Heavenly Father's plan for His children, we know that this mortal life is not a one-act play sandwiched between an unknowable past and an uncertain future." Thus, "because of our knowledge of this plan and other truths that God has revealed, we start with different assumptions than those who do not share our knowledge. As a result, we reach different conclusions on many important subjects that others judge only in terms of their opinions about mortal life."[4] A recent study of the impact of fact-checking revealed that "dueling" facts are frequently driven by different values rather than differences in knowledge.[5] Sometimes evidence supports starting premises, and those premises are strengthened and become knowledge; other times the premises dictate which evidence is considered and presented, making the argument narrow and picky. In an argument, what is not stated is just as important as what is.

An argument assembles information for investigation. It needs to identify which pieces of the past survive and which are missing. Strong arguments tease out multiple possibilities, probabilities, the influence of various causes of an event, and immediate influences and long-term effects. The best arguments address changes over time, the perspectives of participants, and the relevance of sources and conclusions. They explain how the pieces fit together into an interpretation about the entire past. Because arguments about the past are built in the present, they can be analyzed and improved as our understanding moves from good to better to best.

Arguments frequently take one of three common shapes. The

traditional method traces to the Greek philosopher Aristotle, who advocated presenting a claim followed by supporting evidence. The Gospel Topics Essay about whether members of the Church are Christian uses this format to present its information. The first sentence declares the essay's main point: "Members of The Church of Jesus Christ of Latter-day Saints unequivocally affirm themselves to be Christians." The introduction announces three claims, and sections of the essay address each one.[6] By contrast, the Rogerian method (named after American psychologist Carl Rogers) operates in reverse by asking a lot of questions, presenting alternatives, and considering the alternatives before finally drawing a conclusion— its main claim—based on all that has been examined. A third format employs two to four simple statements or premises that are combined in such a way as to deduce a conclusion. "If this . . . and that . . . , then something." Those familiar with the openness and complexity of history tend *not* to use this kind of strict structure, but amateur historians may use this kind of reasoning, which is more common in other fields.

Typically, the content of an argument is presented in some kind of container. It may appear as a personal essay, a letter, an editorial, a review, a lecture, an analysis, a directive, a news story, an article, an announcement, a debate, or a report. In these settings, you'll want to watch for the argument's "signposts." These words, like street signs, direct and orient us through an argument. There are big signposts, like the title, introduction, conclusion, and section headings or breaks. There are also little signposts, including a thesis sentence, usually at the beginning or end; topic sentences in each paragraph; and transition sentences between paragraphs and sections. If you are lucky, there will also be visual signposts, including illustrations, charts, or diagrams. The signposts point you to other important words that form part of the argument.

💬 **Everyday Encounter:**
Getting a Job and Succeeding at Work

No matter your chosen career field, you will achieve more success if you can make and analyze arguments. As a frontline employee, you will be able to organize your thinking and share your expertise persuasively with decision makers. As a leader, you will be able evaluate proposals, consider strategic options, eliminate poor assumptions, and convince others to achieve a vision. Making and evaluating arguments is often what is meant when employers seek people who can "communicate clearly" or "problem solve" or "think critically." In a recent survey of nearly nine hundred executives, 92 percent said soft skills were equally or more important than technical skills, but 89 percent said they have a hard time finding people with these attributes. Making and evaluating arguments are not skills that can be automated or outsourced.[7]

Finding the Argument in a Study

Let's observe how arguments work by examining a classic article by Dean Jessee titled "The Reliability of Joseph Smith's History."[8] First, look for the signposts. The title tells us it will talk about Joseph Smith's history, a massive writing project begun by clerks and scribes under the direction of Joseph and completed after his death. And the title tells us the issue at hand—how reliable is a history prepared by many different people and completed years after the named author was dead? There are no section headings, no keywords, and no abstract. The article has a Rogerian structure; the introduction on page 23 is understated, but there is a good conclusion on pages 44–46 that begins with this topic sentence: "To restate the question raised at the beginning of this study: How reliable is the Joseph Smith *History* as a primary historical source?" Here, the author notes that "Joseph Smith's *History* was lauded for its accuracy by those who produced it." Setting Joseph's history in the context of other nineteenth-century histories, it "compares very well," but times have changed and newer methods for analyzing historical documents by comparing the finished story with original sources reveal that the *History* contains more from the scribes and less of Joseph's "personal expression" and "personality." In short, the *History* gets many (though not all) of the details of the story right, but it should not be considered a firsthand account that reflects the inner thoughts of Joseph Smith.

With this framework, we can quickly peruse the article and understand the structure and content of its argument. Jessee opens by reviewing other histories written in the nineteenth century (pages 24–27) and the conditions of Joseph's writing (pages 27–30)—these observations serve as evidence for his claim that Joseph's history compares well to histories of his time. Jessee then narrates the trial-and-error process by which a series of scribes produced the history (pages 31–36) in order to introduce important evidence for the claim that the work of the scribes contrasts with the personal voice of Joseph. That evidence includes a journal entry written in Joseph Smith's handwriting versus a journal entry written by Willard Richards, writing as if he were Joseph (page 37) and an account of an experience in Zion's Camp from Heber C. Kimball's journal that was transferred into Joseph Smith's first-person words in the published *History* (pages 38–39). Finally, to support his claim that modern historical methods have advanced beyond the work done by the scribes, Jesse examines the combination of four diarists' summaries of Joseph's sermon into a single text (pages 39–40), the elaboration of a single sentence into a paragraph discourse (page 41), and subsequent efforts to remove myths and errors that crept into various editions of the text (pages 42–44).

The results of this comprehensive study by Dean Jessee and other studies by his colleagues who work on The Joseph Smith

Papers Project have prompted changes. Recent talks from the prophets, Church manuals, and the headings of sections in the Doctrine and Covenants are now more careful to point back to earlier manuscript sources on the Joseph Smith Papers website in order to more accurately reflect Joseph's thoughts and teachings.

Analyze an Argument: Dean Jessee's Article

Main Point: Joseph Smith's history was prepared by scribes; it gets many—but not all—of the details right and should not be considered a firsthand account by Joseph Smith (pp. 44–46).

Claim	Claim	Claim
Joseph's history compares well to other histories prepared at the same time.	Work by the scribes contrasts with the personal voice of Joseph Smith.	A modern perspective reveals shortcomings.
Evidence	**Evidence**	**Evidence**
• Review of other histories written in the nineteenth century (pp. 24–27) • Conditions of Joseph's writing (pp. 27–30)	• Scribes worked by trial-and-error (pp. 31–36). • Comparison of journal entries written by Joseph and those written by a clerk (p. 37) • Comparison of the published history to an original source (pp. 38–39)	• Four diaries were merged to create a "single" sermon (pp. 39–40). • A sentence was elaborated into a discourse (p. 41). • B. H. Roberts removed myths (pp. 42–44).

This process of investigation works for book-length studies as well. First, in a book there are additional "signposts," including a table of contents and chapter titles. An introduction or conclusion are the most important places to start to understand a book's shape and claims. Often a chapter of a book will contain a claim and its related evidence. Early chapters of a history book frequently provide background and context before jumping into the analysis. If you are already familiar with the general history, you may be able to read quickly through the early chapters. Read through the book's notes. Doing so will give you a sense of the evidence on which the claims rest.[9]

Arguments Fit within Larger Conversations

After you've found the argument in a book or article, you need to explore how the argument fits within a larger conversation. No book or article or study ever stands alone. Studies are undertaken to answer a question, and frequently the question was posed by other people. Why was Dean Jessee presenting claims supported by evidence about the reliability of Joseph Smith's history? Because previous writers had claimed that the history was unreliable.

Joseph Smith illustrated this conversational aspect in the preparation of his history. The first paragraph of the history observed that there were already "many reports which have been put in circulation by evil-disposed and designing persons, in relation to the rise and progress of The Church of Jesus Christ of Latter-day Saints." The "many reports" raised questions, and Joseph wrote to answer them. And the second verse begins with a huge signpost: "In this history I shall present the various events in relation to this Church, in truth and righteousness, as they have transpired, or as they at present exist" (JS—H 1:1–2). In its introductory comments, Joseph Smith's history describes a conversation and what his history will *do* to enter and advance it.

Frequently, the conversations in which a book or article participate unfold over decades. For example, in 1922, Elder Joseph Fielding Smith asserted in *Essentials in Church History* that the Mountain Meadows Massacre "was the deed of enraged Indians aided by a number of white men." Nearly thirty years later, Juanita Brooks entered the conversation by providing evidence that the massacre was initiated by the Latter-day Saints, not the natives. Sixty years after Brooks, Will Bagley argued that Saints don't act without the prophet's direction, so Brigham Young was responsible for the tragic event. Researching and writing at the same time as Bagley, Ron Walker, Rick Turley, and Glen Leonard demonstrated that the decision was made not by Brigham Young but rather at the local level by the stake president in Cedar City.[10]

As part of a larger conversation, a book or article might *do* any of several things. It might make a bold new claim. It might critique the claims of previous work or answer previous charges. Or it might ask new questions about the past that derive from present needs, values, social problems, or ways of thinking. It might report the discovery of new sources. Some offer modest updates, others "quibble over nuanced issues in old events."[11] The weakest arguments call names or attack the author.[12] Others end up revising previous stories and interpretations. The best consider all of the available sources, stories, and studies.

The areas that host these larger, ongoing conversations between thinkers and across the generations are often called *fields*. And the study of how our knowledge of sources, stories, and studies has developed over time in a field also has a name—*historiography*. "Like medicine, law, or engineering, history is a profession for which scholars spend years learning crucial skills and absorbing bodies of work that help them to interpret the past," observed historian Karin Wulf. "Historians learn from one another and build on each other's work to get an ever clearer, fuller picture of the past."[13] Every book must be evaluated within the context of the larger conversations within its relevant fields.

You Try It

Rumor

I don't need historical experts, arguments, or studies.

Sniff Tests

1. *No citations.* Beware if the author (or publisher) has not taken the time to point you to the evidence—whether through footnotes, endnotes, or an essay on sources.

2. *Argumentation without evidence.* Technically, an argument can appeal to things other than evidence. Such appeals are considered logical fallacies. For example, one might appeal to authority or power (by quoting an authority figure who "says so"), or to the process ("I spent ten years researching this book"), or to tradition ("this is the way it's always been done"), or to the newness ("this is the latest and greatest"), or to common sense ("as everybody knows"), or to nature ("that's the way things are"), or to purity ("no true Latter-day Saint would ever doubt"), or to fear of consequences ("if we allow this, then that will surely follow"). Another way to cover a lack of evidence is to attack an author ("who are you to say that?"), or an author's spiritual standing ("someone with a testimony would not write this"), or an author's gender ("that's what I thought a man would say"), or the circumstances of the statement ("why bring that up now?"). The antidote is "Show me the evidence."

3. *The "definitive" study.* Every study is part of an ongoing conversation. Any one study is rarely definitive.

Real

Arguments based on comprehensive evidence are best.

Key Concepts

1. Studies of history assemble pieces of the past and the stories told about them into arguments that make claims based on evidence.

2. Comprehensive arguments seek all accurate facts, authentic sources, and reliable stories.

3. To find an argument, look for "signposts" that point you to the parts of the argument: the main point or thesis, the supporting claims, and the evidence.

4. Studies engage in larger conversations with previously published books and articles.

Notes

1. Roy Rosenzweig, "Can History Be Open Source? Wikipedia and the Future of the Past," *The Journal of American History* 93, no. 1 (June 2006): 117–46.

2. Richard Bushman, in Michael De Groote, "Wiki Wars: In Battle to Define Beliefs, Mormons and Foes Wage Battle on Wikipedia," *Deseret News*, January 30, 2011.

3. Amy Mitchell, Jeffrey Gottfried, Michael Barthel, and Nami Sumida, "Distinguishing between Factual and Opinion Statements in the News," Pew Research Center, June 18, 2018, https://www.journalism.org/2018/06/18/distinguishing-between-factual-and-opinion-statements-in-the-news/.

4. Dallin H. Oaks, "As He Thinketh in His Heart" (Evening with a General Authority, February 8, 2013), https://www.churchofjesuschrist.org/prophets-and-apostles/unto-all-the-world/as-he-thinketh-in-his-heart.

5. David Barker and Morgan Marietta, "Fact-Checking Can't Do Much When People's 'Dueling Facts' Are Driven by Values Instead of Knowledge," Nieman Lab, May 8, 2019, https://www.niemanlab.org/2019/05/

fact-checking- cant-do-much-when-peoples-dueling-facts-are
-driven-by-values-instead-of-knowledge/.

6. "Are Mormons Christian?" Gospel Topics Essays, The Church of Jesus Christ of Latter-day Saints, https://www.churchofjesuschrist.org/study/manual/gospel- topics-essays/christians.

7. Kate Davidson, "Hard to Find: Workers with Good 'Soft Skills,'" *Wall Street Journal*, August 31, 2016.

8. Dean C. Jessee, "The Reliability of Joseph Smith's History," *Journal of Mormon History* 3 (1976): 23–46.

9. Footnotes can be misused by authors in many ways—they may heap up citations without admitting that the sources disagree (don't mistake quantity for quality), they may omit the sources or studies that present evidence contrary to their thesis (cherry-picking), they may omit the sources or studies on which they rely (plagiarism), or they may hide a partial quotation to suppress inconvenient facts. Pay attention to the notes! Anthony Grafton, *The Footnote: A Curious History* (Cambridge, MA: Harvard University Press, 1997), 100.

10. Joseph Fielding Smith, *Essentials in Church History* (Salt Lake City: Deseret News Press, 1922), 511; Juanita Brooks, *The Mountain Meadows Massacre* (Norman: University of Oklahoma Press, 1950); Will Bagley, *Blood of the Prophets: Brigham Young and the Massacre at Mountain Meadows* (Norman: University of Oklahoma Press, 2012); Ronald W. Walker, Richard E. Turley, and Glen M. Leonard, *Massacre at Mountain Meadows* (New York: Oxford University Press, 2008).

11. Bruce C. Hafen and Marie K. Hafen, *Faith Is Not Blind* (Salt Lake City: Deseret Book, 2018), 31.

12. Paul Graham, "How to Disagree," March 2008, http://www.paulgraham.com/disagree.html; Paul Ratner, "How to Disagree Well: 7 of the Best and Worst Ways to Argue," Big Think, March 16, 2018, http://bigthink.com/paul- ratner/how-to-disagree-well-7-of-the-best-and-worst-ways-to-argue.

13. Karin Wulf, "What Naomi Wolf and Cokie Roberts Teach Us about the Need for Historians," *Washington Post*, June 11, 2019.

PART III
DISPEL THIS

CHAPTER 14

Get Yourself Smart

Mark grew fidgety during the elders quorum lesson. Highly intelligent, he was currently enrolled in a premier program at a prestigious university. All week long he sat with his professors or in the library, wrestling with the toughest questions facing his field. Compared to the dozen or more hours each day he spent engaged in the big ideas of his future profession, this hour on Sunday felt worthless, and he determined to do something about it.

"Today's lesson was a waste of time," Mark complained to the elders quorum president in the foyer after church.

"What do you mean?" the president asked.

"I'm in a great program, and I have to work on it all day every day," he said. "This is the only hour I have each week for spiritual things, and I was not fed!"

Several problems appear on the surface of Mark's comments—he missed the memo about daily study, he assumes that church should feed him without any effort on his part, and he has poor time-management skills. Beneath the surface, it's clear Mark has not yet learned the importance of seeking. The Savior repeatedly implored people to ask, seek, and knock. Each of us must spend time contemplating in our hearts and minds, seeking to understand doctrine.

The investigative skills used to discern what is real and rumor must be nourished and cultivated through a lifetime of study, inquiry, and seeking. You are responsible for getting yourself smart.

You Gotta Read a Lot

It requires a lot of reading to develop a sound understanding of the scriptures, our doctrine, our history, and current events. You cannot read a single scripture passage to learn all there is to know about faith. Truths are scattered throughout the scriptures. It is not uncommon for the Brethren to reread all the standard works while thinking through an issue. President Russell M. Nelson demonstrated this practice when he invited young adults to use the Topical Guide "to study *everything* Jesus said and did as recorded in the standard works."[1] If you want to know the word of God and live "by every word that proceedeth out of the mouth of God" (Matt. 4:4), then you gotta read a lot.

The fulness of our rich doctrine does not fit on a meme or a bumper sticker. Church teachings likewise exist in multiple locations: the scriptures; official declarations and proclamations; and statements by Church leaders in general conference, devotionals, and Church magazines. Further, the doctrine of the Church has been revealed "line upon line," over time, and continues to be received and communicated by Church leaders through these many channels and venues. To understand our doctrine, we have been explicitly counseled *not* to use just a single source.

Elder D. Todd Christofferson emphasized that "a statement made by one leader on a single occasion often represents a personal, though well-considered, opinion, not meant to be official or binding for the whole Church." Elder David A. Bednar elaborated, saying that "attempting to understand a doctrine or principle by examining a single scripture or prophetic statement in isolation from all else that has been revealed on the subject is generally misguided."[2] To understand our doctrine, you gotta read a lot.

Likewise, a complete and accurate knowledge of Church history is not found in a single book. It has been said that "the most dangerous person in the world is the person who has read only one book." The danger lies in assuming that because you know *something*, you must know *everything*. Former assistant Church historian Richard E. Turley often counseled, "Don't study Church history too little."[3] We seek to learn about "things which have been" in order to "be instructed more perfectly in theory, in principle, in doctrine, in the law of the gospel" (D&C 88:78–79). To make sense of myths, rumors, and Church history, you gotta read a lot.

It also requires much reading to keep up with current events. One of the blessings of living prophets is the opportunity for updated teachings and changes. President M. Russell Ballard warned teachers "not to pass along faith-promoting or unsubstantiated rumors or outdated understandings and explanations of our doctrine and practices from the past."[4] Stay up-to-date by reviewing the messages of general conference, teachings of Church leaders in Church magazines and the *Church News*, announcements and information shared in Church emails or through the Church's Newsroom.

Our scriptures, doctrine, and history teach that seeking is a personal responsibility. "The glory of God is intelligence," and it is an individual duty to seek it: "whatever principle of intelligence we attain unto in this life, it will rise with us in the resurrection" (D&C 93:36; 130:18). In a sermon in 1842, Joseph Smith said that "a man is saved no faster than he gets knowledge."[5] More recently, Elder Bednar emphasized an individual's personal responsibility to learn: "We should not expect the Church as an organization to teach or tell us all of the things we need to know and do to become devoted disciples and endure valiantly to the end."[6] This reading and seeking is hard work. Historian Steven C. Harper observed that such seeking "is not for the weak-willed or faint of heart, nor for the intellectually or spiritually lazy."[7] Even though it's hard work, seeking is a mark of true discipleship. In the New Testament, we read that Paul and Silas rejoiced when they learned the Saints in Berea had "received the word with all readiness of mind, and searched the scriptures daily, whether those things were so" (Acts 17:11). Valiant followers of Jesus Christ end up reading a lot.

> ### 💬 Everyday Encounter: Avoiding the Single, Definitive Answer
>
> I recently attended a ward in which every week a speaker or teacher quoted from two former leaders who died 30 years ago. Because it happened every week, I began reading the teacher's manuals and confirmed that the quotations were *not* in the manuals. Why did the speakers continually go to these two sources? It was not just because the men were apostles, because we have apostles today who could be cited. It was not for ease of access, because the internet and Gospel Library app have brought the words of all past and current leaders to our fingertips. Then I began to pay attention to *how* the speakers quoted them. Whatever the topic of the week, the speaker would introduce the quotes as the single, definitive answer on the subject. With a single quote, discussion ended. The approach sought security in a single, definitive response and sidestepped the richness of our doctrine, the ambiguities of the scriptures, and the importance of seeking personal inspiration.

Out of the Best Books

The scripture that encourages us to "seek learning, even by study and also by faith" also guides us where to look—we are to seek faith and wisdom "out of the best books." In another revelation the Lord encouraged the Saints to "become acquainted with all good books" (D&C 88:118; 90:15). What are the best books?

In 2016, President Ballard told seminary and institute teachers that "the 'best books' include the scriptures, the teachings of modern prophets and apostles, and the best LDS scholarship available."[8] How do we recognize the best scholarship available? My general advice is to seek for sources, stories, and studies that are accurate, authentic, reliable, fair, and comprehensive (see chapters 9–13). Seek readable works that present accurate facts and sources, findings that are consistent with evidence, understandings of different contexts, and examinations of all sides of the issues. Look for authors who have earned expertise in the subject and who are transparent about their relationships to their subjects. The "best books" also make a significant impact—they teach correct principles, expand vision and understanding, build wisdom and faith, engage other works in new ways, and offer new perspectives.

How do we understand the truth and benefit from good books that also may include errors? In 1833, while translating the Bible, Joseph inquired what he should do with Apocryphal books included in Latin and Catholic Bibles but not in Protestant versions. "There are many things contained therein that are true," the Lord answered, and "there are many things contained therein that are not true." He counseled Joseph not to translate the books, but added, "Whoso readeth it, let him understand, for the Spirit manifesteth truth; and whoso is enlightened by the Spirit shall obtain benefit therefrom" (D&C 91:1–2, 4–5).

Joseph Smith thus provides an inspiring example of how to seek widely. Early on, he learned from the Bible that he could pray and God would answer, and then he later revised parts of the Bible. He learned the text of the Book of Mormon through the Nephite interpreters and a seer stone, and the text of the book of Abraham in connection with ancient scrolls that had been uncovered with Egyptian mummies. He listened to traveling preachers and then corrected their messages. He participated in Masonic rituals and then moved beyond. He followed his injunction in what is now the thirteenth article of faith—if there was anything virtuous, lovely, of good report, or praiseworthy, no matter where it was found, he sought after those things.

🖥 Best Resources:
Sources for Finding the Best Books

1. *Database of scholarship.* The library at Brigham Young University hosts a searchable database in which you can find a comprehensive list of more than fifteen thousand books and articles on hundreds of topics (**lib.byu.edu/collections/ mormon-bibliography**).

2. *Citations.* The footnotes or endnotes of any book you are currently enjoying will point to other relevant materials of interest.

3. *Google Alert.* You can set up a Google Alert to send you emails about any topic you desire.

Reading and seeking are required to make sense of most topics that generate rumors and myths. Consider the question of where events in the Book of Mormon occurred—this topic has generated a very long conversation that has produced few "best books" and much that fails the sniff tests. When analyzing the author's arguments, the most apparent finding is an *absence* of evidence. Nothing within the Book of Mormon points directly to a place in the Americas recognizable in modern terms. And no archeological discovery in the Americas has yet uncovered a clear reference to a place in the book. During his lifetime, Joseph Smith accepted evidence for connections to *both* the North American Midwest and Central America.[9] In 2019, a Church statement declared that "the Church's only position is that the events the Book of Mormon describes took place in the ancient Americas."[10] After nearly two hundred years of searching, no interpretation has assembled enough evidence to be fully persuasive.

Lacking both direct and contextual evidence, interpreters must make an analogy (see chapter 8) through parallels or "correspondences" to frame a modern landscape with information found in the text. For example, the Book of Mormon refers to minerals, such as copper, and land features, such as rivers, a "small" or "narrow neck of land" (Alma 22:32; Ether 10:20), and a hill called "Ramah" or "Cumorah," where both the Jaredite and Nephite civilizations ended (Ether 15:11; Morm. 6:6). With that information, interpreters reconstruct a generic map of the relationships between places, but the result is very much like the map at the heart of the movie *Indiana Jones and the Last Crusade*—an exciting mystery with no starting place.

The earliest assumptions placed events in the entirety of North and South America (a "hemispheric" view).[11] In the twentieth century, a more limited approach focused on Central America (a "Mesoamerican" view),[12] with a consensus emerging that the small or narrow neck of land corresponded with the Mexican isthmus of Tehuantepec.[13] This view only works if there were two hills named Cumorah—one in the text of the book where the final battles were fought and a second in New York where the plates were buried, named after the original; this interpretation requires Moroni to have walked from Mexico to New York.[14] The idea of a more "limited geography" prompted other theories that place the Nephite experience exclusively in South America,[15] nestled between the Great Lakes,[16] on the Baja Peninsula in Mexico,[17] on the Malay Peninsula in southeast Asia,[18] or in Africa.[19] Some populist theories make appeals to plain-sense reasoning, American patriotism, and distrust of "experts." The "heartland" theory, for instance, begins with the assumption that the Book of Mormon promises of liberty and prosperity can really apply *only* to the United States (and certainly not

Mexico)—Lehi landed in Florida, the Nephites moved inland to Missouri and Iowa, and then the civilization ended in New York, all under the banner of the stars and stripes (which, incidentally, appears frequently in materials promoting the heartland theory).[20]

This landscape of conjecture produces many sniff tests. Lacking direct evidence, interpreters selectively emphasize and omit evidence, promoting one of Joseph Smith's statements while downplaying another or singling out only some Book of Mormon passages. Single-sided treatments offer praise for the interpreter's "brilliance" or "inspiration" and the book's "definitive" treatment. Some interpreters resort to piling up long lists and addenda. You'll find much competitive contention and sniping. There are even conspiracy theories that the Smithsonian uses the Book of Mormon to guide its archeological fieldwork,[21] that the Church is secretly hiding or endorsing an interpretation, and that Moroni intentionally peppered his abridgment with dozens of secret clues about the land because he *wanted* us to find the place.

The "best books" will respect the text of the Book of Mormon, carefully scrutinize evidence from nineteenth-century figures, be written by authors with relevant expertise, and be published by reputable presses. Perhaps the best advice was published by the Church in January 2019: "Individuals may have their own opinions regarding Book of Mormon geography and other such matters about which the Lord has not spoken. However, the First Presidency and Quorum of the Twelve Apostles urge leaders and members not to advocate those personal theories in any setting or manner that would imply either prophetic or Church support for those theories. All parties should strive to avoid contention on these matters."[22] Thus, any answer to the question of Book of Mormon geography currently resides somewhere in the neighborhood of insufficient evidence—"we don't know (and that's okay)." Regardless, true discipleship is built on a testimony of the book's message, not its geography.

A Quest for a Lifetime

The work of seeking widely must, of necessity, be a lifetime quest. You cannot learn everything at once and be finished. Seeking and learning must become part of who we are and how we interact with the world. For missionaries, the quest begins with praying for the needs of investigators and seeking guidance to help them. For busy young parents, the quest involves reading with children and fielding their day-to-day questions. Later stages of life may permit lengthy pondering within temple walls. Opportunities for learning and seeking may surface on work breaks, in transit, in formal classes, and through Church service.

> ### 🔆 Thinking Habit:
> ### Make Seeking a Quest for a Lifetime
>
> 1. Seek the *best books*, characterized by sound methods and significant impacts.
> 2. Cultivate different *varieties* of reading, and match the variety to your current needs.
> 3. Develop a *routine* of taking notes about individual works and overarching topics.

One recommendation for making the most of this quest is to embrace the fact that there are different *varieties* of reading. Sometimes we *browse* through headlines or posts on social media. Other times you might *hunt* through movie listings, looking for a specific show time that fits your schedule. You might *savor* every word and punctuation in a love letter from your significant other. You might study two sources side by side and compare them to identify points of similarity and difference. Learn which kind of reading helps you learn what you desire to learn.

How do you read the scriptures? Do you skim, go line by line, savor every word, or study? One of the Savior's most frequent criticisms was of people who had not even read the scriptures.[23] In His teachings, the Lord "expounded" or "opened" scripture.[24] Other passages link reading with understanding, "giving the sense," remembering, and pondering.[25] Other verbs to describe studying the scriptures include *search, expound* or *explain*, and *connect*.[26] Faith and study combine as we prayerfully feast on the scriptures, read and reflect on multiple sources, make connections between passages and sources, consider information within proper contexts, look for patterns and themes, and draw out relevant lessons. These practices also help us make sense of historical facts and find answers to our questions.

Another recommendation is to develop personalized *routines* for two kinds of note-taking. First, you should take notes about the individual works you read. The quantity of your notes will depend on the kind of reading you are doing, but at minimum you should record the citation and identify the main points, the significant implications, and how the contents connect to you personally.[27] Create a note-taking template that you follow every time. By making it a routine, you train your mind to watch for the most important information. And, instead of spending a lot of time trying to remember where you learned something, you can quickly consult your notes.

Second, you should assemble information from multiple sources, stories, and studies into summaries of different topics. This practice could be as informal as keeping files or folders in which you drop information. You may structure an outline of integrated notes or polish off the information into the text of a talk. President Henry B. Eyring spent the Sundays of his college years writing "outlines of sermons, never given." President Russell M. Nelson encouraged Saints to prepare for the April 2020 general conference by encouraging them to "select your own questions. Design your own plan. Immerse yourself in the glorious light of the Restoration."[28] We can and should design plans of study and record what we have learned.

Lifelong seeking and learning form part of your devotion as a disciple of Jesus Christ. Seeking, learning, and studying—together with serving, ministering, praying, and pondering—provide the nourishment you need to endure to the end.

You Try It

Rumor

The Church should tell me everything I need to know.

Sniff Tests

1. *One definitive answer.* The best answers point not to a single quote or source but to a range of scriptures and teachings rooted in historical contexts.
2. *"I read a book."* The most dangerous person is the one who has read only one book.
3. *No routine for seeking.* Seeking must become part of who we are and part of our habits and routines.

Real

You gotta read a lot.

Key Concepts

1. Seeking and learning are individual responsibilities; we must seek widely to understand the scriptures, Church doctrine, and history.
2. We should seek truth and wisdom out of good books, discerning their truth and benefit.

3. Seeking is a quest for a lifetime, strengthened by routines for reading and note-taking.

Notes

1. Russell M. Nelson, "Drawing the Power of Jesus Christ into Our Lives," *Ensign*, May 2017, 39; emphasis in original.
2. D. Todd Christofferson, "The Doctrine of Christ," *Ensign*, May 2012, 88; David A. Bednar, *Increase in Learning: Spiritual Patterns for Obtaining Your Own Answers* (Salt Lake City: Deseret Book, 2011), xiii.
3. Richard E. Turley, quoted in D. Todd Christofferson, "The Prophet Joseph Smith" (devotional, BYU–Idaho, Rexburg, September 24, 2013), http://www2.byui.edu/Presentations/Transcripts/Devotionals/2013_9_24_Christofferson.htm.
4. M. Russell Ballard, "By Study and by Faith," *Ensign*, December 2016, 27.
5. Joseph Smith, "Discourse, 10 April 1842, as Reported by Wilford Woodruff," p. [146], The Joseph Smith Papers, https://www.josephsmithpapers.org/paper-summary/discourse-10-april-1842-as-reported-by-wilford-woodruff/1.
6. Bednar, *Increase in Learning*, 1.
7. Steven C. Harper, "Seekers Wanted" (lecture, BYU Women's Conference, Provo, UT, April 30, 2015), 6.
8. M. Russell Ballard, "By Study and by Faith," *Ensign*, December 2016, 25, 26.
9. Andrew H. Hedges, "Book of Mormon Geography in the World of Joseph Smith," *Mormon Historical Studies* 8, nos. 1 & 2 (2007): 77–89.
10. "Book of Mormon Geography," Gospel Topics, The Church of Jesus Christ of Latter-day Saints, 2019, https://www.churchofjesuschrist.org/study/manual/gospel- topics/book-of-mormon-geography.
11. See works by George Q. Cannon, George Reynolds, Janne M. Sjodahl, and Joel Ricks.
12. See works by B. H. Roberts, Jesse A. and Jesse N. Washburn, Thomas Ferguson, Fletcher Hammond, and Sidney B. Sperry.
13. See works by John L. Sorenson, Brant A. Gardner, and John L. Lund.
14. A hand-drawn map of Moroni's wanderings is often cited, though

a note on the back of the map states that the unnamed mapmaker got the information thirdhand. "Diagram Showing Moroni's Travels, undated," Church History Library, Salt Lake City.

15. See works by Verla Birrell, Venice Priddis, and Arthur J. Kocherhans.
16. See works by Delbert W. Curtis, Duane R. Aston, and Phyllis Carol Olive.
17. See works by Lynn and David Rosenvall.
18. See works by Ralph A. Olsen.
19. See works by Embaye Melekin.
20. See works by Bruce H. Porter, Rod L. Meldrum, and Jonathan Neville.
21. A 1979 memo from the Museum of Natural History that authoritatively rejects this claim is published in Terryl L. Givens, *By the Hand of Mormon: The American Scripture That Launched a New World Religion* (New York: Oxford University Press, 2002), 115–16.
22. "Book of Mormon Geography," Gospel Topics.
23. See Matt. 12:3, 5; 19:4; 21:6, 42; 22:31; Mark 2:5; 12:10, 26; Luke 6:3; 10:26; 3 Ne. 27:5.
24. For "expounding," see Luke 24:27; 3 Ne. 23:6, 14; 24:1; 26:1–7. For "opening," see Luke 24:32, 45. For declaring scripture fulfilled, see Luke 4:16–22; 3 Ne. 9:16.
25. For reading and understanding, see Matt. 24:15; Mark 13:14; Eph. 3:4; Mosiah 1:4; 3 Ne. 10:14; Morm. 9:8; D&C 57:9; 71:5; 91:4; JS—Matt. 1:2. For reading and giving the sense, see Neh. 8:8. For reading and remembering, see Moro. 10:3. And for reading and pondering, see Josh. 1:8; 2 Ne. 4:15; D&C 138:1, 6–10; JS—H 1:12.
26. For instances of *search*, see John 5:39; Acts 17:11; Jacob 7:23; Mosiah 1:7; Alma 14:1; 17:2; 33:2; 3 Ne. 10:14; 20:11; 23:1; D&C 1:37. For *expound*, see Luke 24:27; Alma 22:13; 3 Ne. 23:6, 14; D&C 24:5, 9; 25:7; 68:1; 71:1; 97:5; 100:11. For *explain*, see Mosiah 27:35; Alma 12:1; D&C 19:7. For *connect*, see 1 Cor. 15:3, 4; James 2:8; Jacob 4:16; D&C 20:41, 69; 24:14. And for *study*, see 2 Tim. 2:15; D&C 11:22; 26:1.
27. Wanda Thibodeaux, "Science Says This Is the Simplest Way to Remember More of What You Read," Inc., February 6, 2018, https://www.inc.com/wanda-thibodeaux/science-says-this-is-simplest-way-to-remember-more-of-what-you-read.html.
28. Henry B. Eyring, "Should I Do Schoolwork on the Sabbath?" *Ensign*, January 1978, 14; Russell M. Nelson, "Closing Remarks," *Ensign*, November 2019, 122.

CHAPTER 15

Don't Say This at Church

"Let's read the chapter of our camp theme!"

The theme "Aim High" was plastered across T-shirts, water bottles, banners, and personal study journals for the stake girls camp along the Wasatch Front. A scripture passage—"I will ascend above the heights of the clouds; I will be like the Most High" (2 Ne. 24:14)—accompanied the theme and was interpreted to mean, "You can accomplish your goals! As a daughter of God, you can become like Him!" Stake leaders emphasized the theme repeatedly in their talks.

Some of the girls began reading chapter 24 in 2 Nephi, and even though Nephi was quoting from Isaiah, they could understand it. They started in verse 1, and as they got closer to verse 14 (the theme of girls camp), they began to grow uneasy. Verse 12 talked about Lucifer, and verse 13 introduced the inner thoughts of his heart. Their camp theme was taken from the words of Lucifer! Stunned, they took their finding to their stake leaders who admitted that they had noticed it too, but only after all of the promotional materials had already been printed. They asked the girls not to tell any of their fellow young women in the stake.

Latter-day Saints love quotes. We share them on social media, in talks, and in lessons to give our messages authority, emphasis, and elegance. Because we hear and share quotes every week, investigating them becomes one of the most common opportunities to improve our thinking and dispel myths.

One benefit of learning to investigate rumors and history is that we become more discerning of false quotes and more precise in our use of statements from scripture and Church leaders. To reach that goal, we need to trace quotes back to their original source. We often need to consider several scriptures and statements on a topic, sometimes reflecting on them again and again, in order to understand Latter-day Saint doctrine and practice more fully.

Tracing a Quote to Its Original Source

Each day we encounter accurate quotes, misquotes, and false quotes in traditional media and on social media, as well as in conversations with family and friends. Seeing a quote on the internet is not enough to justify repeating it. We should trace the quote to its original source, which begins with close reading and questioning—identify *specific* details, follow the details to *specific* sources, and evaluate the reliability of the sources. Does the social media post or sacrament meeting speaker state where the quote came from? If reading a source in print or online, check the footnotes or hyperlinks. Do you know the author of the quote? Do you know the setting—was the statement said in general conference or a passage in a book? If you don't know the setting, you'll need to find out. If you do, you'll need to evaluate. Does the statement come from an authentic and reliable piece of the past, such as a speech, a journal, a letter, or the minutes or report of a meeting?

Frequently, you'll have to modify this general strategy for one of two reasons. First, quotes often get garbled over time, the words changed, the setting misremembered. So you'll need to search not just for exact words but for similar sounding words or the idea expressed in another way. Second, quotes often do not come with a full attribution. The best citation includes four elements—the name of the author, the exact words spoken or written, reference to the original setting, and an original source where the information may be found. If any of those pieces are missing, you'll have to adjust your questions. Sometimes you'll know an author of a quote and the correct wording, so the question is "Did so-and-so really say such-and-such?" Other times you'll know only one of those elements, and be left to ask, "Who said such-and-such?" or "Did so-and-so say something about a topic?"

To find a quote in its original source, you'll often need to search in multiple places. And, no, an internet search engine is not sufficient because it can only search the contents of books and records *if* those contents have been placed online. I've identified some of the best resources in the accompanying box. As you use the resources, you'll get a sense of where to start for particular kinds of quotes. You may have to search several before finding the original source of a quote, or you may search all of them and still come up short. Sometimes the author of a quote turns out to be someone other than the person it was attributed to. Other times you'll discover that the original wording is different (and usually less interesting) than the popularized version.

🖥 Best Resources: Sources for General Authority Quotes

If you think the statement was made in general conference, a few databases provide different options for searching. The LDS General Conference Corpus (**lds-general-conference.org**) contains the full texts of more than ten thousand talks from 1851 to the present and can analyze frequencies of word use. The LDS

Scripture Citation Index (**scriptures.byu.edu**) crosslinks talks to the scriptures cited by the speakers.

The Church's website will not let you limit your search results just to the general conferences, and the search logic that pulls up results on the site is not very precise. Here's a tip. In Google, enter the words "site:ChurchofJesusChrist.org" (without the quotation marks) before your search terms. This allows you to point Google's powerful search capabilities directly at the Church's site.

The Internet Archive (**archive.org**) contains the full text of many Church publications, including the official reports of general conferences as well as old periodicals, such as the *Improvement Era*, *Relief Society Magazine*, and *Millennial Star*. The BYU Speeches website (**speeches.byu.edu**) publishes remarks made in BYU devotionals. Book publishers Deseret Book (**gospelink.com**), the BYU Religious Studies Center (**rsc.byu.edu**), and Signature Books (**signaturebookslibrary.org**) have made full-text electronic versions of many of their publications available online.

Evaluating the Quote in Context

You must follow your search all the way to the original source and, once there, evaluate the original setting. A few examples can illustrate how the original does not always match the popularized version. You may have heard that one day the Saints will walk to Missouri to prepare for the Second Coming. But the closest statement supporting that idea comes from President Joseph F. Smith in 1882, and it is filled with qualifying limitations, such as "some of us may be gathered" and "this is one way to look at it." Another myth related to Missouri claims that for its part in persecuting the early Saints, the state would be destroyed such that "not a yellow dog will be left to wag his tail." The closest we can get to this statement is Amanda Wilcox remembering that Heber C. Kimball told her that Brigham Young said it. However, at the time Wilcox claimed Kimball told her this in Salt Lake City, he was forty-five miles away in Provo. Furthermore, today the state of Missouri hosts two temples, eighteen stakes, and more than seventy thousand members, so any future destruction would harm the Saints as well.[1]

Even if you find the exact words you were looking for, they may not mean what the person quoting them suggests they mean. As a young man growing up outside of Baltimore, I was handed a description of a dream, cited to the journal of Wilford Woodruff, that described Salt Lake City and New York City as decimated by a disease, the White House and Congress empty and in ruins, and dead bodies piled up in Baltimore's Battle Monument Square. The person of trust who shared the dream suggested that this was Wilford Woodruff's vision, and the imagery provoked fear among me and my seminary classmates.

It is accurate that this description of a vision can be found in Wilford Woodruff's journal under the date of June 15, 1878. But several contextual factors suggest Woodruff did not receive the vision. The date of the vision was December 1877, but Woodruff didn't copy it into the journal until six months later, which was unusual for the daily journal keeper (see chapter 9). In the journal entry he mentions having the "strange vision Copied," suggesting it came from another source, and there is a large blank space at the beginning of the description between "I" and "went," suggesting he wanted to write the author's name in later. Also, the clerk who copied the vision wrote "Vision had by" followed by blank. Finally, the text of the vision claimed the recipient was "reading the Revelations in the French language," and Woodruff did not know French. By the 1880s, rumors of the vision attributed it to Joseph F. Smith, who publicly declared it a fraud.[2] Today I wish that my teenage self had known how to discern real and rumor so that I and my fellow early-morning seminary students would not have felt so scared.

One common way quotes get garbled is by forgetting the

original author and citing only the General Authority or other speaker who quoted someone else. Heber J. Grant was quoting poet Ralph Waldo Emerson when he said, "That which we persist in doing becomes easier to do, *not that the nature of the thing has changed but that our power to do has increased.*"[3] David O. McKay was remembering a book by J. E. McCulloch when he declared, "No other success can compensate for failure in the home."[4] Gordon B. Hinckley was quoting journalist Jenkin Lloyd Jones, who said, "Anyone who imagines that bliss is normal is going to waste a lot of time running around shouting that he's been robbed. . . . Life is like an old time rail journey—delays, sidetracks, smoke, dust, cinders, and jolts, interspersed only occasionally by beautiful vistas and thrilling bursts of speed."[5] Dieter F. Uchtdorf quoted St. Francis of Assisi, who said, "Preach the gospel at all times and when necessary, use words."[6] And Stephen Covey made the phrase "Begin with the end in mind" one of his influential habits five years after it had been the title of Russell M. Nelson's BYU devotional.[7]

Sometimes speakers attribute an anonymous quote to someone real. Marjorie Pay Hinckley *never* made a statement about driving up to the pearly gates in a station wagon with peanut butter on her shirt as proof that she really lived. No matter how many Pinterest boards or blogs or columnists recycle the words and attribute them to her, it does not change the fact that those words *do not appear* in her books or writings—even if the sharer says it came from those books. The quote came, instead, through a middle-aged male motivational speaker.[8]

The tendency to misremember the author is not unique among Latter-day Saints. The words attributed to Spiderman "with great power comes great responsibility" appear in the comic book in the mouth of his Uncle Ben and the narrator. Variations of the phrase have been found in the speeches of Winston Churchill (1906) and British parliament member William Lamb (1817), and in a document from the French National Convention (1793). The words were thus not adapted from Doctrine and Covenants 82:3, as some Latter-day Saints have assumed.[9]

Some quotes are simply fabricated. The idea frequently circulates that Brigham Young described single men over age twenty-five as a "menace to society." Not only does the phrase "menace to society" not appear anywhere in Brigham Young's writings or speeches, but the Oxford English Dictionary has not found any use of that phrase before the 1880s (Brigham died in 1877).[10] For many years a quote made the rounds saying that today's youth were generals in the War in Heaven and that people in a future day would bow in their presence. The quote was attributed to multiple speakers, including Neal A. Maxwell, Boyd K. Packer, Thomas S. Monson, and Henry B. Eyring (multiple attributions is a good sniff test). Speaking for his Brethren and as Acting President of the Quorum of the Twelve, President Packer publicly refuted the statement: "I did not make that statement. I do not believe that statement. . . . None of the Brethren made that statement." The quote seems to have originated with another middle-aged male motivational speaker.[11]

Finally, some quotes just don't exist. These phantom or ghost quotes are popular and get printed on home décor and recycled on social media, but they do not appear in any scripture. Jesus did not say "I never said it would be easy. I only said it would be worth it." The Bible does not say "Spare the rod and spoil the child" or "Faith precedes the miracle" or "God helps those who help themselves."

🖥 Best Resources:
Sources for Joseph Smith Quotes

Joseph Smith presents a special case for quotations. On one hand, he is the founding prophet of the Restoration, a revelator and teacher of supreme significance. On the other hand, we do not know everything he ever said. Some of his statements were recorded and then forgotten. Some come from notes of his sayings recorded by others, and many of those long after the fact. Others, such as the *Lectures on Faith*, turn out to have been authored by someone else.[12]

Where should you begin to verify if Joseph Smith really said something? Memories and embellishments of Joseph Smith's words appear in the *Journal of Discourses*, the *History of the Church*, and the widely published volume *Teachings of the Prophet Joseph Smith*. All of these sources should be used cautiously. They are a good place to find words attributed to Joseph but not the best place to verify original sources.

A quick place to start is the volume *Teachings of Presidents of the Church: Joseph Smith*. Each statement was carefully scrutinized before being included in the volume and reflects the best possible sources. The book is available online in formats that allow full-text searching in multiple languages.[13]

The most comprehensive source to verify his statements is the Joseph Smith Papers Project, which gathers all existing Joseph Smith documents and publishes them with both textual and contextual annotation. The project's website (**josephsmithpapers.org**) presents both images and transcriptions of documents from the Church History Library as well as from other libraries and archives.[14]

Selecting the Quote

Latter-day Saints need to not only verify quotations we hear but also select accurate passages to quote as part of our own talks and lessons. Three important elements will make your quotation a success. First, whether you are going to share your quotation verbally or in writing, plan on including a complete attribution that states the name of the author, the exact words, the original setting for the statement, and the source where others can find it. That means you need to record this information at the time you find the quote and then repeat the information each time you share it. The components of a complete attribution fit together like pieces of a puzzle—without one, your quotation is incomplete.

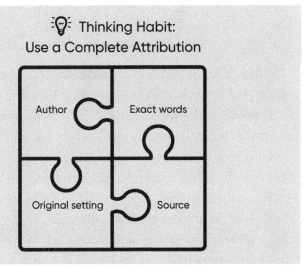

**Thinking Habit:
Use a Complete Attribution**

Author

Exact words

Original setting

Source

Next, you should make sure that the words you quote have the same meaning in the context of your talk or presentation as they had in the original source. If you use the words to mean something different than what they originally meant, you are taking the words *out of context*. If you quote only a few words that support or prove the point you want to make, you are *proof texting*. We often see this with movie reviews. A movie poster or DVD cover will say "Amazing . . . worth watching," but if you were to track down the original review it may read, "This dull movie is far from amazing and is probably not even worth watching."

Finally, introduce your quotation into your talk or lesson by creating a *quotation sandwich*. Begin by setting up the quote with the full attribution and a description of its original context. Next share the words of the quotation. After quoting the passage, provide a sentence explaining why it was important and what it means for the audience.[15] Quotes are pieces of the past, and they do not "speak for themselves." The original author said something at a certain time in a past context. You must connect that past to your present.

💬 Everyday Encounter: Sharing a Quote in Class

Often, a person sitting in a Sunday School class will remember only part of a quote's attribution but then share it anyway, as in "I can't remember who said it, but . . ." Jesus promised that the Holy Ghost will "bring all things to [our] remembrance" (John 14:26). I read that verse to mean that if I am truly inspired to share a quotation for the edification of others, the Holy Ghost will help me remember the complete attribution. If you cannot remember all of the parts of the attribution—the author, the exact words, the setting, and the source—then you are having "a stupor of thought that shall cause you to forget" (D&C 9:9). When this happens to me, I do not share the thought in class, but I do go home and search it out. Frequently, I find that I misremembered the quote or forgot its context. In so doing, I always learn things, which means the thought came to my mind for my edification but not so I could share it with the rest of the class. Later, with the information properly in mind, I often find opportunities to share the message responsibly.

You Try It

Rumor

I can't remember who said this, but . . .

Sniff Tests

1. *Incomplete attribution.* A complete attribution includes the

author, the words, the original setting, and the source. Anything less is not enough!

2. *Quoting out of context.* The person sharing a quotation is responsible to indicate what it meant in its original context and to use it to mean the same thing in our present context.

Real

Every good quote needs an author, the correct wording, the original setting, and the source.

Key Concepts

1. Good quotations come from actual sources and respect original context.

2. Trace a quote to its source by asking questions to identify specific details, follow the details to specific sources, and evaluate the reliability of the sources.

3. Share a complete attribution—the author, the exact words, the original setting, and the source.

Notes

1. Graham W. Doxey, "Missouri Myths," *Ensign*, April 1979, 64–65; "Facts and Statistics: Missouri," Newsroom, The Church of Jesus Christ of Latter-day Saints, https://newsroom.churchofjesuschrist. org/facts-and-statistics/state/missouri.

2. Richard E. Turley, *Victims: The LDS Church and the Mark Hoffman Case* (Urbana: University of Illinois Press, 1992), 16–17.

3. Leon R. Hartshorn, "Heber J. Grant: A Man Without Excuses," *New Era*, January 1972, 45. This quotation does not appear in the complete works of Emerson at http://www.rwe.org/.

4. J. E. McCulloch, *Home: The Savior of Civilization* (Washington, DC: The Southern Cooperative League, 1924), 42.

5. Gordon B. Hinckley, "God Shall Give You Knowledge by His Holy Spirit" (devotional, Brigham Young University, Provo, UT, September 25, 1973), https://speeches.byu.edu/talks/ gordon-b-hinckley_god-shall-give-unto-knowledge-holy-spirit/.

6. Dieter F. Uchtdorf, "Waiting on the Road to Damascus," *Ensign*, May 2011, 77.

7. Russell M. Nelson, "Begin with the End in Mind" (devotional, Brigham Young University, Provo, UT, September 30, 1984), https://speeches.byu.edu/talks/russell-m-nelson_begin-end-mind/; Stephen R. Covey, *The 7 Habits of Highly Effective People: Powerful Lessons in Personal Change* (New York: Simon & Schuster, 1989), habit 2. See also Russell M. Nelson, "As We Go Forward Together," *Ensign*, April 2018, 7.

8. The earliest published source is Jack R. Christianson, *As Good as I Want to Be: A Parent's Guide to Help Your Teen Succeed* (San Diego: ALTI Publishing, 1998), 21–22; Keith A. Erekson, "Pearly Gates and Peanut Butter: Tracing the Source of a Pervasive Quote," *LDS Living*, May/June 2021.

9. "With Great Power Comes Great Responsibility," Wikipedia, accessed November 4, 2020, https://en.wikipedia.org/wiki/With_great_power_comes_great_responsibility.

10. See Jana Riess, "No, Brigham Young Did Not Say that Single Men over the Age of 25 Are a Menace to Society," Religion News Service, May 16, 2018, https://religionnews.com/2018/05/16/no -brigham-young-did-not-say-that- single-men-over-the-age-of-25 -are-a-menace-to-society/.

11. "Church Leader Refutes Quote," *Church News*, April 28, 2001, 5. W. Paul Reeve and Michael Scott Van Wagenen source the quotation to Brad Wilcox, *Tips for Tackling Teenage Troubles* (Salt Lake City: Deseret Book, 1998), 25–27. Reeve and Van Wagenen, eds., *Between Pulpit and Pew: The Supernatural World in Mormon History and Folklore* (Logan: Utah State University Press, 2011), 6–10.

12. Noel B. Reynolds, "The Case for Sidney Rigdon as Author of the Lectures on Faith," *Journal of Mormon History* 31, no. 3 (Fall 2005): 1–41.

13. *Teachings of Presidents of the Church: Joseph Smith* (Salt Lake City: The Church of Jesus Christ of Latter-day Saints, 2007).

14. Nathan N. Waite, "Using the Joseph Smith Papers Website: An Introduction," *Religious Educator* 20, no. 2 (2019): 105–21.

15. Gerald Graff and Cathy Birkenstein, *"They Say/I Say": The Moves that Matter in Academic Writing*, 3rd ed. (New York: W. W. Norton & Company, 2014), 42–51.

CHAPTER 16

Help a Friend in Crisis

A fifty-five-year-old man asked a forty-one-year-old man about the up-and-coming generation of twentysomethings. The inquiring man observed that the younger generation appeared to be "perplexed" with "problems." The other man replied that while some used to struggle in his community, their crises had declined dramatically after a newcomer arrived and began teaching a class at the local institute.

The inquiring man quickly sought an explanation from the new teacher, who offered that the main emphasis of his class was *how* to approach questions and problems. Rather than asking about the Church's position on a social issue, he and his students explored how to answer someone else's question about it. Somehow, this shift in approach from specific issues to methods for explanation, and from focusing on one's own problems to helping another, helped ease the young adults' struggles and strengthened their faith.[1]

———————————————— Q ————————————————

This story is not about millennials or Generation Z.[2] The young adults in this story lived in Boston in the mid-1960s, a time and place that gave them daily exposure to tough questions about the Church's history and then-current positions on racial restrictions and women's rights. When the inquiring man in this story—then-Church Historian Leonard Arrington—asked local history professor Richard Bushman about the challenges facing young adults in 1972, Bushman pointed to the new institute class led by then New England mission president Boyd K. Packer, who taught seventy to eighty young adults attending Harvard, MIT, and other universities in the area.[3]

The story offers several significant lessons as we seek to help friends who struggle with issues related to the Church's history. It illustrates that no single generation holds a unique claim on wrestling with questions about the Church's history and place in contemporary society. A crisis occurs when the tools at hand are insufficient for the task before us. Every aspiring disciple of Jesus Christ must make peace with questions about the past and about our present faith.

My heart goes out to all who struggle with doubts, questions, concerns, and feelings. These struggles invariably involve emotional, intellectual, and spiritual trauma. If only one person were struggling, it would be a great tragedy, but in our day, many suffer in this way. The growing volume—in both size and decibels—rightly prompts the caring concern of friends and loved ones. I have not been called to define Church doctrine and practices, nor have I been trained professionally to address issues of archeology, evolutionary science, or human sexuality. As a historian, my goal here is more modest. I don't aspire to blaze a pathway of faith through a forest of doubts, but I do hope to apply the skills developed throughout this book to clear out the brambles of history that may be a source of entanglement and stumbling.

> ### 🔆 Thinking Habit:
> ### Minister to a Friend in Crisis
>
> • Love and listen to identify specific problems and concerns.
> • Rewrite the script to develop and nourish long-term faith.
> • Make personal peace with the past by learning about how history works, how antagonists operate, how seeking works, and how discipleship develops.

Love and Listen

The most important things you can do for your friend are to love and listen. You love your friend, you have spent time together, you have shared your deeper thoughts and feelings. You also love Jesus Christ, seek to imitate His loving service, and plead for the divine gift of charity. You mourn because your friend struggles; your mourning is not about the eventual outcome but about the pain in the pathway.

Listening with love involves difficult emotional and mental work, but it is a skill that you can develop with practice. We must listen eagerly, be present in the moment when they need to be heard, avoid snap judgments, and allow space.[4]

I don't know which issues trouble your friend. You'll need to find that out by listening. Maybe the question touches near the heart of the Church's message, such as the accounts of the First Vision or the translation of scripture or the role of prophets (who are human). Maybe it stems from something weird or uncertain, such as the strangeness of polygamy, the horrific violence of the Mountain Meadows Massacre, the Black priesthood and temple ban, or the near silence about Mother in Heaven. Maybe there is a familial pain point, through an ancestor who either participated in something unsavory or was excluded from something desirable. There may be deeply personal experiences with a domineering male who makes a Heavenly Father seem distant, with sexual abuse that colors perceptions of polygamy, or with witnessing friends be excluded or insulted for being gay or of a certain race. Perhaps there is concern that past practices will be reinstituted again. Maybe it's a little of all of these and then some. Listen sincerely, lovingly, repeatedly, and well.

You may need to listen deeply, beyond the words your friend expresses. For example, learning that your friend has concerns about plural marriage is usually only part of the process. Sometimes, people have historical questions about plural marriage, such as whether Joseph Smith participated, how many wives or children he had, when the practice began, or when it ended. Underneath such factual questions might be deeper doctrinal questions, such as if prophets can lead the Church astray or why Joseph did not tell Emma about all his marriages. Frequently, the implications are more personal—will the practice be reinstated, will I have to practice plural marriage in the next life, or why do women need their sealings canceled to remarry but men do not? You will need to respond one way to factual questions that trouble the mind about the past, and you will need to respond differently to personal concerns that trouble the heart in the present.

I hope you can help your friend approach the issues in a way that will be the most helpful. Many approaches have been proposed for addressing personal questions and concerns. Each of the approaches has helped someone, but all of them may not help your friend. Indeed, some of the approaches might even harm your friend, and some of the current pain may stem from previous misguided efforts to help. As you listen to your friend, seek to help identify approaches that will nourish.

You may need to be willing to love and listen for decades, granting space and courtesy for your friend to find God. Brigham Young encountered the Book of Mormon in 1830—when the

Church had less than a year of history to consider—and he spent two years deciding to join. It is common to hope that our friends and loved ones will not leave the Church, but I also hope they don't just remain outwardly connected to the Church while inwardly struggling alone. However long the road, I hope that your friend's faith will be nourished through your love and listening, your empathy and support.

Most of all, I hope that your friend will grow closer to Jesus Christ by seeking answers. The Savior has invited each of us to cast our own, individual burdens upon Him, for which He promises rest to our souls. He may cry with us, as He did with Mary and Martha after the death of Lazarus. He may wipe away our tears, as promised in the book of Revelation. He may also remind us that He suffered with us and for us, as He taught Joseph Smith while in Liberty Jail.[5] Help your friend take personal concerns to the Lord. He is the best source of hope, comfort, solace, and strength.

Rewrite the Script

In recent years, individual stories about a personal faith crisis have begun to follow a collective pattern. The story goes something like this: a person participates in Church or seminary or missionary service; the person discovers previously unknown information on the internet or elsewhere that causes confusion; increased reading and searching, coupled with a growing sense of concern, moves to more general questioning about the Church; finally, feelings of guilt or anger force a decision to stay or leave. This pattern has been acknowledged in general conference, blogs and magazine articles, and books.[6]

I obviously cannot comment on every individual experience, but a few things strike me about the pattern that has emerged in the tellings. First, the fact that so many stories fit this pattern suggests that the story itself has become a cultural script (see chapter 4)—a way to give order to thoughts and feelings that are confusing and disorganized. Just like the American Dream script has given a shape to the unarticulated hopes of many, the *faith-crisis script* provides a framework that now shapes understanding. Perhaps unintentionally, the script bears some similarity to the parable of the sower's description of the seed that fell among stony ground and "dureth for a while" until an unanticipated challenge arises (Matt. 13:21).

It is also disconcerting to me that the faith-crisis script rides on so many binaries—good questioning or bad doubting, discovered knowledge versus institutional secrecy, a choice between being true to oneself or to the Church, Church membership or former membership. This dichotomous script is so powerful that it frequently frames the approaches of well-meaning friends who try to help others "deal with doubt" or implore them to "doubt not."

One way to rewrite the script is to replace "or" with "and" (see chapter 5). Ours is not a question of faith *or* doubt, but faith *and* doubt. The scriptures contain stories of people feeling faith and doubt at the same time. My favorite involves a father who asks Jesus to heal his sick child. Jesus said He could, "if thou canst believe." That father replied, "Lord, I believe; help thou mine unbelief" (Mark 9:23–24). Yes, a father seeking healing of his child told Jesus to His face that he believed in Him *and* he also didn't believe. Did Jesus scold the man? Send him away? No, Jesus acknowledged both the father's faith and doubt, and He healed the child, which I believe also helped the father's unbelief.[7]

If we can break free of simplistic binaries, we can rewrite the script by imagining other ways to think about, describe, and give meaning to our experiences seeking to know and trust God. For example, we might see our experience in the age-old context of trials of faith sustained by all who have tried to walk the path of discipleship. "By definition, trials will be trying," noted Elder Neil L. Andersen.[8]

As an alternative, we might see our experience in the context of ancient prophecies that describe our time as "perilous" and populated by "false prophets" who "shall deceive many" because they look and sound accurate—their "lips" draw near to God and their "form" resembles godliness (JS—Matt. 1:9; JS—H 1:19).[9] Or perhaps we might look beyond the *contents* of specific concerns to the *context* of our quest to know God. Alma's metaphor of planting a seed begins with only a "desire to believe" that both gets strengthened and goes "dormant" when the seed sprouts. Later, a different kind of faith is needed—a resilient, long-term faith nourishes the plant and anticipates a more distant future that comes only through our "diligence, and patience, and long-suffering" (Alma 32:27, 34, 43). Perhaps a sense of crisis comes from trying to reapply the short-term faith that succeeded in planting when now the long-term faith is needed to nourish discipleship.

💬 Everyday Encounter:
Why Hasn't the Church Talked about This?

We can replace a conspiracy script ("the Church is hiding things") with a more complete understanding of how information is discovered and distributed ("it's a long story"):

1. Sometimes pieces of the past weren't discovered until recently. Additional accounts of the First Vision surfaced in the 1960s, and a recent project was undertaken to find every source on the Mountain Meadows Massacre.[10]

2. The common teaching technique of identifying principles for application inadvertently omits facts. A lesson that uses the First Vision as a template for receiving personal revelation rarely mentions all the historical accounts.

3. Sometimes certain issues were talked about in now-hard-to-find places, such as the accounts of the First Vision in the *Improvement Era* (1970), the seer stone in the Church's centennial

history (1930) and the children's *Friend* (1974), or the process of translation at a mission presidents seminar (1992).[11]

4. Sometimes errors of fact go unnoticed in the writing, editing, and publishing process. Church curriculum materials or letters about chapel artwork undergo a doctrinal and legal review but not a historical or cultural review.

5. Sometimes powerful artistic portrayals prove both inaccurate and highly influential. Church magazine staff commissioned a painting of the Book of Mormon translation that has appeared more times in Church materials than any other—it erroneously shows the plates sitting uncovered on the table.[12]

6. People draw different conclusions about what is faith promoting, and these judgments, made in the present and influenced by current needs and concerns, have shaped the telling of stories over time. Changes in sensibilities influence what a person or generation deems appropriate for public conversation.

7. Because of its latter-day mission, the Church has prioritized messages about conversion and salvation, which means that information about some historical events or issues receives less priority.

Make Personal Peace with the Past

In the end, every person needs to find her or his own peace with God. I find it significant that the Holy Ghost can bring peace to our minds and hearts: "the peace of God, which passeth all understanding, shall keep your hearts and minds through Christ Jesus" (Philip. 4:7). If your friend's questions are about information or facts, then conversation and study can allow the Holy Ghost to bring assurance, peace of mind, comforting memories, or personal enlightenment.[13] If your friend's concerns involve emotions such as anger or denial, then empathy and prayer can help bring calm feelings so the person can feel the Holy Ghost's peaceful consolation, hope, love, and joy.[14] Ultimately, the peace we find from God becomes "strength, that [we] should suffer no manner of afflictions, save it were swallowed up in the joy of Christ" (Alma 31:38). All of our afflictions—emotional, intellectual, physical, psychological, social, and spiritual—can be swallowed up within our larger personal relationship with Jesus Christ. When we struggle, we lack peace, but He is "The Prince of Peace" (Isa. 9:6).

The problems that people have with Church history may turn out to be more about *history* than about *Church*. If Church members have only ever encountered history in school settings marked by a single textbook, multiple-choice questions, and memorized answers, then they are going to be surprised to learn that history is incomplete, open to interpretation, and different than the present. If their first exposure to these concepts is overlaid with information about the sacred events from our history, then members will be tempted to suspect that the Church is on shaky ground, when in reality that's just how history works. Thus, when questions and concerns are framed as *Church* issues—doubt, weak testimony, or unworthiness—they invariably lead to Church solutions—confession, prayer, or increased devotion (or withdrawal). But if questions and concerns can be framed as *history* issues—examination of sources, differences, and how history works—then we can address the concerns with solutions built on good thinking skills. The problem may not be so much about faith as it is about framing, not so much about testimony as it is about thinking.

The thinking skills and habits introduced in this book can help clarify tough issues about our history. Your friend might need to learn more about facts but almost certainly will benefit by learning more about how history works (chapters 1–8), how antagonists operate (chapters 10 and 12), and how to seek widely and discern accuracy and reliability (chapters 9–14).

Your friend may have to reject either/or framings (chapter 5), be more precise and nuanced (chapter 6), or accept that changes happen (chapter 7) and that it's okay not to know everything (chapter 1). For example, when we consider that the past is gone, then we cherish the multiple accounts of the First Vision and hope another is discovered someday. Knowing that the past was different removes some of the strangeness of using of a seer stone to translate the Book of Mormon; it also helps us see nineteenth-century plural marriages as "horizontal" sealings among contemporaries rather than the current "vertical" links among generations. The habit of identifying what we know and what we don't know helps make sense of the origins of the priesthood ban, and the ability to comprehend that the ban has a long story helps us better understand how the restriction was removed. Plugging things into context does not justify past racism or absolve the perpetrators of the Mountain Meadows Massacre, but it does render a more complete picture. And being aware that our present assumptions distort the past avoids confusion about prophets and the Church.

Your thinking skills ultimately form only part of your path of discipleship. Becoming a disciple of Jesus Christ involves study, prayer, and service. It involves our minds and our hearts, might, and lives. It develops through constancy, patience, and rejoicing. I wish you the very best as you love and listen, rewrite the script, and make personal peace with the past.

💬 Everyday Encounter:
Will Learning Church History Harm Your Testimony?

Frequently, people ask me how studying Church history has strengthened my testimony, or if finding some strange new piece from our past would shake my testimony. This is a puzzling question to me because I did not receive a testimony *from* Church history. I gained my testimony the way that everyone must gain a testimony—by receiving a message in my mind and heart that I recognized as heavenly communication. Are there tough questions about Church history that require humility and our very best thinking? Yes. Will learning about Church history harm a testimony? If Church history does not give testimony, then it should not be able to take testimony away. Studying Church history is not testimony; it is an activity—like listening to music or speaking with a friend—that can serve as a means to other important ends, such as inviting the Spirit, declaring the truth, and witnessing the marvelous works of God.

You Try It

Rumor

My faith crisis means I must quit.

Sniff Tests

1. *"Don't worry about it."* This message is also often worded as "Lean on my testimony" and "Place your concerns 'on a shelf' or 'in a pocket.'" President M. Russell Ballard said, "Gone are the days when a student asked an honest question and a teacher responded, 'Don't worry about it!' Gone are the days when a student raised a sincere concern and a teacher bore his or her testimony as a response intended to avoid the issue."[15] If your friend is drowning, you need to throw a life ring rather than shout out swimming instructions.

2. *Either/or.* Don't get stuck in the cultural script that requires either faith or doubt. The gospel is richer than either/or, and God accepts both our faith and our doubts as we seek to come closer to Him.

3. *"Let's inoculate."* This metaphor is frequently used incorrectly. People use it to encourage protection and prevention. Vaccines work by providing a small dose of a disease now in order to

avoid the full sickness later, but truths about the tough parts of our history should not prevent understanding the full truth. Further, the metaphor sets unhealthy expectations that after a few answers, the problems will go away forever and no future generation will have to make peace with the past. President (and surgeon) Russell M. Nelson taught that "Jesus chooses not to inoculate." The Savior's "method employs no vaccine," he emphasized. "It utilizes the teaching of divine doctrine."[16] We need to eradicate this misused metaphor from our population by simply saying, "Let's teach the truth" or "Let's prepare youth now so they're not surprised later."

Real

Everyone must make personal peace with the past.

Key Concepts

1. The most important things you can do for a friend in crisis are to love and to listen.
2. Rewrite the script to break free of limiting binaries and allow for faith to develop that is built for long-term discipleship.
3. Every person needs to make her or his own peace with God. Encourage your friend to take concerns to the Lord. He is the best source of comfort, solace, and strength.

Notes

1. This story employs the common script of an older generation projecting inadequacies onto a younger one (see chapter 4). It has been used for hundreds of years, with examples that include contrasting the "Greatest Generation" with their slacker children and the present concerns captured in the title *iGen: Why Today's Super-Connected Kids Are Growing Up Less Rebellious, More Tolerant, Less Happy—And Completely Unprepared for Adulthood (and What That Means for the Rest of Us)* by Jean M. Twenge (New York:

Atria Books, 2017). Advertisers have proven especially effective at exploiting generational divides by flattering the elders, criticizing the youngers, and making money for others.

2. Jana Riess, *The Next Mormons: How Millennials Are Changing the LDS Church* (New York: Oxford University Press, 2019); David B. Ostler, *Bridges: Ministering to Those Who Question* (Salt Lake City: Greg Kofford Books, 2019).

3. Gary James Bergera, ed., *Confessions of a Mormon Historian: The Diaries of Leonard J. Arrington, 1971–1999*, 3 vols. (Salt Lake City: Signature Books, 2018), 1:141, 153–54.

4. Russell M. Nelson, "Listen to Learn," *Ensign*, May 1991, 22–25; Rebecca Z. Shafir, *The Zen of Listening: Mindful Communication in the Age of Distraction* (Wheaton, IL: Quest Books, 2000); David Rakel, *The Compassionate Connection: The Healing Power of Empathy and Mindful Listening* (New York: W. W. Norton & Company, 2018).

5. See Matt. 11:38; Ps. 55:22; John 11:29–36; Rev. 21:4; D&C 122:5–8.

6. Dieter F. Uchtdorf, "Learn from Alma and Amulek," *Ensign*, November 2016, 73; Rosemary M. Wixom, "Returning to Faith," *Ensign*, May 2015, 93–95; Jakob R. Jones, "Doubt Not, but Be Believing," *Ensign*, March 2019, 64–69; Patrick Q. Mason, *Planted: Belief and Belonging in an Age of Doubt* (Salt Lake City: Deseret Book, 2015), 11; David B. Marsh, *Doubt Not, but Be Believing: Supporting Loved Ones through Their Trials of Faith* (Springville, UT: Cedar Fort, 2017), 155; Dusty Smith and Kimiko Christensen Hammari, *Trial of Faith: Why a Lawyer Abandoned His Mormon Faith, Argued Against It, and Returned to Defend It* (Springville, Utah: Cedar Fort, 2018).

7. Jeffrey R. Holland, "'Lord, I Believe,'" *Ensign*, May 2013, 93–95.

8. Neil L. Andersen, "Trial of Your Faith," *Ensign*, November 2012, 41.

9. See also Matt. 1:22; 24:11, 24; JS—Matt. 1:22; D&C 123:12; Russell M. Nelson, "Face the Future with Faith," *Ensign*, May 2011, 34–36.

10. Steven C. Harper, *First Vision: Memory and Mormon Origins* (New York: Oxford University Press, 2019), 197–228; Ronald W. Walker,

Richard E. Turley, and Glen M. Leonard, *Massacre at Mountain Meadows* (New York: Oxford University Press, 2008).

11. James B. Allen, "Eight Contemporary Accounts of Joseph Smith's First Vision—What Do We Learn from Them?" *Improvement Era*, April 1970, 4–13; Brigham H. Roberts, *Comprehensive History of The Church of Jesus Christ of Latter-day Saints*, 6 vols. (Salt Lake City: Deseret News Press, 1930), 1:128; "A Peaceful Heart," *Friend*, September 1974, 7; Russell M. Nelson, "A Treasured Testament," *Ensign*, July 1993, 61–65.

12. Del Parson, *Joseph Smith Translating the Book of Mormon* (1996). For a critique of translation artwork, see Richard E. Turley, Mark Ashurst-McGee, and Robin Scott Jensen, "Joseph the Seer," *Ensign*, October 2015, 49–55.

13. See D&C 6:23; 1 Thes. 1:5; John 14:26; D&C 6:15; 11:13; Alma 32:34.

14. See John 14:27; Philip. 4:7; Moro. 8:26; D&C 11:13; Rom. 15:13.

15. M. Russell Ballard, "By Study and by Faith," *Ensign*, December 2016, 22.

16. Russell M. Nelson, "Children of the Covenant," *Ensign*, May 1995, 32.

CHAPTER 17

Know the Dealings of God

"Why should we think about history as incomplete and filled with fallible people?" Whenever I'm asked some form of this important question, I try give the *biggest* possible answer.

"The kind of thinking that engages varieties, complexities, nuances, and ambiguities will help you obtain eternal life." Seeing the expression of disbelief, I explain. "We frequently recite that God's work and glory involve the 'immortality and eternal life' of His children (Moses 1:39). Jesus expounded that 'life eternal' is to 'know thee the only true God, and Jesus Christ, whom thou hast sent' (John 17:3). And modern scripture teaches that 'the salvation of Zion' comes as we 'obtain a knowledge of history' (D&C 93:53). Thus, clear thinking helps us know God as we walk the path of discipleship, on our way to eternal life."

———————————— Q ————————————

A phrase in the Book of Mormon reframed the connection between eternal life and sound thinking for me. In the opening scenes, Nephi made a brief comment about why his brothers failed. Long before Laman and Lemuel tied up Nephi or sought to take their father's life or left the family to establish a godless community, they . . . murmured. Nephi explained, "They did murmur because *they knew not the dealings of that God* who had created them" (1 Ne. 2:12; emphasis added). More than four hundred years later, Zeniff recorded that the Lamanites had become "a wild, and ferocious, and a blood-thirsty people," fueled by anger "because they understood not the dealings of the Lord" (Mosiah 10:12, 14). Understanding God's dealings is clearly a big deal.

We often speak of looking for the *hand* of God in our lives or in our history, but less often do we seek to understand the *dealings* of God. To understand His dealings, we need to know who He is, what He expects, and how He treats His children. Joseph Smith taught that we each, individually, need to understand "the designs and purposes of God in our coming into the world."[1] As we come to understand the dealings of God, we come to know Him, and knowing Him leads to eternal life.

Knowing God

Perhaps nothing is more important to our happiness and progress than what we understand about God. What do you think about God? When you pray, who do you imagine is listening? Do you envision a being who waits, angrily, to cast down thunderbolts of judgment for your sins? Or perhaps a distant deity, who created the world and us and then left us alone? In your mind's eye do you see someone who is forgiving, who cares for the poor and the needy? What we think about God and His dealings shapes how we see His hand in our own lives and in history.

The scriptures affirm that God is "merciful and just" (Alma 50:19). He deals with us "prudently" (Isa. 52:13) and "mercifully" (D&C 111:6). He "fulfill[s] . . . all his words unto the children of men" (Alma 50:19). Joseph Smith taught that "long-suffering, patience, and mercy have ever characterized the dealings of our Heavenly Father towards the humble and penitent."[2]

We must set aside one unhelpful assertion about how God

deals with His children. I frequently encounter people who say that part of the world can be explained by science, reason, and culture while the rest cannot; the former are truths known by study, and the latter are things to be accepted on faith. Among those who try to reconcile science and religion, this approach is often described as seeking a "God of the gaps" because it points to the gaps in our scientific knowledge as places where God must be since there is no scientific explanation. When applied to history, this approach follows events until some "coincidence" cannot be explained—the fog rolled in, the outnumbered army won—and then asserts that God was in the fog. Indeed, one definition of a miracle is something "that is not explained by natural or scientific laws."

This "God of the gaps" or "coincidences" approach bears two significant problems. First, as our understanding of science and history advances, things previously considered unexplainable suddenly become explainable, so things once considered as evidence for God get called into question. Second, this approach implies that God is only operative in our lives if we can't understand His doings. Given the many precious truths we do know about God, I believe we impair our ability to understand Him when we see Him in only what we do not know.

The Dealings of God

God deals with His children in many ways. There have been times in history when God directly intervened in historical events. Jehovah was born and lived on earth. God the Father introduced Jesus at His baptism and to Joseph Smith in the grove. But God talks about His interaction with humans through a metaphor of doing things "without hands" (Dan. 2:34, 45; Mark 14:58; D&C 65:2; 109:72). If we are willing to seek widely, we will discover that God is involved far more and in many more ways than we typically realize.

> ### :💡: Thinking Habit:
> ### Know the Dealings of God
>
> Understand that God deals with us through direct intervention, small means, tender mercies, the Spirit of the Lord, the creation of all things, human agency, the swallowing up of our sufferings, and His tears.

Alma explained that "the Lord God doth work by means to bring about his great and eternal purposes" (Alma 37:7). As examples, he mentioned how Nephite records had been used to convince the Lamanites of the truth and how the Liahona had led Lehi's family through the wilderness. Alma described both the records and the Liahona as being *small means* (Alma 37:41). Other examples of small means include Moses's sticks[3] and the brother of Jared's stones.[4] Each week we consume water and bread to express our willingness to be cleansed.[5] Jesus used saliva and dirt to heal blindness, deafness, and muteness.[6] Joseph Smith translated the Book of Mormon using stones. Sometimes, when people express their concern to me about Joseph Smith's seer stone, I respond that I'd be more worried if God had *not* instructed Joseph to use a stone because its presence is part of "showing that he is the same God yesterday, today, and forever" (D&C 20:12). Because these means are small, we do well to observe Alma's warning to Helaman that some people would think such means to be "foolishness," but he emphasized that "by very small means the Lord doth confound the wise" (Alma 37:7).

A second way to comprehend God's dealings is with the concept of *tender mercies.* One of Nephi's purposes in writing his record was to "show unto [us] that the tender mercies of the Lord are over all those whom he hath chosen, because of their faith, to make them mighty even unto the power of deliverance" (1 Ne. 1:20). Accordingly, his account identifies times when he escaped from Laban's guards, obtained the plates, ate raw meat that tasted good, traveled through the wilderness, survived an ocean voyage, and arrived in the promised land. The Psalmist wrote that God's tender mercies "have been ever of old" and are "over all his works" and "continually preserve me" so "that I may live" (Ps. 25:6; 145:9; 40:11; 119:77).

Elder David A. Bednar explained that tender mercies are "very personal and individualized blessings, strength, protection, assurances, guidance, loving-kindnesses, consolation, support, and spiritual gifts which we receive from and because of and through the Lord Jesus Christ." They are not things that happen to everyone, such as the sun rising on the just and the unjust (that is better characterized as the light of Christ, which is another evidence of God's dealings). Elder Bednar emphasized "that the tender mercies of the Lord are real and that they do not occur randomly or merely by coincidence."[7] Participants in Zion's Camp saw tender mercies in the individuals who volunteered or donated money, by heaven's providing food and water, in the healing of the sick, and through protection from the elements.[8]

The *Holy Ghost* is both a "small" means (it is often described as a small voice) and the bearer of tender and merciful messages. The Holy Ghost can also prompt us to become part of God's dealings, to become an "instrument in the hands of God" (Alma 1:8).[9] One of the fruits of the Spirit is that it leads us to do good, walk humbly, and deal justly. President Spencer W. Kimball taught that "God does notice us and He watches over us, but it is usually through another person that he meets our needs." We recognize tender mercies when someone calls or reaches out to us, and we become part of the process when we reach out to others. Elder Dieter F. Uchtdorf observed that in these situations we become "His hands."[10]

We might also step back to note that everything created by God points to His dealings. Responding to the antichrist Korihor, Alma testified that "*all things* denote there is a God" (Alma 30:44; emphasis added). Alma named the earth, everything on the face of it, its motion, and all of the planets. To begin, all life has its existence and being through the light of Christ.[11] Joseph F. Smith observed, "I am inclined to acknowledge the hand of God in all things. If I see a man inspired with intelligence, with extraordinary ability and wisdom, I say to myself he is indebted to God for that wisdom and ability."[12] In His mercy, God established an earth containing food, clothing, and other resources to be used by humans.[13]

We also see the hand of God any time we see people making choices. *Agency* is a gift of God and He endorses its use.[14] Joseph F. Smith expounded: "When two men give way to their passions, their selfishness and anger, to contend and quarrel with each other, and this quarrel and contention leads to physical strife and violence between them, it has been difficult for me to discover the hand of the Lord in that transaction; other than that the men who thus disagree, quarrel and contend with each other, have received from God the freedom of their own agency to exercise their own intelligence, to judge between the right and the wrong for themselves, and to act according to their own desire."[15] But that does not mean God is responsible for the consequences. "I acknowledge the hand of the Lord in this free agency that he has given to the children of men," President Smith stated, "but I acknowledge the hand of man in the consequences of his own acts."[16] Seeking for people making choices is an important way of finding the hand of God in history.

Sometimes God even permits people to use their agency to act contrary to His expressed desires. God declined Joseph Smith's request to loan the Book of Mormon manuscript pages to Martin Harris, but after repeated efforts, Joseph ultimately received permission to follow his own will, and he later suffered the consequences. The ancient Israelites begged the prophet Samuel to anoint a king like the other nations, even though God had counseled against it. Samuel warned the Israelites of the consequences, but they persisted, their request was granted, and their suffering endured four hundred years. President Ezra Taft Benson referred to this as the "Samuel Principle," explaining, "God wanted it to be otherwise, but within certain bounds he grants unto men according to their desires."[17]

Two final expressions of the dealings of God may not be observed by us until "after the fact." First, the Lord offers a compensatory help that *swallows up* the things we have previously suffered. Elder Neal A. Maxwell explained that "when we are perplexed and stressed, explanatory help is not always immediately forthcoming, but compensatory help will be."[18] While God permits some things to happen, He can also act to preserve people, temper the consequences, or "swallow up" the results. Brigham Young explained this concept with simple clarity: "Man can load his gun to shoot his neighbor, but he cannot make the ball hit him, if the Lord Almighty sees fit to turn it away."[19] We suffer the consequences of others' actions, but in the end the suffering is mitigated by God— the pharaoh's magicians turned their rods into snakes, but Aaron's "swallowed up" the others; the Egyptians chased the Israelites, but the Red Sea swallowed them up; all will die, but "the sting of death is swallowed up in Christ" (Mosiah 16:8).[20]

Second, we should also watch for the *tears of God* in history. The earth's history has been filled with selfishness and brutality, greed and ambition, sadness and tragedy, horror and atrocity, slavery and segregation, racism and discrimination, misuse and abuse of power. The question "Why do bad things happen to good people?" is really better rendered as "Why do awful and horrendous things happen to thousands of millions of people?"[21] When Enoch saw the future sufferings of the world in vision, he was startled also to see Jehovah's tears: "How is it that thou canst weep, seeing thou art holy, and from all eternity to all eternity?" And the Lord responded that the people of the earth "are the workmanship of mine own hands, and I gave unto them their knowledge, in the day I created them; and in the Garden of Eden, gave I unto man his agency," and yet they chose evil (Moses 7:29–33). When we see no respite to our pain, when no swallowing help is apparent, there is immense comfort in knowing that He weeps with us. And, one of the sweetest promises in all of scripture is that one day "God shall wipe away all tears from their eyes; and there shall be no more death, neither sorrow, nor crying, neither shall there be any more pain" (Rev. 21:4).

💬 Everyday Encounter: Making Sense of Suffering

Oversimplified thinking about the dealings of God inhibits our understanding of suffering. For example, if you take the either/or view that God punishes the wicked and preserves the righteous, then righteous people should never suffer and anyone who suffers must be wicked. But, of course, the righteous do suffer, and the wicked also succeed. To resolve the apparent contradiction, some people invent urban legends. After disasters, rumors often circulate, claiming, for instance, that "every building was destroyed except the temple" or that Latter-day Saint missionaries were going to meet downtown on September 11 but were prompted to change their meeting at the last moment. (Both of these stories are false, by the way.[22]) Rather than forcing an either/or narrative, why not allow that righteous people can suffer (and wicked people can prosper)? We must embrace a view of suffering that allows for complexity, contingency, and multiple causes so that we do not blame the victims. God sent us into a fallen physical world, in part, so that we could respond to its physical realities by turning to Him.

The Hand of God Is a Symbol

The dealings of God are symbolized by the scriptural image of "His hand." Jehovah used His hands to create the earth, "the work of my hands." Jesus of Nazareth healed people with His hands, laid His hands on His disciples to give them power and authority, and suffered His hands to be pierced by nails at His Crucifixion. Jehovah's wounded hands are thus a sign that He descended below all things, that He is "the God of Israel," and that He remembers each of us, for we are "graven" on "the palms of [His] hands" (2 Ne. 27:34; 3 Ne. 11:14; 1 Ne. 21:16). His hands are a symbol of justice and punishment, and His stretched out hands a sign of His mercy. For the brother of Jared, seeing the hand of God served as preparation for seeing Him.

Joseph F. Smith taught that "the hand of the Lord may not be visible to all. There may be many who cannot discern the workings of God's will in the progress and development of this great latter-day work, but there are those who see in every hour and in every moment of the existence of the Church, from its beginning until now, the overruling, almighty hand of Him who sent His Only Begotten Son to the world to become a sacrifice for the sin of the world."[23] Such a view is possible if we can see God's dealings in the creation of all things, in the gift of agency and its impacts, in tender mercies and small means, and in swallowing up suffering and wiping away tears.

You Try It

Rumor

God is distant and hard to know.

Sniff Tests

1. *God of the gaps.* God exerts a positive influence as He deals with His children. We will not find Him simply by accounting for everything we can with science and reason and then attributing the leftover to God. If you are trying to find God through the process of elimination, your efforts will come up short.

2. *Headline news.* The dealings of God are small and simple. So small that the smart people may not get it—"by very small

means the Lord doth confound the wise" (Alma 37:7). So small that faithful people may "look beyond the mark" and miss it. If you are watching cable news for evidence of God's dealings, you're looking in the wrong place.

3. *Only a coincidence.* Because God's Spirit whispers and His works are small, you might be tempted to dismiss them as randomness or a coincidence. Look instead to see the indirect ways that God deals with His children.

Real

The hand of God is a symbol for His dealings with His children.

Key Concepts

1. God sometimes deals with His children through direct intervention.

2. More often His dealings are indirect, though tangible intermediary means (such as stones, sticks, water, and saliva), tender mercies, the Holy Ghost, human agency, the swallowing up of suffering, and His weeping for us.

Notes

1. Joseph Smith, in "History, 1838–1856, volume E-1 [1 July 1843–30 April 1844]," p. 1750, The Joseph Smith Papers, https://www.josephsmithpapers.org/paper-summary/history-1838-1856-volume-e-1-1-july-1843-30-april-1844/122.
2. Joseph Smith, "Letter to William W. Phelps, 22 July 1840," The Joseph Smith Papers, https://www.josephsmithpapers.org/paper-summary/letter-to-william-w-phelps-22-july-1840/2.
3. See Ex. 4:1–5, 17, 20–21; 7:8–21; 8:16–19; 9:22–26; 10:12–15; 14:15–18; 17:1–13; Num. 20:7–11; 21:7–9; John 3:14–15.
4. See Ether 3; Ex. 28:12; 35:9, 27; 1 Sam. 23:9–12; 28:6; 30:7–8; Ex. 28:30; Lev. 8:8; Num. 27:21; Deut. 33:8; Ezra 2:63; Neh. 7:65.
5. See 2 Kings 5; D&C 20:77, 79.
6. See John 9:6; Mark 7:33; 8:23.
7. David A. Bednar, "The Tender Mercies of the Lord," *Ensign,* May 2005, 99–102.

8. Matthew C. Godfrey, "'We Believe the Hand of the Lord Is in It': Memories of Divine Intervention in the Zion's Camp Expedition," *BYU Studies Quarterly* 56, no. 4 (2017), 99–132.

9. See 1 Ne. 13:12; Joseph F. Smith, *Gospel Doctrine* (Salt Lake City: The Deseret News, 1919), 497.

10. Spencer W. Kimball, "Small Acts of Service," *Ensign*, December 1974, 5; Dieter F. Uchtdorf, "You Are My Hands," *Ensign*, May 2010, 68.

11. See D&C 88:7–10, 12–13.

12. Joseph F. Smith, *Gospel Doctrine* (Salt Lake City: The Deseret News, 1919), 75.

13. Smith, *Gospel Doctrine*, 288.

14. See 2 Ne. 2:14, 16.

15. Joseph F. Smith, *Improvement Era*, July 1917, 821; Smith, *Gospel Doctrine*, 70.

16. Joseph F. Smith, in James R. Clark, comp., *Messages of the First Presidency of The Church of Jesus Christ of Latter-day Saints*, 6 vols. (Salt Lake City: Bookcraft, 1965–76) 5:70–71.

17. Ezra Taft Benson, "Jesus Christ—Gifts and Expectations," *New Era*, May 1975, 17–18; see also D&C 3, 10; 1 Sam. 8.

18. Neal A. Maxwell, "Swallowed Up in the Will of the Father," *Ensign*, November 1995, 24.

19. Brigham Young, in *Discourses of Brigham Young*, ed. John A Widtsoe (Salt Lake City: Deseret Book, 1954), 63.

20. See also Ex. 7:12; Isa. 25:8; 1 Cor. 15:54; 2 Cor. 5:4; Alma 22:14; 27:28; 36:28; Hel. 8:11; Morm. 7:5; Mosiah 15:7.

21. Smith, *Gospel Doctrine*, 59.

22. It is equally false to assert that temples never survive. See Danielle B. Wagner, "Amazing Footage of Temples Surviving Tornadoes, Fires, and Other Natural Disasters," *LDS Living* (blog), September 2, 2017, http://www.ldsliving.com/Amazing-Footage-of-Temples-Surviving-Tornadoes-Fires-Flooding-and-Other-Natural-Disasters/s/86224.

23. Joseph F. Smith, in Conference Report, April 1904, 2; Smith, *Gospel Doctrine*, 64.

You Take the Next One

Our exploration of rumors and myths and the methods for dispelling them has been moving toward an important objective—to prepare *you* to handle the next one. I cannot predict the issue or the details or the emotions that will be involved, but I am certain that "rumor with [its] thousand tongues [is] all the time employed in circulating falsehoods" (JS—H 1:61). I don't know if it will be a rumored change on the eve of general conference, some old detail from Church history, or a new video on YouTube about the end of the world. It may originate in a well-meaning attempt to share a faith-promoting story, or a conscious effort to provoke a personal crisis, or a chance encounter with previously unheard-of information.

If you have trained well, your investigative skills and habits should immediately kick in, almost as a reflex, and you will begin to survey the *situation*, wondering about when and where the source came from, the author's purpose and intended audience, and the type of information you've found. Did a speaker share a story that feels oversimplified? Have you encountered a document on the internet intended to attack or belittle? Has a family member recommended a book about Church history?

Primed by your anticipatory thinking, you can analyze the

topics and omissions, the argument with its evidence and assumptions, and the structure and form of the work. Evidence is always the key to the *contents*. Does the story rest on sources created at the time of the event, or were the sources created later? Does the website present a long list of anomalies and try to force you into an either/or position? Does the book hide the author's lack of evidence by cherry-picking sources and celebrating coincidences?

The easiest way to perpetuate errors, rumors, and myths is to disconnect facts from their relevant *contexts*. Is the story told without referring to other contemporary occurrences and causes? Has the antagonistic internet post simply plucked a lot of quotations out of the context of the original speaker's time and place? Does the book imagine strained possibilities?

Use the criteria of accuracy, authenticity, reliability, fairness, and comprehensiveness to evaluate historical, usable, or personal *significances*. How complete is the story that is told over the pulpit?[1] How well does the internet writer succeed at being fair and reliable? Are the book's conclusions undermined by its lack of a comprehensive consideration of sources?

If you have learned to question the myths within you, if you are developing strong habits of clear thinking, if you can put the pieces together to discern what is real and what is rumor, you're ready to dispel the next one.

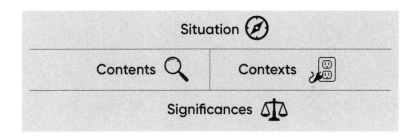

Note

1. As a reward for reading the last endnote of this book, I'll share a secret with you: The first question found in paragraphs two through five of the epilogue was prompted by the story of Brigham Young's transfiguration to look and sound like the martyred Joseph Smith. Sources have been gathered in Lynne Watkins Jorgensen, "The Mantle of the Prophet Joseph Smith Passes to Brother Brigham: One Hundred Twenty-Nine Testimonies of a Collective Spiritual Witness," in *Opening the Heavens: Accounts of Divine Manifestations, 1820–1844*, 2d ed., ed. John W. Welch (Provo, UT: BYU Studies, 2017), 395–429.

Discern Real and Rumor with These Questions

The best investigation occurs through questioning. The better the questions, the better our understanding.

1. Survey the Situation

Before you read, ask questions. You may not be able to answer all of the questions in advance, but getting them into your mind will help you investigate the contents, contexts, and significances.

Time and Place

- When and where was the source, story, or study created?
- Is it related to a specific occasion, such as a meeting or event?

Author

- Who was the author or creator?
- What can you determine about the author's background and perspective? Consider the author's age, gender, race, education, social position, affiliations, values, motives, and biases.

Audience

- Who was the author's intended audience?
- Is the author part of the audience, opposed to the audience, or otherwise related to the audience?

Purpose

- Why did the author prepare this source, story, or study?
- Who benefits from the existence of this source or story?

Type of History

- Is it a piece of the past that remains as a *source* in the present?
- Is it a *story* told by someone who lived through the events or who came later?
- Is it a *study* that considers previous sources and stories?

2. Analyze the Contents $\mathbb{Q}$

Read closely and ask questions about the contents.

Storyline

- What people, events, subjects, times, places, illustrations, images, or metaphors are discussed?
- Who or what is missing or forgotten from this source or story?
- How has the story been simplified? What has been added or exaggerated over time?
- What is left silent, unstated, alluded to, or unanswered?

Structure

- What is presented first, and what is held until the end?
- Is the author visible with a voice and credentials, or hidden behind passive verbs?
- Is the author sincere and objective, gentle and pleading, impatient and demanding, dismissive and condescending, or strident and disapproving?

Argument

- What is the main idea, position, or interpretation?
- What does it ask, claim, reinterpret, defend, or challenge?

• Does the author ignore additional questions or anticipate possible counterclaims?

Evidence

• What evidence does the author present to support the claims?
• Is the evidence observed (firsthand), heard (secondhand), or inferred?
• Are the sources real (authentic), correct (accurate), and complete (comprehensive)?
• Does the author comment on the limitations or inconsistencies of available sources?
• How did the author select the sources, and should other sources also have been considered?
• Does the author cite sources in a way that allows you to locate and evaluate them?

Assumptions and Values

• How does the author conceive of the world, humans, culture, the past, or goodness?
• Does the author presume to share the same language and culture with readers?
• How do assumptions and values shape the purpose and argument?

Script

• Does the specific story follow a more general script?
• Are the story's characters victims, villains, or helpless?
• Does the story evoke larger narratives about America, progress, or culture wars?

Form

• Does the work have citations, illustrations, maps, or an index?
• Does the source require use of a different language or technology?

- Does the source contain notable physical qualities, such as handwriting, seals, annotations, or official stamps?

3. Connect to Contexts

Ask questions that connect the source to other things that occurred before, during, and after its creation.

Situational Context

- Is it a source, a story, or a study?
- When and where was it created?
- What was the author's purpose in addressing this audience?

Historical Context

- What other specific events were happening at the same time, such as wars, political movements, or economic crises?
- What long-term societal, cultural, political, or demographic trends were underway?
- What else was happening during that era in the same types of places, such as in other similar homes or communities?

Literary Context

- How does this source respond to questions, ask questions, or fit into ongoing conversations among authors?
- Does the source use metaphors or symbols or scriptures previously used by others?
- How does it compare to other examples of this type of history?

Material Context

- How was the source produced or distributed in its time or since?
- Where has it been since the author created it? (Provenance)
- Does it exist in a variety of iterations, such as excerpts, copies, transcriptions, or translations?

Ethical Context

- Does it contain information that should be respected due to privacy rights, copyright, or laws and regulations?
- Does it contain information that should be respected for cultural or religious reasons?

Biographical Context

- How does the source, story, or study fit within the life and larger work of its creator?
- Does this source provide any insight into the author's feelings or experiences at a particular time in life?
- Did the author's views change over time?

Eternal Context

- How does it fit within the plan of salvation?
- How does it fit within the gospel of Jesus Christ?

4. Evaluate Significances

After you read, ask evaluating questions.

Basic Evaluation

- What happened? (Description)
- What were they thinking? (Interpretation)
- Why then and there? (Explanation)
- What do we think about that? (Judgment)

Criteria for Evaluation

- Can the information be compared, verified, corroborated, or triangulated from other sources? (Accuracy)
- Was it created in the past by the person who claims to have created it? (Authenticity)
- Is the information consistent and trustworthy? (Reliability)

- Does it consider all relevant information in good faith, without distortion, and in light of vested interests? (Fairness)
- Is it wide enough to address all points of view, deep enough to consider complexities, and thorough in reviewing previous sources and stories? (Comprehensiveness)

Historical Significance

- What were the immediate changes, developments, or consequences of the source or story?
- Were the changes widespread or the impacts long-term, or were precedents set for future actions or interpretations?
- Did people at the time consider it to be important, or did its importance become apparent slowly, over time?

Usable Significance

- Can we use it to document, describe, or illuminate the past?
- From the perspective of today, what does the source mean, why does it matter, how can it be used or applied, and does it relate to current events or trends?
- Can elements from the past be used to frame current activities? (Analogy)

Personal Significance

- Is the author or creator your ancestor?
- How is it relevant or applicable to you in the present?

Dispel These Bad Assumptions

Assumptions frequently surface in conversations, teachings, and writings. Because present assumptions distort the past, they cause harm by contaminating thinking, provoking personal stress, and preventing people from accepting the truth (see chapter 3). This list presents common assumptions about prophets generally, Joseph Smith and the Book of Mormon, the Church, and history.

Prophets

Every statement ever made by a prophet or apostle constitutes the doctrine of the Church. Joseph Smith noted that a prophet is only a prophet when he is speaking as a prophet. Elder D. Todd Christofferson explained that "not every statement made by a Church leader, past or present, necessarily constitutes doctrine." Elder Neil L. Andersen corroborated: "The doctrine is taught by all 15 members of the First Presidency and Quorum of the Twelve. It is not hidden in an obscure paragraph of one talk. True principles are taught frequently and by many."[1]

Prophets know everything about the future. Prophets and seers can know about parts of the future, but no prophet has ever claimed to know everything about everything that will ever happen.

Prophets always receive revelation that is always clear. Sometimes the will of the Lord is very clear, but like every Latter-day Saint, prophets must also study, ponder, pray, and wrestle.

As the "mouthpiece" of the Lord, prophets simply open their mouths and the word of God flows out. Sometimes revelation has come as dictated wording, but prophets also receive inspiration, feelings, and impressions that they then must put into words and actions.

Prophets receive revelation only by kneeling alone and asking for it. Many revelatory experiences certainly happened this way—such as the First Vision—but it is not the only way prophets receive inspiration. Joseph also received revelations with other people—Moroni appeared to him and the Three Witnesses, and he and Sidney Rigdon viewed into the heavens (see D&C 76). As Joseph established the First Presidency (1832), high councils (1834), and the councils of the Twelve and the Seventy (1835), the process of receiving revelation for Church governance expanded from individuals to the collective deliberations of councils.

Prophets speak in mysterious riddles that are only understood later. This assumption of a prophet as a sphinx, riddler, or soothsayer is common in many cultural traditions. Nephi, however, wrote that his "soul delighteth in plainness; for after this manner doth the Lord God work among the children of men" (2 Ne. 31:3).

A prophet must be "a voice crying in the wilderness," who speaks out against evil, social injustice, and oppression. The assumption that prophets must be social-justice reformers leads to a false conclusion that they must publicly denounce all injustice everywhere.

Prophets never make mistakes. The only person to live a mistake-free life was Jesus Christ. Joseph Smith declared, "I never told you I was perfect," and he reported his errors and published his divine rebukes (see JS—H 1:28–29; D&C 3:6–7; 24:2). Elder Dieter F. Uchtdorf admitted that "leaders in the Church have simply made mistakes." President Russell M. Nelson observed of General Authorities: "We recognize them as instruments in the hand of the

Lord, yet realize that they are ordinary human beings. They require haircuts, laundry services, and occasional reminders just like anyone else." And President M. Russell Ballard explained, "Too many people think Church leaders and members should be perfect or nearly perfect. They forget that the Lord's grace is sufficient to accomplish His work through mortals."[2] After correcting an error that had been published by a member of the Twelve who erroneously presented the notes of a member of the First Presidency as a revelation by Joseph Smith, B. H. Roberts observed: "We need not be surprised if we sometimes find [the prophets] mistaken in their conceptions and deductions; just as the generations who succeed us in unfolding in a larger way some of the yet unlearned truths of the Gospel, will find that we have had some misconceptions and made some wrong deductions in our day and time."[3] Latter-day Saint doctrine does not include a provision that a prophet is infallible.

Prophets never get tricked. Isaac's son Jacob came disguised as his brother Esau to receive the birthright blessing, and Jacob later interpreted animal blood on his son Joseph's coat as evidence of his son's death (see Gen. 27:6–10; 37:31–34). After losing the Book of Mormon manuscript, Joseph Smith was told simply, "You cannot always tell the wicked from the righteous" (D&C 10:37).

Prophets never disagree with each other. Prophets bring different perspectives drawn from personal experiences. They counsel together until they reach unanimity. Acts 15 documents this process among the early Apostles. More recently, President M. Russell Ballard has explained, "None of the Twelve are shrinking violets. We each have strong personalities. So when we are unified in a decision, you can rest assured that we have counseled together and come to that decision after much prayer and thoughtful discussion."[4]

When the prophet gives direction, all of the Latter-day Saints immediately follow. This is a frequent claim from opponents of the Church who fear the mass political mobilization of the Saints. It is a conspiracy theory that appeals to antagonist and believer alike, though for different reasons. But many times in the scriptures and Church history the people did not follow the prophet.

Joseph Smith and the Book of Mormon

Joseph should have immediately recorded and shared every detail about the First Vision. This false assumption surfaces in several forms: Any person who saw God would write all of the details down immediately. A teenage boy who saw God would immediately tell everyone about his experience. Any person who had a spiritual experience would forever remember and recite the precise date.[5] Another way of stating this assumption is "As soon as an event occurs, it is immediately and widely known."

Joseph Smith never made mistakes. He made mistakes and did not hide that fact. He admitted his mistakes in his history (see JS—H 1:28–29). He published rebukes from the Lord in the revelations (see, for example, D&C 3:6–7; 24:2). Later in his life he was deceived by persons brought into his inner circle of confidence, including George Hinkle and John C. Bennett.

Joseph Smith used the word translate *the same way that we use it.* No, he did not. His use of the word involved revelation that was received through three different methods—he translated the Book of Mormon by looking into stones, prepared a translation of the Bible by reading the text in English and making inspired changes, and translated the book of Abraham by making notes about Egyptian characters. None of these methods match the way a human translator or Google translates text today. We know little about how his revelatory process interacted with these three physical methods. When asked about the Book of Mormon, he repeatedly explained simply that it was "translated by the gift and power of God."

Joseph Smith's experience is distant from our experience today. I suspect this arises from the way he is portrayed in some paintings and films. President Dallin H. Oaks observed, "When I was a boy, growing up in the Church, I imagined the Prophet Joseph to be old and dignified and distant. But the Joseph Smith I met in my reading and personal research was a man of the frontier—young, emotional, dynamic, and so loved and approachable by his people that they often called him 'Brother Joseph.' My studies strengthened my testimony of his prophetic calling. What a remarkable man!"[6]

Joseph Smith could learn truth from angels but not from Protestant preachers, seer stones, or social clubs. Early on, he learned from the Bible that he could pray and God would answer, and then he later revised parts of the Bible. He learned the text of the Book of Mormon through a seer stone and the text of the Book of Abraham in connection with ancient scrolls uncovered with Egyptian mummies. He listened to preachers and then corrected their messages. He participated in Masonry and gleaned from its practices. He followed his injunction in what is now the thirteenth article of faith—if there was anything virtuous, lovely, of good report, or praiseworthy, no matter where it was found, he sought after those things.

The Book of Mormon people are the ancestors of all modern Native Americans. This assumption arose in the nineteenth century and found its way into the introduction of the Book of Mormon. Recently, the introduction was changed to say that the descendants of Lehi are "among the ancestors" of Native Americans.[7]

The Book of Mormon presents early American ideas as the will of God. Embedded in this assumption is the idea that Joseph Smith drew the ideas in the book from his cultural surroundings. Historian Richard Bushman noted that the book actually runs counter to American ideals of the past and present: "The *Book of Mormon* proposes a new purpose for America: becoming a realm of righteousness rather than an empire of liberty. Against increasing wealth and inequality, the *Book of Mormon* advocates the cause of the poor. . . . Against republican government, it proposes righteous rule by judges and kings under God's law . . . ; against nationalism, a universal Israel. It foresees disaster for the nation if the love of riches, resistance to revelation, and Gentile civilization prevail over righteousness, revelation, and Israel."[8]

The Church

The Church is complete. The doctrine and practices of the Church are not complete but get revealed "line upon line" as part of an "ongoing restoration." Jesus declared the church to be "living." Elder J. Devn Cornish explained, "We read the Lord's own statement that this Church is 'the only true and living church upon the face of the whole earth' (D&C 1:30). So it may seem reasonable to expect that the history of the true Church portray unerring leaders successfully implementing a sequence of revealed directions progressing to a perfect organization that is widely welcomed and embraced. But that is neither what the scriptures describe nor what our history represents, because the perfecting of the Church as an organization was not the Lord's primary purpose."[9]

Leaders and members of the Church make no errors and have no disagreements. This assumption is laughable when stated, but when unstated it permeates so much of gossip and criticism about our brothers and sisters who give dull talks, forget to show up for chapel cleaning assignments, or make errors of judgment. "We will be thrilled by what we find in our history," explained Elder J. Devn Cornish, "if we expect it to demonstrate how the process of the Restoration not only established the Lord's true Church on earth but also provided the experiences by which its leaders and members could grow toward perfection as they learned from their triumphs and their mistakes."[10]

The true Church does not change. This assumption gets phrased many ways: "Because God is unchanging, His church is unchanging" or "This Church is the exact same church as existed in the meridian of time." This is simply not true. Joseph Smith promised that the Lord "will yet reveal many great and important things pertaining to the Kingdom of God" (A of F 1:9). Church leaders can be inspired to change policies in place for 130 years (the priesthood ban), 60 years (plural marriage), or 3 years (baptisms for children of LGBTQ parents). The Restoration is ongoing, and the "hastening of the work" suggests we'll see more changes more quickly. How can a changing church be considered true? Elder Cornish explained, "It means that we may have complete confidence in the validity of the restored priesthood authority, the saving ordinances, the revealed doctrine, the scriptures, and the united quorums of the Twelve Apostles and the First Presidency. It means that we may know that the Savior Himself directs the Church and that the Holy Ghost will bear witness to all sincere seekers of the truth of these things. It means that by striving to keep the covenants associated with the ordinances, and continually repenting, even imperfect but sincere people like you and me will live in celestial glory with God and Christ and our families forever, through the Atonement of Jesus Christ."[11]

A change in Church practice represents the silent correction of a mistake. The Church changes because people change, needs change, technology changes, and society changes. God reveals His will "unto [His] servants in their weakness, after the manner of their language, that they might come to understanding" (D&C 1:24). The announcement of two-hour church acknowledged that most social events no longer last that long (except football games).[12] Changes happen because the work moves forward.

The Church should teach me everything about everything. This assumption often appears in reverse, as in "Why didn't I hear about that at church?" Elder David A. Bednar explained: "Each and every member of The Church of Jesus Christ of Latter-day Saints bears a *personal* responsibility to learn and live the truths of the Savior's restored gospel and to receive by proper authority the ordinances of salvation. We should not expect the Church as an organization to teach or tell us all of the things we need to know and do to become devoted disciples and endure valiantly to the end."[13] You are responsible for your own salvation, learning, and seeking.

The truth is only in the Church. We do not own all truth. Other churches, traditions, cultures, and belief systems have much to offer that is virtuous, lovely, of good report, and praiseworthy (see A of F 1:13). The Holy Ghost bears witness of all truth, wherever it is found (whether in a Protestant church service or a math class).

Before 1830 (especially during the Dark Ages), the earth was filled with darkness and the absence of truth. This assumption is often built as a counterpoint—if the fulness of the gospel was restored then there must have been a total absence of the gospel before. To make the truth brighter, the assumer makes the precursor darker. The centuries before the Restoration, however, witnessed profound developments in science, education, politics, art, social progress, and religion. During the Middle Ages, God continued to interact with humanity, prompting and inspiring women and men in their daily lives and public works. Countless acts of sincere religious devotion in many faith traditions from this era can teach us much about how we should approach our own faith.

The Church should act at the forefront of efforts to achieve equality and social justice. The *General Handbook* explains that "Jesus Christ established His Church to enable individuals and families to do the work of salvation and exaltation."[14] In practice, the Church as an institution acts unadventurously to maintain its ability to carry out the work of salvation. The Church establishes working relationships with nations to grant formal recognition, facilitate visas and building permits, and comply with relevant laws and regulations; it is "subject" to nations "in obeying, honoring, and sustaining the law" (A of F 1:12). Yet the "Spirit of God, which is also the spirit of freedom" does lead individual citizens—within the Church and without—to "do justly" and "judge righteously" and "be anxiously engaged" in good causes in their communities (Alma 61:15; D&C 11:12; 58:27).

History

Today things are worse than they were in the "good old days." Typically not. Later generations experience developments in science, hygiene, health, and quality of life. We can make judgments about changes on various issues over time. For example, the twenty-first century witnesses a more open embrace of sexual immorality, but smoking is no longer as socially acceptable as it once was. The sins of racism and sexism are hopefully on the decline. Adam Miller described our romanticized assumptions about Church history as "softly lit watercolor felt-board versions of scripture stories and church history" that need to be replaced by the "messy, vibrant, and inconvenient truths that characterize God's real work with real people."[15]

Whatever we cannot explain today must have been "the hand of God." Sometimes we just can't explain things now, but later when a new document surfaces, we have a better understanding. The hand of God can be seen in small means, tender mercies, the work of the Holy Ghost, the creation of all things, and human agency.

Asking questions demonstrates a lack of faith. The scriptures are filled with charges to ask, seek, and knock; to ask "in faith, nothing wavering" (James 1:6) while "believing that ye shall receive" (JST, Mark 9:45; Enos 1:15; D&C 8:1); and to ask "with an honest heart," "with a sincere heart, [and] with real intent" (D&C 8:1; Moro. 10:4). Robert L. Millet reassured that asking questions is not "unusual, inappropriate, or a sign of cynicism or even weakness."[16] And Sheri Dew encouraged Latter-day Saints to "ask with the assumption that there are answers." This shifts the conversation from

"Here's something I don't understand, so the gospel must not be true" to "Here's something I don't understand, but I wonder what the Lord or His prophets will teach us."[17]

Every question has a complete and satisfying answer. Sometimes the answer is "I don't know" or "Not yet." President M. Russell Ballard said, "We need to do better in responding to honest questions. Although we may not be able to answer every question about the cosmos or about our history, doctrine, and practices, we can provide many answers to those who are sincere. When we don't know the answer, we can search answers together—a shared search that may bring us closer to each other and closer to God."[18]

Notes

1. D. Todd Christofferson, "The Doctrine of Christ," *Ensign*, May 2012, 88; Neil L. Andersen, "Trial of Your Faith," *Ensign*, November 2012, 41.

2. Joseph Smith, in *Teachings of Presidents of the Church: Joseph Smith* (Salt Lake City, The Church of Jesus Christ of Latter-day Saints, 2007), 522; Dieter F. Uchtdorf, "Come, Join with Us," *Ensign*, November 2013, 22; Russell M. Nelson, "Honoring the Priesthood," *Ensign*, May 1993, 39; M. Russell Ballard, "God Is at the Helm," *Ensign,* November 2015, 24–25.

3. B. H. Roberts, *New Witnesses for God II. The Book of Mormon*, 3 vols. (Salt Lake City: Deseret News, 1909), 3:503–4.

4. M. Russell Ballard, "Be Still, and Know That I Am God" (CES Devotional for Young Adults, San Diego, CA, May 4, 2014), https://www.churchofjesuschrist.org/broadcasts/article/ces-devotionals/2014/01/be-still-and-know-that-i-am-god.

5. See Steven C. Harper, *Joseph Smith's First Vision: A Guide to the Historical Accounts* (Salt Lake City: Deseret Book, 2012), 3–12.

6. Dallin H. Oaks, "Joseph, the Man and the Prophet," *Ensign*, May 1996.

7. See "Book of Mormon and DNA Studies," Gospel Topics Essays, The Church of Jesus Christ of Latter-day Saints, 2014, https://www.churchofjesuschrist.org/study/manual/gospel-topics-essays/book-of-mormon-and-dna-studies.

8. Richard Lyman Bushman, *Joseph Smith: Rough Stone Rolling* (New York: Alfred A. Knopf, 2005), 105.

9. J. Devn Cornish, "The True Church: 'For the Perfecting of the Saints,'" *Ensign*, September 2018, 60.

10. Cornish, "The True Church," 60.

11. Cornish, "The True Church," 60–61.

12. Quentin L. Cook, "Deep and Lasting Conversion to Heavenly Father and the Lord Jesus Christ," *Ensign*, November 2018, 11, endnote 2.

13. David A. Bednar, *Increase in Learning: Spiritual Patterns for Obtaining Your Own Answers* (Salt Lake City, Utah: Deseret Book, 2011), 1.

14. *General Handbook: Serving in The Church of Jesus Christ of Latter-day Saints* (Salt Lake City: The Church of Jesus Christ of Latter-day Saints, 2020), 1.3.

15. Adam S. Miller, *Letters to a Young Mormon* (Provo, UT: Neal A. Maxwell Institute for Religious Scholarship, 2014), 49.

16. Robert L. Millet, *Holding Fast: Dealing with Doubt in the Latter Days* (Salt Lake City: Deseret Book, 2008), 11.

17. Sheri Dew, *Worth the Wrestle* (Salt Lake City: Deseret Book, 2017), 8–9.

18. M. Russell Ballard, "An Epistle from an Apostle," *Ensign*, September 2019, 25.

The Sniff Tests

Sniff Tests are clues that something just isn't right. Like the Lamanite queen in the Book of Mormon, you can tell when something stinks or not (see Alma 19:1–12). You don't need to know every fact to recognize these warning signs.

Survey the Situation

- "History is like school and science." (chap. 1)
- "Hindsight is 20/20." (chap. 1)
- Hiding the interpretive process (chap. 4)
- "We'll await the judgment of history." (chap. 4)
- Debunking (chap. 6)
- No attempt at analysis (chap. 9)
- No provenance (chap. 10)
- No routine for seeking (chap. 14)

Analyze the Contents

- Nothing missing (chap. 1)
- One definitive answer (chap. 14)
- No evidence (chap. 2)
- No source (chap. 11)
- No citations (chap. 13)
- Argumentation without evidence (chap. 13)
- A single piece of evidence (chap. 2)
- Narrowly selected evidence (chap. 2)
- Vague evidence (chap. 2)
- Vague attribution (chap. 11)
- Incomplete attribution (chap. 15)

- More emotion than evidence (chap. 3)
- Oversimplification (chap. 5)
- Reduction (chap. 6)
- Only two options or sides (chap. 5)
- "True facts are light and pure" (chap. 5).
- "True facts are dark and insidious" (chap. 5).
- Vague or conflicting details (chap. 11)
- "What a weird thing!" (chap. 12)
- "A lot of weird things!" (chap. 13)

Connect to Contexts

- Omission (chap. 5)
- True but incomplete (chap. 6)
- "I read a book" (chap. 14).
- Taking history out of context (chap. 7)
- Taking scripture out of context (chap. 7)
- Quoting out of context (chap. 15)
- "The past was just like the present" (chap. 7).
- "The past was nothing like the present" (chap. 7).
- No attempt at corroboration (chap. 9)

Evaluate Significances

- "The past is in the past" (chap. 1).
- Exaggerated descriptions (chap. 3) Superlatives (chap. 8)
- Coincidences (chap. 8
- More coincidences (chap. 8)
- Only a coincidence (chap. 17)
- Incomplete analogies (chap. 8)
- Too good to be true (chap. 10)
- "Something dark connects them!" (chap. 12).
- "You can go on being duped or choose the truth" (chap. 12).
- Either/or (chap. 16)
- "Put your concerns 'on a shelf'" (chap. 12).
- "Don't worry about it" (chap. 16).
- "Let's inoculate" (chap. 16).
- The definitive study (chap. 13)
- Headline news (chap. 17)
- God of the gaps (chap. 17)

Acknowledgments

The ideas in *Real vs. Rumor* developed over the past three decades in classrooms, presentations, and conversations with thousands of people. The concepts began to take their current shape in 2016 as I prepared an article for the *Ensign* magazine, an accompanying essay for the Church's website, and a story for the *Church News*.[1] The articles prompted invitations to discuss the ideas further with young adults, seminary teachers, college professors, business leaders, and many others at Latter-day Saint conferences, firesides, family reunions, and events.

I am grateful for many mentors and colleagues who shared their time and expertise over the years, through conversation, counsel, and encouragement: Susan S. Rugh, Richard E. Bennett, and J. Gary Daynes; David Thelen, Ed Linenthal, James H. Madison, Eric Sandweiss, and Stephen J. Stein; Alan Booth, Sean Brawley, Lendol Calder, David Pace, T. Mills Kelly, Leah Showkow, and Sam Wineburg. This book has benefitted from the questions and feedback of Jeff Anderson, Jeffrey K. Anderson, Jennifer Barkdull, Anne Berryhill, Jay Burton, Emily Crumpton, Matthew Godfrey, Matthew J. Grow, Jeff Haddon, Steve Harper, John Heath, Kate Holbrook, Jenny Lund, Matthew McBride, Spencer McBride, Alan Morrell, Joan Nay, Reid L. Neilson, Sadie Nellis, Sharon Nielson,

Jenny Hale Pulsipher, Ben Pykles, Jenny Reeder, Paul Reeve, Eric Paul Rogers, Emily Stanford Schultz, Richard Turley, Emily Utt, Lis Allen Walker, Paul Westover, and Jed Woodworth. Those who prefer to go unmentioned are certainly not unthanked.

Carolyn Erekson has strengthened every idea that appears in this book and improved every page of its manuscript. Her comprehensive knowledge of the scriptures and the words of the living prophets are retrieved more quickly and precisely than any search algorithm yet invented. Insightful conversations with Emily, Alyse, Haley, and Lyndie have made me smarter and happier.

Note

1. See "Understanding Church History by Study and Faith," *Ensign*, February 2017, 56–59; "A Pattern for Learning Church History by Study and Faith," Church History, The Church of Jesus Christ of Latter-day Saints, April 12, 2017, https://history.churchofjesuschrist.org/article/a-pattern-for-learning-church-history-by-study-and-faith; "Honor the Pioneers by Telling Better Stories," *Church News*, July 10, 2016.

Index

About the Author

KEITH A. EREKSON is an award-winning author, teacher, and public historian, who serves as the director of the Church History Library of The Church of Jesus Christ of Latter-day Saints. He has researched and published on topics including politics, hoaxes, Abraham Lincoln, Elvis Presley, and Church history. He is a talented public speaker with a passion for helping history make sense. He grew up in Baltimore, served a mission in Brazil, and earned a PhD in history and a master's in business administration. He lives near Salt Lake City, Utah, with his wife and children.